W9-BVO-184

The New York Times

COUNTRY
WEEKEND
COOKBOOK

The New York Times

COUNTRY WEEKEND COOKBOOK

FOREWORD BY

MARK BITTMAN

EDITED BY

LINDA AMSTER

ILLUSTRATED WITH PHOTOGRAPHS FROM THE PAGES OF The New York Times

ST. MARTIN'S PRESS ❧ NEW YORK

www.stmartins.com

Book design and composition by Ralph Fowler / rlf design

Photographs are courtesy of *The New York Times* and the following photographers whose work can be seen on the listed pages:

Daniel J. van Ackere: 60, 214; Michelle V. Agins: 170; Paul O. Boisvert: 87; Robert Caplin: 160; Tony Cenicola: v (opposite copyright page), xv, 1, 30, 35, 39, 44, 73, 109, 115, 119, 137, 159, 167, 168, 193, 195, 196, 221, 234; Don Hogan Charles: 148; Peter Da Silva: 88; Joe Fornabaio: xi, 8, 22; Gordon M. Grant: ii (frontispiece), 29, 32, 180, 235; Chester Higgins, Jr.: 5; Jodi Hilton: 225; David Karp: 164; Naum Kazhdan: 59; John Lei: 104; Thomas McDonald: vii (contents page); Mike Mergen: 187; Ozier Mohammad: 199; Paxton: xi, 37, 141, 207, 229; Jonathan Player: 75; Judith Pszenica: 72; Anne Raver: xvi; Trace Rozhon: 233; Andrew Scrivani: 2, 16, 20, 41, 52, 77, 91, 117, 122, 125, 126, 128, 131, 138, 144, 162, 163, 173, 174, 179, 184–185, 198, 201, 202, 213, 260; Robert Stolarik: 71; Les Stone: xii (opposite Foreword), 132–133; Evan Sung: 7; Michael Tomkins: 38; Jim Wilson: 51, 58, 81, 107, 219.

ISBN-13: 978-0-312-35939-3
ISBN-10: 0-312-35939-X

First Edition: May 2007
10 9 8 7 6 5 4 3 2 1

With loving thoughts of

Elizabeth and Richard Levine
Terry and Charles Tolk
Jane and Lyndon Woodside
Mort Sheinman

and cherished memories
of country weekends
together that were
"the best."

CONTENTS

ACKNOWLEDGMENTS

My deepest gratitude to the dozens of accomplished chefs, restaurateurs, cookbook writers and other fine cooks for their splendid recipes and for the graciousness and enthusiasm with which they agreed to contribute to this volume. I am also immensely indebted to the talented and generous reporters at *The New York Times* for their exceptional recipes, which first appeared under their bylines in the paper's Dining In/Dining Out section: Melissa Clark, Florence Fabricant, Amanda Hesser, Moira Hodgson, Julia Moskin and Kim Severson. No *New York Times* cookbook compilation would be complete without recipes by Craig Claiborne, the late, great food editor, and I am honored to include a selection of his signature dishes in this book. I am also very thankful for many recipes from Bryan Miller, Molly O'Neill, Jacques Pépin, the late Pierre Franey and other writers who regularly contributed to the paper's food pages.

Mark Bittman occupies a special place in my pantheon of food professionals—not just for the recipes that are reprinted here, which are outstanding country weekend fare, but also for his Foreword, which so enhances this book. It is a thrill to have my name associated with his.

I am very grateful to *The Times*'s small-but-mighty book development staff for their collegiality, encouragement and assistance. Mike Levitas played a vital role from the inception of the book to the final stage of securing reprint permissions. Alex Ward offered valued guidance and assurance that smoothed my way. The invaluable Tomi Murata could always be counted upon to problem-solve with calm and friendly efficiency.

I have special admiration for another *Times* colleague, Phyllis Collazo, of the photo sales department, who culled the paper's archives with uncanny knowledge and unfailing good humor to locate many of the glorious pictures that grace these pages.

I am in awe of Michael Flamini, my extraordinarily enthusiastic and creative editor at St. Martin's Press, for envisioning and creating a cookbook that would be a feast for the eyes as well as the palate, and for his brilliant organization of the recipes. His influence throughout the development of the manuscript is reflected on every page of the book.

The rest of the team at St. Martin's Press could not have been more professional or accommodating. Thanks especially to Vicki Lame, who handled a myriad of details with great competence and cheer, to Leah Stewart, the excellent copy editor, to James Sinclair, RLF Design and to Adriana Coada for transforming the messy manuscript into this beautiful volume.

Abiding affection to Carol Auerbach, Nancy Ford Charles, Carol Coburn, Ethel Christin, Helen Doctorow, Barbara Goldsmith, Maxine Jaffe, Elizabeth Levine, James Meyerson, Jane Slotin, Terry Tolk, Laurie Wilson and Jane Woodside for their interest and support, which sustained me from first to last, and loving thanks to Harold Stone for cheering me on.

Very special thanks to Phyllis Yellin, a lifelong friend with a degree in Food and Nutrition from Cornell University, for generously giving of her time and knowledge to shape the book and especially for taking on the daunting challenge of preparing the Recipe Planner (pages 237–255) and doing it so superbly.

Boundless gratitude to my dear friend Judy Knipe, an accomplished cookbook writer and editor, who gave unstintingly of her time, encouragement and expertise to shape the book. I could not have compiled it without her collaboration.

Most heartfelt and loving appreciation of all to Mort Sheinman, who sets the gold standard not just as an editor but, more important, in profound ways that make him an immense and enduring blessing in my life.

PREFACE

Weekends are a time to cook for pleasure. So here's a book of recipes to inspire you, not tire you.

When the workweek ends, it's the signal to relax, to exhale, to take off the shoes and shake off the stress. And there's no better place to savor the luxury of weekend leisure than a country getaway.

That's especially true at mealtime. The ambience of a natural setting—a beach or brook, a meadow or mountain—inspires more relaxed cooking and more enjoyable eating. Inevitably, there's no lack of family and friends who are eager to share this bounty of country life and fare.

Whether you're preparing meals for yourself or meals for a houseful of guests, carefree, weekend cooking is your goal—and the purpose of this collection, too. The organization of the chapters, for example, follows the progression of what might be a typical weekend—Quick Meals After a Long Ride, then Breakfast/Brunch dishes before A Visit to the Farm Stand and then recipes for Lunch, and, finally, the Main Event—Dinner.

Another aid to easier cooking is the handy Recipe Planner on page 237. Arranged by course, the ingenious chart lets you see at a glance which dishes best suit your schedule and your meal plan. For example, if you want an unusually speedy and delicious entrée to serve to company, the chart will quickly point you to Salmon with Hot Mustard Glaze and to Daniel Boulud's Hanger Steak with Shallots, two of many recipes that can be prepared in thirty minutes. If you'd like a brunch dish that can be assembled the night before and popped into the oven the following morning, the chart will lead you to Brasserie's Orange French Toast, Nigella Lawson's Bacon-and-Egg Bake and Mollie Katzen's Amazing Overnight Waffles.

There are dozens of quick recipes like these that can be on the table in an hour or less. For more ambitious fare and for your convenience, another column highlights scores of dishes that can be partially prepared at your leisure, then set aside for anywhere from a short time to a few days—during which you're free to go off and enjoy yourself—with only the final cooking to do before serving. Other columns will point you to dishes that can feed a crowd and to suggestions for recipes to serve when company's coming.

The tempting recipes that grace this collection—and the food pages of *The New York Times,* from which they are reprinted—were created by celebrated chefs and restaurateurs, noted cookbook authors, outstanding home cooks and, of course, by *The Times*'s own acclaimed food writers and columnists. They showcase the produce and other fresh ingredients so readily available at the farm stands and local markets near weekend homes.

Whatever your mood or palate, simple or sophisticated, you'll find recipes that appeal—from classic family favorites (for example, Rose Levy Beranbaum's Buttermilk Blueberry Pancakes, Alice Waters's Baked Goat Cheese with Lettuce Salad, Zuni Café's Roasted Fillet of Beef with Black Pepper, Larry Forgione's Old-Fashioned Strawberry Shortcake) to dishes with an innovative flair (a few: French Laundry's Gazpacho, Le Bernardin's Fresh and Smoked Salmon Spread, Mario Batali's Wood-Grilled Veal Chops with Lemon-Oregano Jam, Pierre Hermé's Bittersweet Chocolate Sorbet).

So, put yourself in a country state of mind as you leaf through the recipes and glorious photos in the following pages. Then enjoy yourself in the kitchen. And, afterward, bask in the bounty of warm feelings that come from wonderful food, family and friendship at your weekend table.

—Linda Amster

FOREWORD

By Mark Bittman

The Times did not invent the idea of weekend entertaining, of course, but it's hard to imagine a better collection of weekend-oriented recipes by a more accomplished group of food writers and chefs than the one you're holding. Perhaps this isn't surprising, given the history of *The Times*'s food pages and the strong tradition of readers entertaining not only in their homes but in their weekend retreats.

Nearly forty years ago, Craig Claiborne just about single-handedly popularized the notion of making chefs' recipes available to a large public audience—*The Times*'s readership, and more, by collecting those and other recipes in book form—and *The Times*'s staff has been following in his footsteps ever since.

It was Claiborne who hooked up with Pierre Franey, and urged the paper to hire him—one of the best-known French chefs in the history of New

York—to generate weekly recipes. And it was *The Times* that recognized that chefs' recipes, great as they are, must be standardized and vetted in order to be useful to the public.

So it is that tradition that makes this collection exceptional, not only for the talent and imagination of the recipe creators but for the process. First, look at their sources: the names here read like a who's who of cooking for the last couple of generations. (And, as everyone knows, the last couple of generations have been the most important in the history of American cooking.)

Equally important, when you think about it, is that this is among the best possible ways to assemble a cookbook (at least from the admittedly prejudiced view of a *Times* food writer). Here are recipes that have been run through the filter of my colleagues (and me), the incomparable editing staff at *The Times*, and the paper's unimaginably large and critical audience. These recipes have been scrutinized and tested by the best and by the most demanding.

Add to all of this that the concept is one that makes perfect sense, far more than that of most collections, and you have a real winner.

For reasons that have to do with the origins of food sections (in most papers, the "women's" pages), and the way in which food sections came of age, the history of recipes in newspapers followed two courses: one was recipes for daily cooking, and the other was recipes for entertaining.

Until the introduction of Franey's *60-Minute Gourmet*, *The Times*'s food pages were, for better or worse, of the latter category. In fact they were somewhat effete, geared not toward the housewife (to use an archaic but once valid term) but toward the woman and, increasingly, man, who cooked recreationally.

Whatever one did for food on weekdays, the Wednesday recipes were clipped and reserved for weekends, when there was time to tackle them. This was the style when I was learning to cook, in the '60s and '70s; Friday afternoons and Saturday mornings were given to shopping and prep, and Saturday evenings were for entertaining. *Cuisine* was *haute* and almost exclusively French.

By the mid-70s that had changed, and Franey—aided in his writing by Claiborne, Bryan Miller and Rick Flaste (who has been a part of every major improvement in *The Times*'s coverage of food for the last twenty years, and continues in that role)—began to simplify and popularize not only the French tradition that was in his blood but the cuisines of other countries. (I daresay, though I can't prove, that Franey was the first French chef to publicly endorse the use of then-exotic and non-French ingredients like soy sauce and chili powder.)

Things have progressed from there. The '80s saw the addition of recipes by America's first superstar chefs: Jacques Pépin, Alice Waters, Michael Romano and Jasper White, to name a few (they're all represented here). The next two decades added Eric Ripert, Daniel Boulud, Jean-Georges Vongerichten, Rick Bayless and more (they're all here, too). All of these chefs have had their work understood and codified by top food writers, many of whom remain regular *Times* contributors: Florence Fabricant, Molly O'Neill, Amanda Hesser, and dozens of others.

The result is a stunning collection of recipes, including some of my favorites: Craig's venerable Bluefish Cooked in Foil (an August dish if ever there was one); Alfred Portale's classic Tuna Burgers; Grill-Roasted Cornish Hens from John Willoughby and Chris Schlesinger; Julie Sahni's Tandoori Chicken; and Daniel Boulud's trusty Hanger Steak. The desserts are equally appealing: try, for example, Tom Colicchio's Roasted Summer Fruit, Pierre Hermé's Bittersweet Chocolate Sorbet, or my own Freeform Fruit Tart.

The work of these luminaries has been appreciated, understood and brilliantly organized by Linda Amster and Michael Flamini. The unprecedented Recipe Planner chart (see page 237) will allow you to plan your meals with ease. Even the chapter structure is logical (I think the slightly sad-sounding "Back to the City" is ultra-smart).

This combination of great material and great organization is rare, so enjoy it.

ABOUT RECIPE CREDITS

Most of the recipes in this book are reprinted from articles in *The New York Times*. Below each recipe you will find the name of the person who wrote the article in which it appeared. Recipes that have only the byline credit were created by that *Times* writer.

Names of restaurateurs, chefs and cookbook writers who contributed to this book are given in the titles of their recipes and/or in the "adapted" line beneath. They are identified as they were at the time of the article—not necessarily as they are now, since some chefs are no longer at restaurants with which they were once associated, and some restaurants have closed. Similarly, the identities of people who contributed personal recipes are given as they appeared in the paper and may have changed since their original publication.

The only recipes that are not taken from *The Times* are those reprinted from *The Best of Craig Claiborne* and are credited to that book.

One final note: An arrow before a recipe title indicates a component that can be used in the preparation of other dishes.

RECIPES FOR
APPETIZERS AND CANAPÉS

FRICO'S BEAN PURÉE WITH ROSEMARY AND LEMON

Adapted from Frico Bar, New York City

This purée is very versatile: you can use it as a dip for breadsticks, pita or other bread, or for raw vegetables. Or spread it on sandwiches, or make it the centerpiece of a plate of lightly and simply cooked vegetables (carrots, green beans, turnips, asparagus, potatoes, or cauliflower). Or roll smoked salmon or thinly sliced cooked vegetables around a bit of the purée, and serve them as hors d'oeuvres.

2 cups cooked white beans, like cannellini, drained but moist (see Note)
1 to 2 cloves garlic, peeled
Salt and freshly ground black pepper
¼ cup plus 1 tablespoon extra virgin olive oil
2 teaspoons minced fresh rosemary
Grated rind of 2 lemons

1. Put the beans in the container of a food processor with 1 clove of garlic and a healthy pinch of salt. Turn the machine on, and add the ½ cup olive oil in a steady stream through the feed tube; process until the mixture is smooth. Taste, and add more garlic if you like; then purée the mixture again.

2. Place the mixture in a bowl, and use a wooden spoon to beat in the rosemary, lemon zest and the remaining tablespoon of olive oil. Taste, and add more salt and pepper as needed. Use immediately, or refrigerate for as long as 3 days.

Yield: 2 cups

Time: 10 minutes if using canned beans

Note: This purée can be made in about 10 minutes with canned beans. Use almost two full 15-ounce cans, drained. But, like most bean dishes, the purée is best made with freshly cooked dried beans. For dried beans: cook the beans in enough unsalted water to cover them (presoaking is unnecessary), with a couple of bay leaves, until very tender. Cooked beans can be successfully frozen in their water for later use.

Mark Bittman

RICOTTA WITH GARLICKY TOMATO-BASIL SPREAD

1 (6-ounce) jar sun-dried tomatoes packed in olive oil
4 medium tomatoes, seeded and chopped coarsely
2 cloves garlic, skinned (green part removed)
1 cup loosely packed fresh basil or flat-leaf parsley leaves
Coarse salt and freshly ground pepper
2 pounds ricotta cheese
Sprig of basil or parsley to garnish

1. Combine the sun-dried tomatoes, fresh tomatoes, garlic and basil in a food processor. Blend to a smooth purée and season to taste.

2. Place the ricotta in a mound on a large round plate. Spoon the tomato mixture around the edge. Garnish the cheese with a sprig of basil.

Yield: About 5 cups

Time: 20 minutes

Moira Hodgson

LE BERNARDIN'S FRESH AND SMOKED SALMON SPREAD

Adapted from *Le Bernardin Cookbook: Four-Star Simplicity*

1 bottle dry white wine
2 tablespoons chopped shallots
1 teaspoon fine sea salt, plus more to taste
2 pounds fresh salmon fillet, fat trimmed,
    cut in 1-inch cubes
6 ounces smoked salmon, fat trimmed,
    cut into tiny dice
2 tablespoons thinly sliced fresh chives
1/3 cup fresh lemon juice
1 cup mayonnaise, homemade or prepared
1/4 teaspoon freshly ground white pepper
Toasted baguette slices, for serving

1. Place the wine, shallots and 1 teaspoon of the salt in a large saucepan and bring to a boil. Add the fresh salmon and poach for 40 seconds. Drain in a sieve and run cold water over the fish just to stop the cooking. Drain well and refrigerate until cold, at least 1½ hours. Discard the poaching liquid.

2. Place the smoked salmon in a large bowl and stir in the chives. Add the poached salmon and, using the side of a wooden spoon, shred the salmon as you mix. Stir in the lemon juice, mayonnaise and white pepper. Add sea salt to taste.

3. Refrigerate up to 6 hours, then serve with toasted baguettes.

Yield: 4 cups (8 to 12 servings)

Time: 20 minutes, plus 1½ hours refrigeration, plus up to 6 hours additional refrigeration

Florence Fabricant

TUNA TAPENADE

Adapted from *A Can of Tuna*

Tapenade may be stored, covered, in the refrigerator for up to a week, but should be allowed to warm to room temperature before serving.

2 cloves garlic, peeled
4 anchovy fillets
2 tablespoons capers, drained
3 tablespoons extra virgin olive oil
2 teaspoons Dijon mustard
1½ teaspoons fresh thyme, chopped, or
    ½ teaspoon dried
1 tablespoon Cognac or good-quality brandy
1 cup pitted, oil-cured black olives (about 40)
1 (6-ounce) can chunk light tuna packed in
    water or olive oil

1. With the motor of a food processor running, drop the garlic down the feed tube and purée. Stop the machine, remove the top and scrape down the sides of the bowl. Add the anchovies and capers. Purée, and scrape down the sides of the bowl again.

2. Add the oil, mustard, thyme, Cognac and half the olives. Purée again. Add the remaining olives and tuna, and pulse until the mixture is well combined but still slightly chunky. Spread on baguettes or crackers, or use as a vegetable dip.

Yield: About 1 cup

Time: About 20 minutes

Sam Gugino

Nueva York Clam Dip

NUEVA YORK
CLAM DIP

A garlicky clam dip, studded with bacon and spiced with cilantro and a chipotle pepper, that complements tostada chips, celery, jicama or other crudités.

1 (12-ounce bottle) light lager beer
18 littleneck clams, scrubbed
4 slices bacon, chopped
3 tablespoons minced onion
2 cloves garlic, minced
8 ounces cream cheese, at room temperature
3 tablespoons Mexican crema or sour cream
3 tablespoons chopped fresh cilantro
1 chipotle pepper in adobo sauce
   (with clinging sauce), minced
Juice of ½ lime
Several dashes habanero hot sauce or
   Tabasco sauce
½ red bell pepper, finely diced
3 scallions, thinly sliced

1. Pour the beer into a wide saucepan large enough to hold clams in one layer. Place over high heat and bring to a boil. Add the clams, cover and cook until the clams open, 3 to 5 minutes.

2. Using a slotted spoon, transfer the clams to a bowl, discarding any unopened clams. Reserve 2 tablespoons of the cooking liquid and discard the remainder. When the clams are cool, remove them from their shells and mince.

3. In a large skillet over medium heat, fry the bacon until crisp; transfer to paper towels to drain. Add the onion and garlic to the skillet and sauté until the garlic is golden and the onions are softened, about 1 minute.

4. In a medium bowl, whisk together the cream cheese and crema or sour cream. Add the reserved clam cooking liquid, bacon, onions and garlic, clams, cilantro, chipotle pepper, lime juice and hot sauce.

Stir to combine. Garnish with the red bell pepper and scallions. If desired, serve with potato or tostada chips, or assorted dipping vegetables like cherry tomatoes, celery and jicama.

Yield: About 2 cups (8 servings)

Time: 30 minutes

Julie Powell

PIERRE FRANEY'S LEMONY CHICKPEA AND TUNA SPREAD

1 (15-ounce) can of chickpeas, drained
⅓ cup sesame paste (tahini), stirred well
1 clove garlic, peeled
2 scallions, chopped
¼ cup water
½ teaspoon sesame oil
1 teaspoon ground cumin
¼ cup chopped fresh cilantro
⅓ cup canned water-packed tuna, drained
2 tablespoons fresh lemon juice
Tabasco to taste
Salt and freshly ground black pepper to taste

Combine all ingredients in the bowl of a food processor. Purée to a coarse texture. Cover and keep cool. Serve on croutons, crackers or bread.

Yield: About 2 cups

Time: 10 minutes

Pierre Franey

BLUE SMOKE'S DEVILED EGGS

Adapted from Kenny Callaghan

10 large eggs
1 teaspoon champagne vinegar
½ teaspoon dry mustard, preferably Colman's
2 teaspoons Dijon mustard
¼ teaspoon cayenne pepper
7 tablespoons mayonnaise
¼ teaspoon curry powder (optional)
Salt and freshly ground black pepper

1. Place the eggs in a 4-quart saucepan, and cover with cold water. Place over high heat, and bring to a full boil; reduce the heat to low, and simmer 9 minutes. Remove the eggs from the water, and run under cold water until cool enough to handle. Gently crack the shells, and peel the eggs under cold running water.

2. Cut a small slice from both ends of the eggs so they will sit flat on a plate when halved. Halve the eggs crosswise, and gently remove the yolks. Set the cup-shaped whites aside.

3. In a small food processor combine the yolks, vinegar, dry mustard, Dijon mustard, cayenne and mayonnaise. Blend until smooth. Taste, and add curry powder if desired. Season to taste with salt and pepper.

4. Place the yolk mixture in a pastry bag with a star tip. Pipe the mixture into the egg-white cups in the shape of rosettes. Place in a covered container and refrigerate until ready to serve.

Yield: 5 to 6 servings

Time: 25 minutes

Alex Witchel

Blue Smoke's Deviled Eggs

FIG AND ANCHOVY CROSTINI

The sweet figs and the salty anchovies are an un-usual and winning combination.

6 fresh ripe figs, quartered

1 large garlic clove

3 oil-packed anchovies, well rinsed

1 baguette, sliced in ¼-inch-thick rounds

3 tablespoons olive oil

Freshly ground black pepper

1 tablespoon small capers, rinsed, or
    shavings of Parmesan cheese

1. Place the figs, garlic and anchovies in a food pro-cessor, and pulse until just blended.

2. Toast the bread slices on both sides, and brush with olive oil.

3. Spread about 1 tablespoon of fig mixture on each slice, and grind a bit of black pepper over the top. Garnish with a few capers or a shaving of Parme-san cheese. Serve immediately.

Yield: 6 servings

Time: 10 minutes

Erica De Mane

MARINATED WHITE ANCHOVIES WITH BASIL AND LEMON ZEST

½ pound marinated white anchovies
2 tablespoons chopped fresh basil
1 tablespoon good extra virgin olive oil
1 teaspoon grated lemon zest
Freshly ground black pepper

Combine all the ingredients in a bowl and toss well. Let rest for 10 minutes. Serve with toothpicks and cocktail napkins.

Yield: 6 to 8 servings

Time: 5 minutes, plus 10 minutes' resting

Melissa Clark

TARAMOSALATA CANAPÉS

1 seedless hothouse cucumber
1 cup taramosalata (Greek fish roe dip)
2 ounces salmon roe
Dill sprigs, for garnish

Slice the cucumber into ¼-inch-thick rounds. Spoon some taramosalata on top of each round, and top with salmon roe. Garnish with dill.

Yield: 8 servings

Time: 10 minutes

Melissa Clark

Opposite:
Clockwise from upper left: Prosciutto-Wrapped Peaches, Taramosalata Canapés, Marinated White Anchovies with Basil and Lemon Zest, Shrimp with Lime Pickle and Mint, Cheese Board of Aged Cantal and Young Pecorino and Romaine Hearts with Ripe Époisses.

MUSHROOM CEVICHE

Adapted from *The Art of South American Cooking*

1 pound small white button mushrooms
¼ cup extra virgin olive oil
1½ cups fresh lemon juice
2 cloves garlic, peeled and crushed
½-inch piece fresh ginger, minced
1 jalapeño pepper, seeded and finely chopped
Coarse salt
¼ cup finely chopped scallions
2 tablespoons chopped fresh dill
¼ cup finely minced red bell pepper

1. Place the mushrooms in a bowl and toss with the olive oil. In another bowl, combine the lemon juice, garlic, ginger, jalapeño pepper and salt to taste. Add the mushrooms, and marinate 30 minutes at room temperature.

2. Add the scallions and dill, and marinate for another 30 minutes. Check the seasonings, sprinkle with the minced red pepper and serve.

Yield: 6 to 8 servings

Time: 15 minutes, plus 1 hour marinating

Florence Fabricant

SHRIMP WITH LIME PICKLE AND MINT

1 pound cooked, shelled shrimp
3 tablespoons chopped lime pickle
    (available in Indian markets)
2 tablespoons chopped fresh mint

Combine all the ingredients in a bowl and toss well. Let rest for 20 minutes. Serve with toothpicks and cocktail napkins.

Yield: 8 servings

Time: 5 minutes, plus 20 minutes' resting

Melissa Clark

ROMAINE HEARTS AND RIPE ÉPOISSES OR CAMEMBERT

2 romaine lettuce hearts
1 box ripe, runny Époisses or Camembert cheese
(about 8.8 ounces)

Separate well-washed lettuce leaves, discarding the core and bottom. Leaving the cheese in its wooden box, use a spoon to scoop off the top orange crust. Instruct your guests to dip the lettuce leaves into the cheese.

Yield: 6 to 8 servings

Time: 5 minutes

Melissa Clark

CHEESE BOARD OF AGED CANTAL AND YOUNG PECORINO

1 pound aged Cantal or other firm, nutty cheese
1 pound semisoft pecorino Romano,
under 6 months old
Walnut oil or hazelnut oil, for drizzling
¼ cup chopped toasted walnuts
Aged balsamic vinegar, for drizzling

Cut the rind off the Cantal, if necessary. Cut both cheeses into bite-size chunks. Arrange them on a platter or board, keeping different cheeses on opposite sides of the platter. Drizzle the Cantal with the walnut oil or hazelnut oil, and sprinkle with the toasted walnuts. Drizzle the pecorino with balsamic vinegar. Serve with toothpicks.

Yield: 8 servings

Time: 5 minutes

Melissa Clark

PROSCIUTTO-WRAPPED PEACHES

4 ripe peaches
¼ pound prosciutto

Halve and pit the peaches. Cut the halves lengthwise into thirds; you should have 24 wedges. Tear the prosciutto into 24 pieces (lengthwise is best) and wrap each slice around a peach wedge.

Yield: 8 servings

Time: 10 minutes

Melissa Clark

LA CARAVELLE'S CITRUS GRAVLAX

Adapted from Cyril Renaud

2 cups salt
2 cups sugar
Grated zest of 2 oranges, 2 lemons,
2 limes and 2 grapefruit
2 tablespoons juniper berries
1 tablespoon cracked coriander seeds
1 bunch dill, stems and all, roughly chopped
2 tablespoons gin
1 (2- to 3-pound) fillet of salmon, pinbones
removed

1. Mix together the salt, sugar, zests, juniper, coriander, dill and gin. Place the salmon, skin side down, on a large sheet of plastic wrap. Cover the flesh side of the salmon with the salt mixture, making sure to coat it completely.

2. Wrap the fish well in the plastic wrap and refrigerate for 12 to 24 hours.

3. Unwrap the salmon, and rinse off the cure. Dry the fish, then slice on the bias. Serve plain or with

lemon wedges, crème fraîche, sour cream or light vinaigrette.

Yield: At least 12 servings

Time: 30 minutes, plus refrigeration for 12 to 24 hours

Note: The longer the gravlax sits, the drier and stronger flavored it will become. If you are planning to serve the gravlax unsauced, allow it to ripen in the refrigerator for 24 hours.

Mark Bittman

SMOKED TROUT CANAPÉS WITH LEMON-CHIVE SAUCE

A quick and addictive canapé of smoked trout on toasted baguette, topped with dollops of an easy-to-make lemon-chive crème fraîche. You can also serve the trout and sauce on a bed of fresh greens as an appetizer course.

2 medium smoked trout
¼ cup mayonnaise
¼ cup sour cream
¼ cup crème fraîche
Finely grated zest of 2 lemons
2 teaspoons lemon juice
1½ teaspoons snipped fresh chives
2 tablespoons minced fresh dill
1 baguette, sliced

1. Cut the head and tail from the trout. Peel back the skin and, using a fork, gently lift the meat from the bones. Pick over the fillets for any remaining bones.

2. In small bowl, combine the mayonnaise, sour cream, crème fraîche, lemon zest, lemon juice, chives and dill. Mix well.

3. Place a piece of trout on a slice of baguette, and top with a dollop of sauce. Repeat with remaining trout, and arrange on a platter.

Yield: 10 to 12 hors d'oeuvre servings on baguette slices, or 2 to 4 appetizer servings on greens

Time: 20 minutes

Celia Barbour

SCANDINAVIAN SHRIMP

A festive hors d'oeuvre for a cocktail party, these shrimp are also a treat when served, along with the marinated onions, as either an appetizer or heaped on greens as the centerpiece of an elegant salad. The shrimp are so flavorful that they do not need any sauce.

For the Shrimp
½ cup celery tops
¼ cup mixed pickling spice
1 to 3 tablespoons salt (the more salt, the brinier the water)
2 to 2½ pounds large fresh shrimp in the shell
2 cups mild onions, sliced horizontally into ¼-inch-thick rings
7 to 8 whole bay leaves

For the Marinade
1½ cups salad oil (not olive oil)
¼ cup white vinegar
1½ teaspoons salt
2½ teaspoons celery seed
3 tablespoons bottled capers, preferably small, and juice
2 dashes Tabasco sauce, or more to taste

1. Bring 3 quarts of cold water to a boil. Add the celery tops, pickling spice and salt and bring back to boil. Add the shrimp and cook until all the shrimp

turn pink, about 5 minutes. Do not overcook. Drain the shrimp in a colander, running cold water over them to stop the cooking. Ignore the celery and pickling spices that stick to the shrimp; they will be discarded with the shells when you peel the shrimp.

2. Prepare the marinade: Combine the salad oil, vinegar, salt, celery seed, capers with caper juice and Tabasco. Stir well.

3. Shell the shrimp and, if desired, devein. Place a layer of onion in a large bowl, then a layer of shrimp, then a bay leaf and repeat the layers until all the ingredients are used. Stir the marinade again and pour it over the shrimp-onion layers. Cover with plastic wrap and refrigerate at least 24 hours. Serve with toothpicks as an hors d'oeurvre or with the marinated onions, if you like, as either an appetizer course or with greens and other ingredients of your choice in a salad.

Yield: 10 servings

Time: 1 hour preparation, 24 hours or more refrigeration

Note: To save time and effort, you might want to invest in a shrimp sheller, a gadget that simplifies this cumbersome job.

Craig Claiborne

ECUADOREAN SEVICHE "MARTINI"

Adapted from Bistro Latino, New York City

½ pound fresh tuna, cut in ½-inch cubes
½ pound sea or bay scallops, cut in ½-inch cubes
½ pound medium shrimp, shelled, deveined, and halved
Juice of 3 limes
Juice of 1 lemon
Juice of 1 orange
1 ripe Hass avocado, peeled and diced in ½-inch cubes
⅓ cup finely diced red onion
1 cup peeled, finely diced, seeded tomatoes
1 cup tomato juice
½ cup ketchup
½ teaspoon Tabasco sauce or to taste
Salt and freshly ground black pepper to taste
⅓ cup coarsely chopped fresh cilantro leaves

1. Combine the tuna, scallops and shrimp in a bowl. Fold in the citrus juices. Cover and refrigerate for 12 hours.

2. Just before serving, drain off the liquid from the seafood and discard it. Place the seafood in a mixing bowl, and add the remaining ingredients.

3. If desired, serve in martini glasses that have been chilled.

Yield: 6 servings

Time: 45 minutes, plus 12 hours' marinating

Florence Fabricant

FLORENCE FABRICANT'S SOUFFLÉED CRABMEAT CANAPÉS

Florence Fabricant: "This recipe can do double duty, either as a delicious open-face, knife-and-fork sandwich at lunch, or cut in small pieces and served as hors d'oeuvres. It's my adaptation of the simple mixture of crabmeat and mayonnaise, lightened with beaten egg whites and baked, that we could not stop eating many years ago at the home of a cousin in California. She used canned crabmeat and fortunately had plenty of it on hand since we polished off dozens of these delicious bites. I use fresh, pasteurized crabmeat for this recipe; the costly jumbo lump variety is not necessary."

6 slices country bread, ½ inch thick
2 large eggs, separated
Juice of ½ lemon
½ teaspoon salt
3 ½ tablespoons pesto, homemade or bought
6 tablespoons extra virgin olive oil
¾ pound lump crabmeat
Paprika

1. Preheat the oven to 425 degrees. Place the rack in the center of the oven. Lightly toast the bread and place on a foil-lined baking sheet.

2. Place the egg yolks, 1 tablespoon lemon juice, the salt and ½ tablespoon pesto in the food processor or a bowl. While processing or whisking constantly, slowly drizzle in the olive oil; continue mixing until thickened to a mayonnaise. Transfer to a clean bowl and mix in the crabmeat. Stir in the remaining lemon juice.

4. In another bowl, beat the egg whites until they hold peaks. Fold the egg whites into the crabmeat mixture.

5. Spread the toast with the remaining pesto and top each slice with the crabmeat mixture, covering it completely. Lightly dust with paprika. Bake 15 minutes, or until puffed and browned. Cut each slice in half and serve for lunch or as a first course, or cut each slice in 6 pieces and pass as hors d'oeuvres.

Yield: 12 large canapés, or 36 small hors d'oeuvres
Time: 35 minutes

Florence Fabricant

OYSTER PIGS IN BLANKETS

Adapted from *The Big Oyster*

16 thin slices bacon (1 pound)
16 plump shucked oysters
Lemon wedges, for serving

1. Place a strip of bacon on a work surface. Place an oyster in the middle, wrap the bacon around the oyster and secure with a toothpick. Repeat with the remaining oysters and bacon.

2. Place a large skillet over medium heat. Fry the bacon-wrapped oysters until the bacon is golden brown, turning them once. Drain briefly, then serve with the lemon wedges.

Yield: 16 pieces
Time: 20 minutes

Florence Fabricant

RHODE ISLAND STUFFIES

Adapted from The New England Clam Shack Cookbook

These clams are ideal fare for an informal party. They can be prepared ahead, then refrigerated or frozen, with a final baking just before serving.

3 tablespoons extra virgin olive oil

10 to 12 slices bacon, minced

8 cloves garlic, minced

1 cup finely chopped celery

1 cup finely chopped onion

2 quarts shucked hardshell clams with juice, chopped

½ cup chopped fresh parsley

¼ cup lemon juice

2 tablespoons hot pepper sauce

2 tablespoons Worcestershire sauce

½ cup (1 stick) unsalted butter, cut in 10 slices

6 to 8 cups panko (Japanese bread crumbs)

24 to 30 clean quahog shells (3 to 4 inches across) or 48 cherrystone clam shells

Paprika, for dusting

Lemon wedges, for serving

1. Heat the oil in a very large skillet or saute pan. Add the bacon, garlic, celery and onion and cook over medium heat, stirring frequently, until the bacon renders its fat and the vegetables soften, 10 to 15 minutes. Spoon off excess fat. Add the clams, parsley, lemon juice, hot pepper sauce and Worcestershire sauce. Increase the heat to high, and cook until the mixture just starts to simmer. Reduce the heat to low.

2. Add the butter and 6 cups of the crumbs. Cook gently, stirring and adding more crumbs as needed to absorb most of the liquid. The mixture should hold its shape but not be dry. Remove from heat and pack into the shells, filling them generously. Refrigerate the stuffed clams until 30 minutes

before serving. The stuffed clams can be frozen before baking.

3. Preheat the oven to 425 degrees. Place the clams on a baking sheet and bake until the filling is heated through and lightly browned, 25 to 30 minutes, or about 45 minutes if frozen. If the clams are not browned enough they can be finished briefly under a broiler. Dust with paprika and serve with lemon wedges.

Yield: 12 to 24 servings

Time: 1 hour, plus 25 to 45 minutes in the oven

Florence Fabricant

MARK BITTMAN'S POLPETTI

Adapted from The Best Recipes in the World

These little meatballs can be mixed a day or so in advance and refrigerated, then sautéed at the last minute. They can be baked, too, on a rimmed sheet at 450 degrees for about 20 minutes, but they won't be as crisp. For that matter, they can be cooked in advance and reheated, or served warm. If you make them tiny, they're perfect toothpick food.

½ pound each ground veal and pork, or any combination of ground meats

1 egg

¼ cup freshly grated Parmesan cheese

¼ cup chopped fresh parsley leaves

¼ cup minced onion

Salt and pepper

2 tablespoons extra virgin olive oil

Flour for dredging

1. Combine the meat in a bowl with the egg, cheese, parsley, onion and salt and pepper to taste. Mix well. Form into balls of any size; tiny ones (½ inch in diameter) are nice but take longer.

2. Put the oil in a large skillet. Turn the heat to medium. One by one, dredge the meatballs in flour and add them to the oil. Cook, turning as necessary, until nicely browned all over, 10 to 15 minutes. Serve hot or at room temperature.

Yield: 6 to 8 servings

Time: 30 minutes

Mark Bittman

MARK BITTMAN'S GOUGÈRES

Adapted from The Best Recipes in the World

These rich but airy cheese morsels are easy to prepare and can be made up to an hour or so in advance, then served hot, warm or at room temperature. No wonder that they are the pre-amuse-bouche of choice at many high-end restaurants and are a favorite on the party circuit.

> 4 tablespoons (½ stick) butter
> ½ teaspoon salt
> 1½ cups (about 7 ounces) all-purpose flour
> 3 eggs
> 1 cup freshly grated Emmenthal, Gruyère, Cantal or Cheddar cheese
> 1 cup freshly grated Parmesan or other hard cheese

1. Lightly grease two baking sheets and preheat the oven to 425 degrees.

2. In a medium saucepan, combine 1 cup water, the butter and salt. Turn the heat to medium-high and bring to a boil. Cook, stirring, until the butter melts. Add the flour all at once and cook, stirring constantly, until the dough holds together in a ball, 5 minutes or less. The dough will get stiffer as you stir; keep stirring until the dough is smooth. Transfer the batter to a large mixing bowl or the workbowl of a standing mixer.

3. Add the eggs one at a time, beating hard after each addition (this is a little bit of work; a hand mixer will probably not be powerful enough). Stop beating when the mixture is glossy. Stir in the cheeses.

4. Drop teaspoonfuls onto the baking sheets and bake until puffed and lightly browned, 10 to 15 minutes. Serve hot, warm or at room temperature.

Yield: 30 to 40 gougères

Time: About 30 minutes

Mark Bittman

MARK BITTMAN'S ASIAN CORN FRITTERS

Adapted from The Best Recipes in the World

These Asian-style corn fritters can be made a few minutes ahead and kept hot in a low oven, or served warm. Like all fried food, they're best about a minute out of the oil, drained and sprinkled with salt. Make them for people with whom you are comfortable enough to stand around in the kitchen while you cook—informal entertaining at its best.

> 2 fresh Anaheim or poblano chilies
> 1 serrano, or 1 or 2 Thai (bird) chilies, seeded and minced, or 1 teaspoon red pepper flakes, or to taste
> 3 cups corn from cob (5 or 6 ears), or use frozen
> 1 egg
> ½ cup flour
> ½ teaspoon ground coriander
> 1 teaspoon ground cumin
> ½ cup fresh cilantro leaves
> Salt and pepper to taste
> Corn, grapeseed, canola or other neutral oil, as needed

1. Roast the whole, fresh chilies in a dry skillet, broiler or on a grill until lightly charred all over. Cool, then peel, stem and seed. Combine in the work bowl of a food processor with the serrano or Thai chilies and 2 cups of corn; process until quite smooth, about 1 minute, stopping the machine to scrape down the sides, if necessary.

2. In a bowl, combine the purée with the remaining corn kernels, egg, flour, spices, cilantro and salt and pepper. The mixture should hold together when you clump it; if it does not, add a little more flour.

3. Put at least 2 inches of oil in a deep saucepan or skillet and turn the heat to medium-high; bring to 350 degrees (a pinch of flour will sizzle). Use a spoon or your hands to form the batter into fritters the size of golf balls or smaller; gently slide them into the oil and fry until golden brown, turning once, about 4 minutes. Serve immediately.

Yield: 6 to 8 servings

Time: 30 minutes

Mark Bittman

MARK BITTMAN'S GRILLED CHICKEN WINGS, ASIAN-STYLE

Adapted from *The Best Recipes in the World*

These are the kind of chicken wings served as bar food in much of Japan—lightly seasoned but not really sauced. They are better served warm or at room temperature than hot, because as finger food they can be tricky to handle when they're at a finger-burning temperature. So roast them in advance and keep them warm, or reheat them gently.

3 tablespoons soy sauce
2 tablespoons sake
2 tablespoons mirin or honey
3 scallions, trimmed and roughly chopped
2 garlic cloves, peeled and chopped
1 inch-long piece fresh ginger, peeled and chopped
3 pounds chicken wings, wing tips removed, drumettes and wings separated

1. In a large baking dish, mix together everything but the chicken wings. Add the wings and turn to coat, then cover with plastic wrap and refrigerate for at least 2 hours, or as long as overnight. Turn the wings occasionally in the marinade.

2. Start a charcoal or wood fire or preheat a gas grill or broiler; the fire should be only moderately hot and the rack should be about 6 inches from the heat source. If you are going to broil the wings, line the dish with foil.

3. Remove the wings from the marinade and put on a grill or in a broiler. Cook for about 10 minutes on each side, remove from heat and serve within 20 minutes.

Yield: 6 to 8 servings

Time: 40 minutes, plus at least 2 hours' marinating

Mark Bittman

JAMES O'SHEA'S SPICY CHICKEN WINGS

Adapted from the West Street Grill, Litchfield, CT

1 medium onion, coarsely chopped
Juice of 1 lemon
1-inch piece of fresh ginger, grated
3 tablespoons sun-dried tomato paste
1½ tablespoons medium-hot curry powder
½ teaspoon red pepper flakes (or to taste)

Continued

Opposite:
Finger food for a crowd: peppery Asian corn fritters, cheese gougères and grilled wings

1 to 2 tablespoons peanut or vegetable oil

5 pounds chicken wings, preferably small and organic, wing tips removed, drumettes and wings separated

1. Combine all the ingredients except for the chicken in a food processor and purée to a paste. Coat the wings thoroughly with the mixture and allow them to marinate in the refrigerator for 2 to 3 hours (overnight is even better). Remove the wings from the refrigerator several hours before cooking and, if desired, toss them in additional paste.

2. Preheat a broiler or grill. If you are going to broil the wings, line the pan with foil. Place the chicken wings on a rack 6 inches from the heat source and cook over moderate heat until they are done, about 20 minutes, turning occasionally. Check to make sure they are thoroughly cooked.

3. Remove the wings from the grill and arrange them single file without overlapping, so that they remain crisp. Serve within 20 minutes. These wings are very flavorful by themselves. But if you like, serve them with chutneys, chili sauces, freshly cut limes and/or various salted nuts. Or make an intense dark green dip by mixing all-natural Greek yogurt with cilantro paste to taste and, for even more kick, 1 or 2 tablespoons of mango paste (see Sources, page 259).

Yield: 18 to 26 pieces, depending on the size of the wings

Total time: 20 minutes hands-on, 2 to 3 hours or overnight for marinating

Note: This dish also may be prepared with a 3½-pound chicken cut into eight pieces, with the skin removed (except from the wings) or with boneless, skinless chicken breasts. You may wish to make a double batch of the paste—either to slather on the wings before grilling or to reserve for another meal. It freezes well and also can be refrigerated for up to 2 weeks.

Moira Hodgson

NIGELLA LAWSON'S CHICKEN SATAY

4 skinless, boneless chicken breast halves

½ teaspoon ground cinnamon

½ teaspoon ground turmeric

1 teaspoon ground cumin

1 teaspoon ground coriander

1 teaspoon sugar

2 tablespoons salted, roasted peanuts

¼ cup peanut oil

6 scallions, trimmed

Zest of 1 lemon, removed in strips

1. Cut the chicken breast halves lengthwise into long strips, about 5 from each breast half. Place in a freezer storage bag and set aside.

2. In a food processor, combine all the remaining ingredients. Process to make a smooth paste. Add to the bag of chicken, seal the bag, and mix well so that the chicken is well coated. Refrigerate for at least 2 hours, preferably overnight.

3. About an hour before cooking, soak 10 bamboo skewers in water. Preheat a grill or broiler. Thread two long strips of chicken onto each skewer. Grill or broil until lightly browned and crisp on the edges.

Yield: 10 skewers

Time: About 25 minutes, plus 2 hours' marinating

Nigella Lawson

➤ VONG'S PEANUT SAUCE

Adapted from Vong, New York City

Peanut sauce is rich and sweet, as well as spicy. It stands up well to beef and pork, for which it can be used as a sauce or a dip, or as a dip for raw vegetables or shellfish. You can also swirl it into a puréed vegetable soup, or use it as a base for a marinade that will sweeten and add a hint of spice to lamb, pork, grilled swordfish and chicken—even to vegetables.

½ cup shelled, unsalted, roasted
  peanuts
1 tablespoon peanut oil
2 teaspoons red curry paste
1 teaspoon sugar
1 cup unsweetened coconut milk
2 teaspoons soy sauce
1 tablespoon fresh lime juice

1. Grind the peanuts in a food processor. Set aside.

2. Heat the oil in a medium saucepan over low heat. Add the curry paste and stir for about 1 minute. Whisk in the sugar, coconut milk and peanuts.

3. Bring to a boil, whisking constantly. Remove from the heat and whisk in the soy sauce and lime juice. Serve warm.

Yield: 1½ cups

Time: 10 minutes

Molly O'Neill

MOLLY O'NEILL'S BEEF OR PORK SATAY

¼ cup white wine
¼ cup nuoc mam (Vietnamese fish sauce)
1 tablespoon peanut oil
1 tablespoon fresh lime juice
2 large cloves garlic, peeled and chopped
1 pound boneless pork loin or flank steak
About 3 dozen bamboo skewers, soaked in
  water
Peanut Sauce (recipe above)

1. Combine the white wine, nuoc mam, peanut oil, lime juice and garlic and put in a nonreactive shallow dish.

2. If using pork, trim off any excess fat, and cut into thin strips about 3 inches long and ¾ inch wide. If using flank steak, cut across the grain into thin strips.

3. Place the meat in the dish and toss with the marinade. Refrigerate for 1 to 2 hours.

4. Preheat a grill or broiler. Thread each piece of meat onto a skewer, making an S pattern. Grill or broil, turning the skewers once, until the pork is just cooked through, or until the beef is browned but still pink inside. Place on a platter and serve hot with peanut sauce for dipping (see above).

Yield: About 3 dozen skewers

Time: 30 minutes plus 1 to 2 hours' refrigeration

Molly O'Neill

MANGO-JICAMA GUACAMOLE

Adapted from Patricio Sandoval of Mercadito, New York City

2 large avocados
½ cup Spanish onion, diced
1 cup tomatoes, diced
1 tablespoon serrano chilies, minced
1 tablespoon roughly chopped fresh cilantro
1 teaspoon salt
1 tablespoon lime juice
2 tablespoons adobo sauce from canned
  chipotles (save the peppers for another use)
½ cup jicama, diced
½ cup mango, diced

1. Slice the avocados in half, remove the pits and scoop out the flesh into a large bowl. Mash, add the rest of the ingredients and stir to combine.

2. Serve with tortilla chips.

Yield: About 3½ cups

Time: 10 minutes

Dana Bowen

DIANA KENNEDY'S CLASSIC GUACAMOLE

Adapted from *My Mexican Kitchen*

Diana Kennedy, the cookbook author who has spent 40-plus years unraveling the mysteries of Mexican cuisine, says the word *guacamole* stems from the Aztec *ahuacamulli,* or avocado mash. She favors a less-is-more guacamole, to draw attention to the avocados which, when ripe, "are really so delicious in their own right." The most popular avocado for guacamole is Hass, a buttery, thin-skinned California native.

3 tablespoons white onion, finely chopped, plus another tablespoon for garnish

4 serrano chilies (seeds and all), finely chopped or to taste

3 tablespoons roughly chopped fresh cilantro, plus another tablespoon for garnish

Sea salt

3 avocados

½ cup tomatoes, finely chopped, plus ¼ cup tomato for garnish

1. Put the onion, chilies, cilantro and salt to taste into a molcajete (lava stone mortar), and crush to

a paste. Or purée in a blender and transfer to a mixing bowl.

2. Cut the avocados in half, and without peeling, remove the pit, and squeeze out the flesh. Mash the avocado into the onion-serrano base and mix well. Stir in the ½ cup of tomatoes.

3. Sprinkle the surface with the garnishes: ¼ cup chopped tomato, finely chopped onion and a tablespoon of finely chopped cilantro. Serve immediately.

Yield: about 2½ cups

Time: 10 minutes

Dana Bowen

NINFA'S CREAMY GUACAMOLE

Not a guacamole for purists, but a tasty, creamier version of the avocado dip.

> 3 medium tomatoes (green or red),
>   coarsely chopped
> 4 large tomatillos, husks removed,
>   coarsely chopped
> 2 fresh jalapeño peppers, stems removed
>   and coarsely chopped
> 3 cloves garlic
> 3 avocados
> 1½ cups sour cream
> 1 tablespoon fresh cilantro, minced
> 1 teaspoon salt

1. In a medium saucepan, bring the tomatoes, tomatillos, jalapeños, garlic, and 2 cups water to a boil. Reduce the heat and simmer until the tomatillos are soft, about 10 minutes. Drain the mixture, and reserve 1 cup of the cooking liquid.

2. Slice the avocados in half, remove the pits, and scoop out the flesh into a blender. Add the tomatillo mixture, sour cream, cilantro, and salt. Purée until smooth. If the mixture is too thick, slowly add a little of the reserved cooking liquid.

3. Transfer to a bowl and serve with tortilla chips or warmed tortillas.

Yield: about 5 cups

Time: 25 minutes

Dana Bowen

NIGELLA LAWSON'S PARMESAN DISKS

These crunchy cheese disks couldn't be simpler to make and are perfect for those times when you'd like to accessorize a soup or a salad or, perhaps, just savor a snack.

8 tablespoons freshly grated Parmesan cheese

1. Preheat the oven to 425 degrees. Use a tablespoon to make 8 evenly spaced mounds of cheese on a nonstick baking sheet. Pat each mound into a flat cohesive disk.

2. Place the baking sheet in the oven until the cheese has melted and is just beginning to brown, 3 or 4 minutes. Remove from oven and allow to sit for 1 minute, then transfer to paper towels until cooled and crunchy.

Yield: 8 disks

Time: 10 minutes

Nigella Lawson

Opposite:
Diana Kennedy's Classic Guacamole

RECIPES FOR
COCKTAILS

LA CARAVELLE'S KIR ROYALE 38

Adapted from La Caravelle, New York City

1 teaspoon Cognac
1 teaspoon Grand Marnier
6 to 8 ounces champagne
½ orange slice

Pour the Cognac and Grand Marnier into the bottom of a champagne flute. Fill the glass with champagne, and garnish with the orange slice.

Yield: 1 aperitif

Time: 5 minutes

William Grimes

THE RED CAR'S FRAGOLA

Adapted from Red Car, New York City

½ cup plus 2 tablespoons sliced ripe, sweet
    strawberries
1 teaspoon sugar, or more to taste
22 ounces, plus 2 tablespoons Prosecco, chilled

1. In a bowl, combine the strawberries with sugar and 2 tablespoons Prosecco. Using a fork, crush the strawberries to a rough pulp. Taste. If the strawberries are not sweet, add a touch more sugar; the mixture should not be too sweet. Place in the refrigerator for 2 hours.

2. Divide the strawberry mixture among four champagne glasses. Pour the chilled Prosecco on top. Serve.

Yield: 4 cocktails

Time: 5 minutes, plus 2 hours' macerating

Amanda Hesser

GIN AND TONIC BY THE PITCHER

Adapted from Andrea Cecchini

5 limes, at room temperature
16 ounces of gin
Cracked ice
1 liter tonic water, chilled

1. Knead 4 of the limes by rolling them firmly under the heel of your hand on a cutting board, to bring the citrus oil to the surface of the skin. Then halve and juice the limes. Slice the used rinds into thin strips and put them in a large pitcher.

2. Pour the gin over the rinds, and muddle for 2 minutes. Add the lime juice, and let stand for 5 minutes.

3. Fill the pitcher halfway with ice. Slowly add the tonic, pouring it gingerly, on a slant, down the side of the pitcher. Stir carefully, preferably with a glass wand, just to distribute the gin (you don't want to jostle the fizz out of the tonic). Pour into tall highball glasses that have been chilled in the freezer. Garnish with lime rounds cut from the remaining lime.

Yield: 4 servings

Time: 15 minutes

Note: Tanqueray is recommended for its punchy botanicals and authority; it is 94 proof to the more common 80, making it perfect for a G and T.

Toby Cecchini

HORSERADISH VODKA

Adapted from Dylan Prime, New York City

At Dylan Prime in TriBeCa, vodka is infused with fresh horseradish, celery seeds and whole black peppercorns. It is the foundation of what the bar calls a "Bloodless Mary," served in a martini glass garnished with a julienne of celery and rimmed with celery salt (see recipe, page 26). The first evocative whiff is followed by a rush of sinus-clearing heat.

> 2 ounces fresh horseradish root
> 1 (750-milliliter) bottle of vodka
> 1 tablespoon celery seed
> 2 tablespoons black peppercorns

1. Peel the horseradish and cut into fine shreds with a vegetable peeler. Uncap the vodka, pour off 1 cup and reserve. Using a funnel, add the celery seeds and peppercorns to the bottle. Add the horseradish, then top off the bottle with the reserved vodka. Let stand at room temperature for 24 hours.

2. Strain the vodka through a fine sieve to remove the celery seeds and fine particles. Chill completely before serving.

Yield: 700 milliliters

Time: About 15 minutes, plus 24 hours

Matt Lee and Ted Lee

VODKA OR GIN GIMLET

Adapted from Fifty Seven Fifty Seven Bar at the Four Seasons Hotel, New York City

> 4 ounces vodka (or gin if you insist)
> ½ ounce fresh lime juice
> ½ ounce Rose's Lime Juice
> 1 thin lime wedge

Combine the liquid ingredients in a cocktail shaker with ice. Shake, and strain into a martini glass. Garnish with the lime wedge.

Yield: 1 serving

Time: 5 minutes

William L. Hamilton

THE MARTINI

Adapted from John Conti

> 3 ounces of gin
> ½ ounce of dry vermouth
> Green olive

1. Chill a 7-ounce martini glass by filling it with ice and water. Fill a professional bartender's glass, or a tall 16-ounce glass, two-thirds full with ice.

2. Add the gin and vermouth to the bartender's glass. Slide a long-necked spoon—preferably one that is bent slightly so that it will follow the sides of the glass—and twirl it gently, as opposed to agitating, keeping the spoon close to the side of the glass as you swirl the ice.

3. Stir until the glass frosts, about 20 seconds. Empty the ice water from the martini glass. Strain the contents of the bartender's glass into it, using a circular motion so that the liquid doesn't splash. Garnish with the olive.

Yield: 1 serving

Time: 5 minutes

William L. Hamilton

JAMES BOND MARTINI

Adapted from Merchants, New York City

1½ ounces Smirnoff vodka
1½ ounces Tanqueray gin
½ ounce Martini & Rossi extra-dry
  vermouth
½ ounce Lillet Blanc
Twist of lemon peel

1. Combine the vodka, gin, vermouth and Lillet in a cocktail shaker partly filled with ice. Shake briefly. Or stir briefly in a pitcher containing ice.

2. Strain into a chilled martini glass, and garnish with the lemon twist.

Yield: 1 serving

Time: 5 minutes

Florence Fabricant

SAKETINI

Adapted from Mirez, New York City

1 to 2 ounces Chung Ha Korean sake
  (other types of clear sake can be
  substituted)
4 to 5 ounces Tanqueray vodka
1 slice cucumber, unpeeled

1. Combine the sake and vodka in a cocktail shaker partly filled with ice. Shake briefly. Or stir briefly in a pitcher containing ice. Proportions of sake and vodka can be adjusted.

2. Strain into a chilled martini glass, and garnish with the cucumber.

Yield: 1 serving

Time: 5 minutes

Florence Fabricant

WATERMELON MARTINI

Adapted from the Cub Room, New York City

1 pound (about 3½ cups) watermelon cubes,
  seeded
4 ounces lemon vodka

1. Using a blender, purée the watermelon until smooth. Place a fine strainer over a bowl, and strain the watermelon purée; reserve the juice, and discard any remaining pulp.

2. In a metal cocktail shaker half filled with ice, combine the vodka and 1 cup watermelon juice. Shake well, and strain into two 7¼-ounce chilled martini glasses.

Yield: 2 drinks

Time: 10 minutes

Florence Fabricant

FLORIDIAN

Adapted from Asia de Cuba, New York City

2⅔ ounces orange vodka
1 ounce Cointreau or Triple Sec
4 splashes sour mix
2 splashes cranberry juice
2 twists of orange peel

1. In a metal cocktail shaker half filled with ice, combine the vodka, Cointreau, sour mix and cranberry juice.

2. Shake well, and strain into two martini glasses. Garnish each drink with a twist of orange peel.

Yield: 2 servings

Time: 5 minutes

Florence Fabricant

BLOODLESS MARY

Adapted from Dylan Prime, New York City

> Celery salt
> 2 ounces horseradish-infused vodka,
>   well chilled
> 1 celery stalk

Dip the rim of a martini glass in water, then in celery salt to coat. Add chilled vodka. Garnish with celery cut into a very fine julienne on a mandoline or with a vegetable peeler. Serve.

Yield: 1 cocktail

Time: 5 minutes

Matt Lee and Ted Lee

COYOTE CAFE'S BLOODY MARIAS

Adapted from Coyote Cafe, Santa Fe

> 3 serrano chilies
> 12 ounces gold tequila
> 1 bunch cilantro
> 46 ounces tomato juice
> 1 teaspoon salt
> 6 ounces freshly squeezed lime juice
> 1 lime, sliced

Finely chop the serranos and allow them to macerate in the tequila for 10 minutes. Finely chop the cilantro and mix all the ingredients in a cocktail shaker or pitcher with ice. Pour through a strainer into wine or martini glasses and garnish each with a slice of lime.

Yield: 12 cocktails

Time: 15 minutes

Robert Clark

JUNIPEROTIVO

Adapted from Monzu, New York City

> 4 large mint leaves
> ½ ounce simple syrup (see Note below)
> 1½ ounces Junipero, or other gin
> ½ ounce lime juice
> ¼ ounce pomegranate syrup

1. In a mixing glass, using a spoon, crush 2 mint leaves in the simple syrup, and add gin, lime juice and pomegranate syrup.

2. Pour into an ice-filled shaker. Shake well, and strain into a chilled cocktail glass. To garnish, float the 2 remaining mint leaves on the surface of the drink.

Yield: 1 aperitif

Time: 15 minutes

Note: To make simple syrup, in a small saucepan boil 1 cup water and 1 cup sugar, stirring occasionally until sugar is dissolved and liquid is clear, about 5 minutes. Let cool before using. Store refrigerated for up to a week.

William Grimes

'21' CLUB'S SOUTHSIDE

Adapted from '21' Club, New York City

4 ounces gin (or vodka, rum or bourbon)
3 ounces fresh lemon juice
4 teaspoons sugar, or to taste
Club soda, optional
4 sprigs fresh mint

Place the gin, lemon juice and sugar in a shaker half filled with ice cubes. Shake well and pour into a glass along with ice, or pour into a tall glass and top off with club soda. Garnish with mint.

Yield: 2 drinks

Time: 10 minutes

Florence Fabricant

GRAMERCY TAVERN'S KAFFIR LIME COCKTAIL

Adapted from Nick Mautone

15 kaffir lime leaves, plus more for serving
1½ cups honey
4 limes, halved
1 liter pure cactus tequila, such as Porfidio

1. Place the leaves in a large, sealable container. Pour 1 cup boiling water over them and steep 5 minutes. Add the honey. (Kaffir lime leaves are available at specialty markets, see Sources, page 259.)

2. Juice the limes; add the juice and skins to the kaffir mix. Add the tequila, seal the container and shake vigorously. Steep at least 3 days, occasionally shaking gently. (Mixture will keep indefinitely in a refrigerator.)

3. For each drink, fill a cocktail shaker with ice. Add ¼ cup tequila mixture and shake well. Fill a cocktail glass halfway with ice and strain the chilled tequila mixture into it. Float a kaffir lime leaf on top and serve.

Yield: About 1½ liters or 24 servings

Time: 5 minutes, plus 3 days' steeping

Melissa Clark

RAMOS GIN FIZZ

These are the ingredients of the New Orleans refresher, invented approximately 100 years ago.

1 cup crushed ice
1 egg white
3 ounces milk
1¼ ounces gin
1 tablespoon fresh lemon juice
½ tablespoon fresh lime juice
1 teaspoon superfine sugar
3 drops orange flower water (available at specialty food stores)

1. Place all the ingredients in a large cocktail shaker and shake vigorously for two and one-half to three minutes, mainly to break up the egg white, which produces the foam.

2. Strain the mixture into an 8-ounce highball glass and serve with a straw.

Yield: 1 drink

Time: 5 minutes

Howard Goldberg

TEQUILA SUNRISE

Apparently the tequila sunrise, a Mexican enlivener, first appeared during Prohibition.

> 3 ounces fresh orange juice
> 1½ ounces tequila
> ½ ounce fresh lime juice
> ½ ounce grenadine
> 1 cup crushed ice
> Slice of lime

1. Put all the ingredients except the ice and the slice of lime in a cocktail shaker and shake until well combined.

2. Place the ice in an 8-ounce highball glass and pour the drink over it. Garnish with the slice of lime.

Yield: 1 drink

Time: 5 minutes

Howard Goldberg

THE DAIQUIRI

Although the daiquiri was created in 1900 in Santiago de Cuba, a slightly enhanced version, served at the Floridita bar in Havana, was made famous by Ernest Hemingway. It consisted of the following recipe, to which one-quarter ounce of maraschino was added.

> 1 cup crushed ice
> Juice of ½ lime, freshly squeezed
> 1 teaspoon sugar
> 1½ ounces light rum

1. Place the ice, lime juice, and sugar in a large cocktail shaker and shake until the ingredients are cold.

2. Add the rum and shake until the sides of the shaker frost.

3. Strain into a 4½-ounce martini glass.

Yield: 1 drink

Time: 5 minutes

Howard Goldberg

POMEGRANATE DAIQUIRI

Adapted from Soho House, New York City

> 1 teaspoon pomegranate syrup or molasses
> 2 ounces Montecristo rum (or other dark rum)
> 2 ounces orange juice
> Pomegranate seeds, optional

Pour the ingredients into a shaker filled partly with ice, shake and pour the contents, unstrained, into a rocks glass. Garnish with pomegranate seeds, if desired.

Yield: 1 cocktail

Time: 5 minutes

John Hyland

MANGO MOJITO

Adapted from Son Cubano, New York City

For the Mojito

> 1 tablespoon mango purée (recipe follows)
> 1 tablespoon sugar
> ½ lime
> 4 fresh mint leaves
> 3 ounces light rum
> 1½ ounces mango rum (or substitute with
>   1 tablespoon mango purée and 1 ounce
>   light rum)
> 1 slice ripe mango, skin on, for garnish

For the Mango Purée

> 1 ripe mango, peeled and cut into small chunks
> 6 ounces canned or bottled mango juice

1. For the mango purée: combine the mango chunks and mango juice in a blender and purée.

2. In a shaker, combine 1 tablespoon purée with the sugar, lime and mint and mash with a muddler or wooden spoon. Add ice and the rums. Cover and shake vigorously. Strain into a chilled martini glass. Garnish with the mango slice.

Yield: 1 cocktail

Time: 5 minutes

John Hyland

CHERRY CAIPIRINHA

Adapted from Blackbird, New York City

1 lime, quartered, or more to taste

10 pitted cherries, preferably sour cherries, plus
    2 stemmed whole cherries, for garnish

2 ounces simple syrup (see Note, page 26)

4 ounces cachaça

1. Place the lime and pitted sour cherries in a mixing glass or cocktail shaker. Add the syrup and

muddle (lightly crush) the lime pieces and cherries. If using sweet cherries, add an additional lime. Add the cachaça and 1½ cups of cracked ice. Shake well.

2. Pour the contents into two Old-Fashioned glasses and serve each garnished with a cherry.

Yield: 2 drinks

Time: 10 minutes

Florence Fabricant

TI-PUNCH

Adapted from Brandy Library, New York City

4 ounces white rum, preferably La Favorite
1½ ounces fresh lime juice
1 ounce cane syrup or simple syrup (see Note, page 26)
2 lime wedges
Sparkling water or club soda, optional

Combine the rum, lime juice and syrup in a shaker, add ice, and stir. Pour, with the ice, into large wineglasses. Add lime. If desired, add sparkling water.

Yield: 2 cocktails

Time: 5 minutes

Florence Fabricant

COFFEE SHOP'S CAIPIRINHA

Adapted from Coffee Shop, New York City

Cachaça (kah-SHAH-sah), an unrefined clear spirit distilled from sugarcane, is the national beverage of Brazil. Clear, 80-proof cachaça, made in Brazil from sugarcane grown in the country's northeast, tastes like pure alcohol with a distinct burnt sugar–molasses flavor. Add some lime juice and rinds, a little sugar and some ice, shake vigorously, pour into a lowball glass and you have a *caipirinha* (kuy-per-REEN-yah; the name means "little country guy"), a kind of dacquiri with guts.

Ice cubes
1 lime
1 tablespoon granulated sugar
2 ounces cachaça

Fill an 8- to 10-ounce lowball glass with ice cubes. Cut a lime in quarters or eighths, squeeze the juice into the glass and add the squeezed rinds. Add the sugar and cachaça. Transfer to a cocktail shaker (or put a large plastic cup over the glass) and shake vigorously for half a minute. Pour back into the glass and serve.

Yield: 1 drink

Time: 5 minutes

Suzanne Hamlin

COFFEE SHOP'S BATIDA

A *batida*, whose name means "beaten" in Portuguese, is a fanciful version of a caipirinha, a combination of cachaça, fruit nectar and crushed ice, mixed in a blender and often served in a soda-fountain glass with a straw. Just about any fresh or bottled fruit nectar, particularly tropical, will do.

8 ounces crushed ice
½ cup guava, mango or passion fruit nectar
2 ounces cachaça
Dash of sugar to taste

Fill an 8- to 10-ounce soda-fountain glass with ice and add nectar, cachaça and sugar. Pour into a blender and blend briefly. Pour back into the glass and serve with a straw.

Yield: 1 drink

Time: 5 minutes

Suzanne Hamlin

THE OLD-FASHIONED

1 teaspoon superfine sugar or 2 tablespoons
    simple syrup (see Note, page 26)
4 dashes Angostura bitters
1 half orange, sliced
2 to 3 ounces bourbon or rye whiskey
1 lemon twist
1 maraschino cherry

In a double-rocks (Old-Fashioned) glass, combine the sugar and bitters. Add a couple of teaspoons of hot water, and stir together until sugar is dissolved. Add the orange slices, and mull until well mixed. Fill a glass with ice, top with bourbon, and stir well. Garnish with the lemon peel, twisted to release oil, and the cherry.

Yield: 1 serving

Time: 5 minutes

Toby Cecchini

THE CUKE

Adapted from Adam Frank

6 limes, rinsed
1 cup packed mint leaves, stems removed,
    plus 6 sprigs for garnish
3 unwaxed cucumbers
1/2 cup sugar
2 cups vodka or gin, preferably Hendrick's gin
Sparkling water

1. Thinly slice 3 limes and place in a pitcher. Juice the remaining 3 limes and add the juice to the pitcher. Add the mint leaves. Slice 2 cucumbers and add; then add the sugar. Muddle the ingredients. Add the vodka or gin. Place in the refrigerator to steep for 30 minutes or longer.

2. Peel the remaining cucumber and cut lengthwise into 6 spears.

3. Fill 6 highball or other large glasses with ice. Strain the mixture from the pitcher into each. Top with a splash of sparkling water, garnish each glass with a sprig of mint and a cucumber spear, and serve.

Yield: 6 servings

Time: 15 minutes, plus 30 minutes' chilling

Peter Meehan

The Cuke

FIVE-SPICE RUM

Adapted from AZ, New York City

1 (750-milliliter) bottle of dark rum
1 cinnamon stick
4 whole cloves
1 star anise
¼ teaspoon fennel seeds
Pinch of Sichuan peppercorns

1. Uncap the rum, and add the spices. Replace the cap and shake the bottle well, then let stand at room temperature for 48 hours.

2. Strain the rum through a fine sieve, and discard the spices. Serve in highball glasses straight up, chilled or on the rocks. (To make AZ's Dark and Ztormy cocktail, pour the rum into a highball glass, add a splash of ginger beer and garnish with a wedge of lime.)

Yield: 8 drinks

Time: 2 minutes, plus 48 hours for infusion

Matt Lee and Ted Lee

PEACH SAKE

Adapted from Above, New York City

2 to 3 ripe peaches
1 liter sake, chilled

1. Cut the peaches in half, and remove the stones but not the skins. Slice the peaches thinly, and place in a large Mason jar or pitcher. Pour the sake over the peaches, cover and refrigerate for 24 hours.

2. Strain the sake through cheesecloth into a clean decanter, reserving the peaches. Serve immediately, with 3 or 4 peach slices in each glass, or refrigerate the sake and peaches in separate containers for later use. Infused sake will keep 4 to 5 days in a sealed bottle in the refrigerator. Peaches will keep 3 days.

Yield: 1 liter

Time: 10 minutes, plus 24 hours for infusion

Matt Lee and Ted Lee

DANIEL BOULUD'S FRESH FRUIT PUNCH

3 cups freshly squeezed grapefruit juice
    (about 3 grapefruits)
3 cups freshly squeezed orange juice
    (about 6 oranges)
3 tablespoons freshly squeezed lemon juice
    (about 1 lemon)
1½ cups finely diced very ripe fresh pineapple
1½ cups finely diced ripe banana,
    about 3 (5-ounce) bananas
4 tablespoons grenadine
4 tablespoons sugar

1. Combine the ingredients in a food processor or blender. Blend as thoroughly as possible. This can be done in batches.

2. Set a medium-size strainer over a mixing bowl. Pour the mixture into the strainer and let it drip into the bowl. Press the inside of the strainer with the sides of a rubber or plastic spatula to extract as much liquid as possible from the fruit solids. Discard the solids. Chill the liquid overnight.

Yield: 8 to 10 servings

Time: 15 minutes

Craig Claiborne

ICED TEA CONCENTRATE

Adapted from John Harvey

> 4.4 ounces loose tea (preferably Earl Grey, Darjeeling, Orange Pekoe, or English Breakfast, mixed with a little Jasmine for extra flavor).

1. Place the tea in the center of a well-laundered bandanna or handkerchief or in several layers of cheesecloth. Tie or pin so that the tea is securely contained in fabric but has plenty of room to expand when wet.

2. In a large pot, bring 5 quarts water to a boil. Remove from heat, and add the bundle of tea. Allow to steep for 20 to 30 minutes, stirring gently once or twice to release the flavor.

3. Remove the bundle of tea, and decant liquid into two 2-quart canning jars with plastic lids. Refrigerate until needed, up to three weeks.

Yield: 4 quarts concentrate

Time: 10 minutes, plus 30 minutes' steeping

QUICK ICED TEA

> 2½ cups iced tea concentrate (see recipe above)
> ½ cup freshly squeezed lemon juice, or to taste
> 1 teaspoon fruit syrup, or to taste, optional (see Note)
> 2 tablespoons sugar or ¾ teaspoon artificial sweetener, or to taste

1. In a large pitcher, combine the iced tea concentrate with 5 cups cold water.

2. Add the lemon juice, fruit syrup, if desired, and sugar or sweetener. Mix well, and adjust the flavorings to taste. Pour into ice-filled glasses, and serve.

Yield: 2 quarts

Time: 5 minutes

Note: David Colman recommends peach, passion fruit, apricot, black currant, mango, kiwi and cranberry flavors. For information about where to purchase fruit-flavored concentrates, see Sources, page 259.

David Colman

UNION SQUARE CAFÉ'S LEMONADE WITH LEMONGRASS AND DRIED LEMON

Adapted from Daniel Silverman

Daniel Silverman at Union Square Café simply heightens the pure lemon flavor by adding dried lemons and lemongrass.

> 2 cups sugar
> 1 stalk lemongrass, chopped
> 1 dried lemon (see Note)
> 3 cups fresh lemon juice (about 24 lemons)

1. Combine the sugar, lemongrass and dried lemon in a saucepan. Add 2 cups water, and bring the mixture to a boil. Simmer 5 to 7 minutes or until the dried lemon is tender. Using a spoon, squash the lemon against the side of the pan.

2. Turn off heat, and let the mixture rest for 10 minutes, then strain it into a pitcher. Add the lemon juice and 6 cups cold water. Chill until thoroughly cold, at least 2 hours. Serve over ice.

Yield: 8 to 10 servings

Time: 25 minutes, plus chilling

Note: Dried lemons are available at Middle Eastern markets (see Sources, page 259).

Melissa Clark

GINGER-BERRY LEMONADE

Adapted from Gotham Bar and Grill, New York City

At Gotham Bar and Grill, the house lemonade is flavored with fresh ginger and whatever berries are in season. The ginger lends a peppery note to the combination, whether strawberries, raspberries or both are used.

3 cups sugar
1¼ cups coarsely chopped fresh ginger
1 cup sliced fresh strawberries or raspberries, or a combination
4 cups fresh lemon juice (about 32 lemons)
Lemon slices, for garnish

1. In a large saucepan over high heat, combine the sugar and ginger with 8 cups water. Bring to a boil, stirring occasionally until the sugar dissolves. Boil for 15 minutes.

2. Remove from the heat, and let cool for 15 minutes. Strain through a fine sieve, discarding the solids, and refrigerate until well chilled.

3. Set aside about one-third of the berries for garnish. In a blender or food processor, process the remaining berries until smooth. Strain the purée through a mesh sieve, pressing the berries with the back of a wooden spoon to extract as much juice as possible. Discard the solids.

4. In a pitcher, combine the ginger syrup, strained berries and lemon juice. Serve over ice, garnished with reserved berries and lemon slices.

Yield: 12 servings

Time: 50 minutes, plus chilling

Melissa Clark

WATERMELON-GAZPACHO COOLER

3 very ripe tomatoes, cored and seeded
4 cups seedless watermelon, cut into 2-inch chunks
½ large Vidalia onion, or other sweet onion, peeled and cut into 1-inch chunks
1 medium cucumber, peeled, seeded, and cut into large chunks
1 clove garlic, peeled and minced
¼ cup packed fresh basil leaves
¼ cup extra virgin olive oil
1½ tablespoons fresh lemon juice, or more to taste
Coarse sea salt or kosher salt
Coarsely ground black pepper

1. In a blender, combine the tomatoes and the watermelon. Purée for about 30 seconds. Add the onion, cucumber, garlic, basil, olive oil, lemon juice and salt and pepper to taste. Purée until very smooth, about 2 minutes.

2. Adjust the lemon juice and salt and pepper to taste. If necessary, thin with water until loose enough to drink from a glass.

3. Refrigerate until thoroughly chilled, about 2 hours. Place 2 ice cubes in each of six tall glasses. Fill the glasses with gazpacho, and serve.

Yield: 6 servings (6 cups)

Time: 10 minutes, plus 2 hours' chilling time

Amanda Hesser

QUICK SUPPERS
AFTER A LONG TRIP

RECIPES FOR
QUICK SUPPERS

OYSTER AND CORN CHOWDER

Adapted from *The Best of Craig Claiborne*

2 tablespoons unsalted butter

½ cup grated onion

1 large garlic clove, peeled and chopped fine

4 scallions, white and light green, finely chopped

1½ cups milk

1 cup heavy cream

Salt to taste

¼ teaspoon freshly ground pepper

About 1 cup oyster liquor or clam juice

1 dozen fairly large oysters, cut into halves (see Note)

2 cups fresh corn kernels (cut from 4 to 5 ears corn)

1 tablespoon chopped fresh chives

1. Melt the butter in a heavy saucepan and add the grated onion, garlic and scallions. Cook over medium heat for 1 minute.

2. Add the milk and cream and bring to a boil.

3. Add the salt, pepper, oyster liquor or clam juice, oysters and corn kernels. Bring to a boil. Remove from the heat and let sit for 5 minutes.

4. Serve sprinkled with chives.

Yield: **4 servings**

Time: **45 minutes**

Note: Use freshly shucked oysters; canned oysters tend to curdle the milk mixture.

HUBERT KELLER'S COCONUT MILK SOUP WITH GINGER, LEMONGRASS AND BASIL

Adapted from Fleur de Lys, San Francisco

3½ cups canned unsweetened coconut milk, shaken well

1 small stalk celery, diced

3 fresh lemongrass stalks, chopped

2 teaspoons finely chopped ginger

3 tablespoons plus 1 teaspoon fresh lemon juice

2 teaspoons chopped garlic

4 teaspoons coarsely chopped fresh cilantro

⅔ cup dry white wine

Salt and freshly ground pepper to taste

2 teaspoons olive oil

1 small onion, thinly sliced

1 small carrot, peeled and thinly sliced

1 small leek, trimmed, julienned, and washed

10 coarsely chopped fresh basil leaves

4 teaspoons finely chopped fresh chives

1 small tomato, peeled, seeded and chopped

1. Place the coconut milk, celery, lemongrass, ginger, lemon juice, garlic, cilantro, white wine and salt and pepper to taste in a large saucepan over medium-high heat. Bring to a boil. Reduce the heat and simmer for 15 minutes. Strain through a fine sieve.

2. Heat the olive oil in a large saucepan. Add the onion, carrot and leek and cook for 2 minutes. Season with salt and pepper. Add the coconut broth and bring to a boil. Reduce the heat to a bare simmer and cook for 6 minutes. Stir in the basil, chives and tomato and bring to a boil. Ladle into 4 soup bowls and serve immediately.

Yield: 4 servings

Time: 50 minutes

Molly O'Neill

FRITTATA OF SMOKED SALMON AND LEEKS

 3 to 4 tablespoons olive oil or butter
 2 cups chopped leeks (4 to 6 large leeks)
 6 eggs, beaten
 ½ pound smoked salmon, diced
 1 tablespoon chopped fresh chives
 Salt and freshly ground black pepper

1. Heat 3 tablespoons of the oil in a heavy 9-inch skillet. A well-seasoned, cast-iron skillet or a professional-quality nonstick skillet works best. Add the leeks and cook very slowly, covered, until they are tender but not brown.

2. Meanwhile mix the eggs with the salmon and chives. Season to taste with salt and pepper. You will probably need very little salt. When the leeks are tender remove them from the skillet with a slotted spoon, leaving as much of the oil as possible in the skillet. Add the leeks to the egg mixture.

3. If necessary, add additional oil to the skillet to coat it. Reheat the skillet and pour in the egg mixture, tipping the pan to fill it evenly.

4. Cook the eggs over medium heat 5 to 7 minutes, until they are set and golden brown on the bottom but still creamy on top. Using a spatula, loosen the frittata around the sides of the pan and, if necessary, along the bottom.

5. Place a platter larger than the skillet upside down over the skillet. Using potholders or mitts, hold both the platter and the skillet tightly together and turn them over to invert the frittata onto the platter. Then quickly slide the frittata, uncooked side down, back into the skillet. Continue cooking until the underside is set, another 3 minutes or so.

6. Serve directly from the skillet or transfer the frittata to a serving platter. Serve it hot, warm or cooled to room temperature.

Yield: 4 to 6 servings

Time: 30 minutes

Florence Fabricant

JAMES BEARD'S PLEASANT PASTA WITH PEAS, PARMESAN AND PROSCIUTTO

Adapted from *The Fannie Farmer Cookbook*

 Salt
 1 pound spaghetti
 1 (10-ounce) package frozen peas
 4 tablespoons butter
 ½ pound thinly sliced prosciutto di Parma,
  rolled up and cut in ¼-inch-wide strips
 ⅔ cup heavy cream
 Freshly ground black pepper
 ½ to ¾ cup grated Parmesan cheese, or
  more as needed

Opposite:
James Beard's Pleasant Pasta

1. Bring a large pot of lightly salted water to a boil. Add the pasta, and cook until just tender. While the pasta cooks, combine the peas and 1 cup water in a small saucepan. Bring to a boil, and stir until peas are thoroughly heated. Drain and set aside.

2. Drain the pasta, return it to the pot and toss with the butter. Add the peas, prosciutto and cream.

Toss to mix well and to separate prosciutto strips. Season with salt and pepper to taste. Add Parmesan to taste, and toss again. Serve piping hot, passing more Parmesan separately at the table.

Yield: 4 servings

Time: 20 minutes

Alex Witchel

SPRING RISOTTO

Sea salt

¾ pound asparagus, trimmed

¼ cup each sliced fresh chives, packed
    fresh tarragon leaves, and packed
    fresh flat-leaf parsley leaves

Coarsely ground black pepper

¼ cup extra virgin olive oil

5 cups chicken broth

1 clove garlic, peeled

1 cup Arborio rice

⅓ cup white wine

2 tablespoons butter

1 cup freshly grated Parmesan
    cheese

1. Fill a large pot with water and season generously with salt. Bring to a boil. Add the asparagus and cook for 90 seconds. Plunge the asparagus into ice water to stop the cooking. Dry well and cut into ½-inch pieces.

2. Put the chives, tarragon leaves and parsley into a food processor. Add a pinch of salt and pepper. With the machine on, add the oil through the feed tube. Purée until a coarse paste forms.

3. Bring the chicken broth to a simmer and add the garlic. Place a medium saucepan over medium heat. Add enough oil to film the base. Add the rice and stir to coat it. Continue stirring until lightly toasted, then pour in the wine and cook until it is absorbed.

4. Begin ladling in broth, ½ cup at a time, stirring until each addition is absorbed. Cook until the rice is al dente, but quite loose. Discard the garlic. Remove from the heat, and stir in the herb oil, then the butter and asparagus. Spoon onto plates and shower with cheese.

Yield: 4 servings

Time: 1 hour

Amanda Hesser

MARK BITTMAN'S PASTA WITH CORN, ZUCCHINI AND TOMATOES

This dish is flexible not only in its flavorings but in its ingredients. You can use onions, garlic, or shallots, singly or in combination; add green beans (or even fresh limas) to the mix; substitute eggplant for the zucchini. Think of it as a delicious mélange of whatever is on hand. The cooking is straightforward and there is no ahead-of-time anything. Shuck the corn and cut the kernels off the cob: do this with a sharp knife in a shallow bowl placed in the sink to maximize yield and minimize mess. Set a pot of water to boil, and start the kernels cooking in a skillet; you want them to brown nicely. Meanwhile, dice the zucchini or summer squash, the onion or whatever else you are using. The tomatoes go into the pan last.

Salt

3 tablespoons extra virgin olive oil, or
    2 tablespoons oil and 1 tablespoon butter

1 cup corn kernels (2 or 3 ears)

1 cup diced zucchini or summer squash (2 or 3
    small vegetables)

Freshly ground pepper

1 medium onion or 3 or 4 shallots, diced

¼ teaspoon minced garlic, optional

1 or 2 sprigs tarragon

4 plum or 2 large tomatoes, diced

1 pound cut pasta, such as penne

1. Set a large pot of water to boil and salt it. Put 2 tablespoons oil in a large skillet over medium-high heat and add corn. Cook, stirring occasionally, until the corn begins to brown. Add the zucchini and some salt and pepper. Cook, stirring occasionally, until the zucchini begins to brown.

2. Add the onion or shallots and garlic if you are using it. Cook, stirring occasionally, until the onion

softens, about 5 minutes. Add the tarragon and cook for 30 seconds, then add the tomatoes. Put the pasta in the boiling water and cook until tender but not mushy, 10 to 15 minutes.

3. While the pasta cooks, continue to cook the sauce, reducing the heat when the tomatoes begin to break down. If the sauce dries out (with plum tomatoes, this is likely), add some pasta cooking water, about ½ cup at a time. When the pasta is done, drain it, toss with sauce and remaining oil or butter and serve immediately.

Yield: 4 servings

Time: 30 minutes

Mark Bittman

PENNE WITH GARDEN VEGETABLES

Other seasonal vegetables can be substituted for the ones in this recipe. Lightly steamed green beans, broccoli or cauliflower broken into small pieces work well in place of the zucchini; shredded spinach or other greens can take the place of the eggplant.

1 medium sweet bell pepper, red or yellow
1 small eggplant
1 clove garlic, coarsely chopped
½ cup extra virgin olive oil
2 small or 1 medium zucchini
3 tablespoons minced fresh green herbs, such as flat-leaf parsley, basil, chives or a combination
Sea salt to taste
1 pound penne, or other short, stubby pasta
¾ to 1 cup tomato sauce, homemade or a good-quality commercial tomato sauce

1. Core and seed the pepper and cut it into ¼-inch strips. Cut the eggplant into ½-inch cubes or smaller.

2. In a large frying pan, sauté the garlic and peppers in 2 tablespoons olive oil over medium-low heat until they are very soft. Remove and set aside in a medium bowl. Add the remaining oil to the pan, and raise the heat to medium-high. Add the eggplant, and brown quickly, removing the cubes as they brown and adding them to the peppers.

3. While the vegetables cook, cut the zucchini in half lengthwise, and then slice it about ½-inch thick. Add the zucchini pieces to the pan, brown quickly on both sides, and add them to the eggplant and peppers.

4. Remove the pan from the heat, and immediately stir the minced herbs into the hot oil. Pour over the vegetables and keep warm.

5. Bring 5 to 6 quarts water to a rolling boil. Add at least 2 tablespoons salt and then the pasta.

6. While the pasta is cooking, warm the tomato sauce in a separate pan.

7. Start testing the pasta at 6 minutes. When the pasta is done, drain it and turn it immediately into a preheated bowl. Mix rapidly with the hot tomato sauce. (Or drain the pasta when it is not quite done, and finish cooking in the sauce.) When the sauce is thoroughly mixed in, add the sautéed vegetables, and mix lightly. Serve immediately.

Yield: 6 servings

Time: 40 minutes

Nancy Harmon Jenkins

NIGELLA LAWSON'S SPAGHETTI WITH RAW TOMATO SAUCE

(Spaghetti al Sugo Crudo)

Adapted from *Forever Summer*

Raw tomatoes are peeled, seeded, and chopped, then left to steep with a little sugar, some salt, pepper, a bruised garlic clove and good olive oil. If your tomatoes are fresh and fat and ripe—and they will be, increasingly, as the weeks pass into summer—you'll find that there is perhaps no finer way to dress pasta. And by all means add cubes of fresh buffalo mozzarella to the soused tomatoes before you add the hot pasta, if you want.

2½ pounds ripe tomatoes
1 teaspoon sugar
Maldon or other sea salt
Freshly ground black pepper
1 clove garlic, peeled and lightly smashed
½ cup extra virgin olive oil
1 pound uncooked spaghetti

1. Bring a large pot of water to a boil. Add the tomatoes, simmer for 10 seconds and drain. Peel, core and halve the tomatoes, discarding the seeds and liquid. Chop the tomato pulp finely and place in a medium bowl. Add the sugar, and season with salt and pepper to taste.

2. Add the garlic and olive oil, and whisk until blended. Cover with plastic wrap, and allow to sit

at room temperature for at least 30 minutes and up to 8 hours. Discard the garlic.

3. Bring a large pot of lightly salted water to a boil, and add the spaghetti. Cook until al dente, and drain well. Add the tomato mixture to the hot pasta, and mix until the pasta is evenly coated with sauce. Serve immediately.

Yield: 4 servings

Time: 20 minutes, plus 30 minutes' to 8 hours' marinating

Nigella Lawson

SPAGHETTI WITH SCALLOPS, LEMON AND BREAD CRUMBS

In Italy, homemade bread crumbs often take the place of grated cheese in pasta dishes. This is especially true with seafood sauces, since Italians consider the marriage of fish and cheese to be odd. Traditionally, stale loaves are grated by hand, and the coarse crumbs are toasted in a skillet to a rich golden-brown color. A food processor fitted with a metal blade speeds the grating. Homemade bread crumbs are coarser and more flavorful than commercial varieties.

2 cups stale bread cut into ½-inch cubes

1 pound spaghetti

Salt to taste

6 tablespoons olive oil

3 medium garlic cloves, minced

2 tablespoons lemon juice

2 tablespoons minced fresh flat-leaf parsley leaves

½ teaspoon red pepper flakes, or to taste

1 pound sea scallops, tendons discarded, cut into ¾-inch cubes

1. Bring 4 quarts of water to a boil in a large pot.

2. Place the bread cubes in a food processor fitted with the metal blade, and grind into coarse crumbs, about 1 minute. Place the bread crumbs in a large skillet set over medium heat. Toast, shaking the pan often, until the crumbs are golden brown. Remove the crumbs from the pan, and set aside.

3. Add the spaghetti and salt, to taste, to the boiling water.

4. While the pasta is cooking, briefly heat the oil in the empty skillet. Add the garlic, and cook until golden, about 1 minute. Stir in the lemon juice, parsley, red pepper flakes and salt to taste. Cook for 30 seconds. Add the scallops, and cook, stirring often, until they are opaque and cooked through, 3 to 4 minutes. Do not overcook the scallops. Adjust seasonings and keep the sauce warm.

5. Drain the spaghetti when al dente, but do not shake bone dry. Transfer the spaghetti, still dripping with a little cooking water, to a large bowl, and toss with the scallop sauce. Sprinkle with the bread crumbs and toss well. Divide pasta into individual bowls, and serve immediately.

Yield: 4 servings

Time: 30 minutes

Florence Fabricant

SESAME NOODLES WITH FRESH VEGETABLES

This can be served hot or cold, with vegetables or plain.

½ pound Chinese egg noodles, vermicelli or angel hair pasta

For the Dressing

2 scallions, trimmed and chopped, including green parts

⅓ cup vegetable or chicken broth

¼ cup smooth peanut butter, preferably sugar- and salt-free

¼ cup cider vinegar or rice wine vinegar

½ cup low-sodium soy sauce

2 teaspoons dark (toasted) sesame oil

And some or all of the following:

1 cucumber, peeled, seeded and cut into small pieces

1 cup sliced red radishes

1 bunch scallions, trimmed and cut in thin rounds, including more of the green parts

1 cup bean sprouts

1 carrot, shredded

1 cup snow peas

½ cup roughly chopped fresh cilantro

¼ cup toasted sesame seeds

1. Bring a large pot of salted water to a boil. Add the noodles and boil for 3 to 4 minutes, until tender. Drain in a colander, then cool under running water. Shake the noodles dry and transfer to a large, shallow bowl.

2. Blend all the ingredients in a blender or food processor. Pour over the noodles, turning until completely mixed.

3. If serving immediately, add any or all of the remaining ingredients, mix well, and serve. Or cover and chill; mix in the additions right before serving.

Yield: 4 to 6 servings

Time: 30 minutes, plus chilling, if desired.

Suzanne Hamlin

SPICY GINGER AND LEMON CHICKEN

The sweet, spicy mixture of this recipe has an unusual flavor that goes well with the chicken. The dish can be made ahead and reheated at serving time.

2 tablespoons olive oil

6 chicken legs (about 4 pounds), with skin and tips of drumsticks removed

1 teaspoon salt

1 teaspoon chili powder

1 teaspoon cumin powder

½ teaspoon dried thyme leaves

¼ teaspoon cayenne pepper

1 tablespoon flour

6 pieces lemon zest, cut with a vegetable peeler

6 pieces orange zest, cut with a vegetable peeler

¼ cup fresh ginger pieces (washed, but not peeled)

4 cloves garlic, peeled

1 cup sweet apple cider

1. Heat the oil in a large saucepan until hot but not smoking. Add the chicken legs in one layer, and brown them over medium to high heat, turning occasionally, for 15 minutes.

2. Add the rest of the ingredients, bring the mixture to a boil, reduce the heat to low, cover and

cook gently for 15 minutes. Serve, 1 leg per person, with some of the cooking juices.

Yield: 6 servings

Time: 35 minutes

Jacques Pépin

MARK BITTMAN'S CHICKEN KEBAB, TURKISH STYLE

2 large onions, peeled
2 tablespoons extra virgin olive oil
Juice of 1 lemon
1 tablespoon minced garlic
Salt and pepper to taste
3 bay leaves, crumbled
1 tablespoon fresh marjoram or oregano leaves,
    or 1 teaspoon dried oregano
1½ pounds boneless chicken thighs or legs,
    cut into 1½-inch chunks
Lemon wedges or ground sumac (see Sources,
    page 259)

1. Start a charcoal or wood fire or heat a gas grill. The fire should be moderately hot and the rack about 4 inches from the heat source. Mince 1 onion, and combine it in a large bowl with the oil, lemon juice, garlic, salt, pepper, bay leaves and marjoram or oregano. Taste, and adjust seasoning. Marinate the chicken in this mixture for at least a few minutes, or overnight in the refrigerator.

2. If using wooden skewers, soak them in water to cover for a few minutes. Cut the remaining onion into quarters, then separate it into large pieces. Thread the chicken and onion alternately onto skewers, leaving a little space between the pieces.

3. Grill the kebabs, turning as each side browns, and brushing with the remaining marinade, for

about 12 to 15 minutes, or until the chicken is cooked through. Serve with lemon wedges or sprinkle with a bit of sumac.

Yield: 4 servings

Time: 45 minutes, plus marinating from a few minutes to overnight

Mark Bittman

CHICKEN TAGINE WITH CHICKPEAS AND RAISINS

This chicken dish is based on the Morrocan spicy stew that is simmered in a tagine, an earthenware pot with a conical lid, but an ordinary casserole dish with a cover will do the job. Pieces of chicken are cooked with chickpeas and raisins and served in a sauce that is spiced with turmeric and saffron that is a deep golden orange. Using canned chickpeas, you can have a tasty, one-pot dish on the table within an hour.

1 chicken, quartered
1 tablespoon olive oil
2 cloves garlic, minced
1 onion, thinly sliced
1 teaspoon ground turmeric
1 cinnamon stick
1 pinch saffron
Salt and pepper to taste
½ cup raisins
¼ cup fresh flat-leaf parsley or cilantro,
    chopped
1 (20-ounce) can chickpeas

1. Brown the chicken in the oil. Add the garlic, onion, turmeric, cinnamon, saffron, salt and pepper. Cover and simmer, stirring occasionally to prevent the chicken from sticking to the bottom of the pan. Cook for 20 minutes.

2. Add the raisins, parsley or cilantro and chickpeas. Mix well. Cover and simmer for 20 to 30 minutes, or until the chicken is tender. Adjust the seasoning and serve.

Yield: 4 servings

Time: 1 hour

Moira Hodgson

'21' CLUB HAMBURGER

Adapted from Anne Rosenzweig

8 tablespoons butter at room temperature
1 tablespoon finely chopped fresh thyme
2 tablespoons finely chopped fresh basil
1 tablespoon finely chopped fresh flat-leaf
    parsley
12 ounces freshly ground choice chuck
    (preferably with a 22-percent fat content)
Salt to taste, if desired
Freshly ground pepper to taste
2 slices Italian country bread, each
    slice about ½ inch in thickness and
    5 inches in diameter
3 tablespoons olive oil
2 to 4 thin slices red, ripe tomatoes
2 thin slices red onion
2 teaspoons freshly squeezed lemon juice

1. Combine the butter, chopped thyme, 1 tablespoon chopped fresh basil and chopped fresh parsley. Blend well. Place the mixture on a rectangle of waxed paper or aluminum foil and roll it into a sausage shape about 1 inch in diameter. Place in the freezer for an hour or longer, until it is frozen. This butter may be used a portion at a time and refrozen.

2. Preheat a gas or charcoal broiler to high.

3. Shape the meat into a round ball without kneading. With your finger, make a partial indentation through the center of the ball. Shove 1 tablespoon of frozen butter into the center of the ball and press to close the opening. Flatten the meat into a patty shape about ¾ inch thick. Sprinkle on both sides with salt and pepper. Place the meat on the grill and cook about 4 minutes until it is well seared on one side; turn the meat and cook about 4 minutes longer, or to the desired degree of doneness.

4. Brush the bread slices on one side with 1 tablespoon of olive oil. Place the slices oiled side down on the grill and cook briefly until lightly toasted. Turn and cook briefly on the second side.

5. Meanwhile, as the meat cooks, place the tomato and onion slices in a small bowl and sprinkle with the remaining 2 tablespoons of oil, the lemon juice, salt, pepper and remaining tablespoon of chopped fresh basil. Toss briefly.

6. Place a slice of the warm grilled bread on a dinner plate, place the hamburger in the center and cover with the second slice of bread. Serve the tomato and onion slices on the side to be added to the hamburger as desired. At '21' Club, tomato ketchup is served only on request. The hamburger is also served with freshly cooked gaufrette potatoes on the side.

Yield: 1 hamburger

Time: 30 minutes, plus 1 hour to freeze the herb butter

Note: The herb butter may also be used to sauté poultry or over vegetables.

Craig Claiborne and Pierre Franey

CRAIG CLAIBORNE'S FAVORITE HAMBURGERS

Craig Claiborne preferred a simple burger, made with ground round steak, cooked in a heavy cast-iron skillet and seasoned with Worcestershire sauce, lemon juice, and finely chopped parsley.

1½ pounds freshly ground round steak
Salt to taste, if desired
Freshly ground pepper to taste
4 tablespoons butter
4 hamburger buns
1 teaspoon Worcestershire sauce
¼ cup finely chopped fresh flat-leaf parsley
2 tablespoons lemon juice
4 ¼-inch-thick slices of onion, preferably Vidalia onion or red onion

1. Divide the meat into four equal portions and shape each portion. Press each portion as gently as possible, just enough so that it holds together.

2. Sprinkle the bottom of a heavy skillet, preferably a cast-iron skillet, lightly with salt, if used. Heat the skillet until it is hot and almost smoking. Add the patties and sear well on one side, about 2 minutes. Using a pancake turner, turn the patties and reduce the heat to moderate. Cook on the second side 2 or 3 minutes, or to the desired degree of doneness.

3. If desired, sprinkle each hamburger with salt and pepper and top each with 1 tablespoon of butter.

4. Meanwhile, toast the cut sides of each bun until they are lightly browned. Arrange the bun halves, cut side up, on four dinner plates. Sprinkle each patty with ¼ teaspoon Worcestershire sauce, 1 tablespoon parsley and ½ tablespoon lemon juice. Add 1 onion slice atop each hamburger. Top each serving with the remaining toasted bun halves, cut side down. Serve with tomato ketchup.

Yield: 4 hamburgers

Time: 15 minutes

Craig Claiborne and Pierre Franey

MIDDLE-EASTERN-STYLE LAMB BURGERS WITH DRIED FIG AND MINT RELISH

For the lamb

1½ pounds ground lamb
¼ cup roughly chopped fresh flat-leaf parsley
2 tablespoons minced garlic
2 tablespoons toasted coriander seeds
2 teaspoons red pepper flakes
1 tablespoon ground cumin
Salt and freshly ground black pepper
2 large pita rounds, halved
1 tablespoon olive oil
Relish (recipe follows)

1. Light a fire in the grill, or heat the broiler.

2. In a large bowl, combine the lamb, parsley, garlic, coriander, red pepper flakes, cumin, salt and pepper. Mix well with your hands until the mixture has an even consistency, then form into 4 patties.

3. Grill the patties over a medium hot fire, or broil, until done the way you like them. Halfway through the cooking time, brush the pita rounds with the olive oil, place them on the grill and cook to desired doneness.

4. Remove the patties from heat; place inside pita halves, along with a tablespoon or two of the relish, and serve, passing any remaining relish separately.

Yield: 4 servings

Time: 15 minutes, plus grilling time to desired doneness

➤ DRIED FIG AND MINT RELISH

 ½ cup finely chopped dried figs
 ¼ cup roughly chopped fresh mint
 Juice of 1 lemon
 1 tablespoon honey
 Salt and freshly ground black pepper

Combine the figs, mint, lemon juice, honey, and salt and pepper to taste. Mix well and set aside.

Yield: ¾ cup

Time: 10 minutes

Note: This relish is an excellent complement to lamb roasts and chops.

John Willoughby and Chris Schlesinger

GRILLED STEAK WITH HERB SALAD

Adapted from Traci Des Jardins

For the Herb Salad (see Note)

 1 cup per serving of frisée, baby arugula, sliced fennel, tarragon, chives or chervil, or other fresh tender herbs
 Extra virgin olive oil
 Red wine vinegar
 Salt and freshly ground black pepper

For the Grilled Steak

 Vegetable oil, for oiling grill rack
 4 (16-ounce) T-bone or rib-eye steaks, preferably grass-fed beef
 Kosher salt and black pepper
 3 tablespoons butter
 5 cloves garlic, peeled
 ¼ cup packed fresh thyme stems
 Fleur de sel
 Salsa verde (recipe follows)

1. In a large mixing bowl, combine the salad greens. Cover and refrigerate.

2. Prepare a fire of mesquite charcoal; burn down until coals are white. Push the coals to the side of the cooking area. Clean the grill rack with a wire brush, then lightly oil the rack.

3. While the grill heats, season the steaks well on both sides with salt and pepper. In a small saucepan, combine the butter, garlic and thyme over very low heat. Set aside.

4. Place the steaks on the grill until seared, about 5 minutes. Flip the steaks over and brush with the herbed butter. Allow the steaks to sear again for a few minutes, then flip and brush again with butter. Continue until the steaks are grilled to taste: 125 degrees on an instant-read thermometer for rare, 130 degrees for medium-rare or 135 degrees for medium. (Grass-fed beef cooks more quickly than grain-fed beef.)

5. Remove the steaks from the grill and allow to rest for 10 minutes before seasoning again and serving. Dress the salad with olive oil and vinegar and salt and pepper to taste.

6. To serve, thinly slice the steaks. Place a portion of salad in the center of each serving plate and surround with sliced steak. Sprinkle with a little *fleur de sel,* and garnish each plate with a spoonful of salsa verde.

Yield: 4 to 8 servings

Time: About 30 minutes, plus time for heating the grill

Note: The herb salad is made to the taste of the cook. Some will want more greens, others more herbs.

➢ SALSA VERDE

¼ cup finely chopped fresh flat-leaf parsley
3 tablespoons each finely chopped fresh
   chervil, chives, and tarragon
1 shallot, minced
3 tablespoons chopped capers
3 tablespoons finely chopped anchovies
Finely grated zest of 1 lemon
½ cup extra virgin olive oil
1 tablespoon red wine vinegar
Salt and pepper to taste

Combine all ingredients and season to taste with salt and pepper. Serve with steaks.

Yield: 2 cups

Time: 15 minutes

Kim Severson

Grilled Steak with Herb Salad

JIM FOBEL'S RIB-EYE STEAKS WITH WATERCRESS

Adapted from *The Food & Wine Annual Cookbook 2004*

2 rib-eye steaks (10- to 12-ounces each),
   about 1 inch thick
1 tablespoon coarsely ground black pepper
Salt
¼ cup dry red wine
2 tablespoons unsalted butter
2 large bunches watercress, stemmed

1. Season the steaks on both sides with pepper, lightly patting it on. Place a large cast-iron skillet over medium-high heat. Season the steaks with salt, then place in a dry skillet. Sear the steaks without moving them until they are brown and crusty on the undersides (about 4 minutes for medium-rare meat; adjust to taste). Turn the steaks, and sear for 4 minutes more. Transfer steaks to a serving platter.

2. Pour off any excess fat, and add wine to the skillet. Cook over low heat until the wine is reduced by half, about 30 seconds. Pour the wine reduction over the steaks.

3. Wipe out the skillet, and return it to medium-low heat. Melt the butter in the skillet, and add the watercress. Increase heat to high, and toss watercress until wilted, about 1 minute. Season to taste with salt, and arrange around the steaks. To serve, cut the steaks in half. Place a portion on each of four plates, accompanied by a serving of watercress.

Yield: 4 servings

Time: 15 minutes

William Grimes

Opposite:
Jim Fobel's Rib-Eye Steaks with Watercress

DANIEL BOULUD'S HANGER STEAK WITH SHALLOTS

Adapted from *Café Boulud Cookbook*

1 tablespoon vegetable oil
6 hanger steaks (6 to 7 ounces each)
Salt and freshly ground white pepper
2 tablespoons unsalted butter
8 medium shallots, peeled and thinly sliced
2 tablespoons red wine vinegar
½ cup dry red wine
2 tablespoons finely chopped fresh flat-leaf
   parsley

1. Place a large, heavy skillet over high heat. Add the oil. Season the steaks with salt and pepper and sear, turning once, to the desired degree of doneness, about 6 minutes for medium rare. You may not be able to cook all the steaks at once. Transfer to a warm serving dish.

2. Lower the heat to medium and add 1 tablespoon of the butter. Add the shallots and cook, stirring, 3 minutes, until soft but not brown. Add the vinegar and cook until it evaporates; then add the wine. Boil until reduced by half. Remove the pan from heat and swirl in the remaining butter; then stir in the parsley.

3. Slice the steaks, and serve with the sauce poured over.

Yield: 6 servings

Time: 30 minutes

Florence Fabricant

GRILLED DOUBLE-THICK PORK CHOPS WITH SOUTHERN FLAVORS

4 double-thick rib or loin pork chops
2 tablespoons vegetable oil
Salt and freshly ground black pepper
1 large yellow onion, peeled and diced
2 tablespoons minced fresh ginger
2 tablespoons minced garlic
½ cup rum
¼ cup red wine vinegar
½ cup ketchup
¼ cup molasses
1 tablespoon ground allspice
Pinch of ground mace

1. Build a small fire in one side of a covered charcoal grill, using enough charcoal to fill a shoe box. It will take about 40 minutes for the charcoal to reach the right temperature.

2. Meanwhile, rub the chops lightly with 1 tablespoon of the oil, sprinkle with salt and pepper to taste and set aside.

3. In a small saucepan over medium heat, heat the other tablespoon of oil until hot but not smoking. Add the onions and sauté, stirring occasionally, until transparent, about 5 to 7 minutes. Add the ginger and garlic, and sauté, stirring, for 1 minute. Add the rum, vinegar, ketchup, molasses, allspice and mace, and bring to a boil. As soon as the mixture begins to boil, reduce the heat to low and simmer gently for 5 minutes, stirring frequently. Remove from the heat and set aside.

4. Place the chops on the grill directly over a hot fire and cook for 3 to 4 minutes per side. When they are nicely seared, move them to the side of the grill with no fire and let them cook slowly, uncovered, about 10 minutes per side. During the last minute of cooking, brush the chops with the sauce. Cut into one chop to make sure it is cooked through and just lightly pink at the center. Remove from the grill and serve drizzled with any extra sauce.

Yield: 4 servings

Time: 45 minutes

John Willoughby and Chris Schlesinger

EASY SALMON WITH HOT-MUSTARD GLAZE

Adapted from David Kinch, Manresa, Los Gatos, CA

This dish, marrying sweet and spice against the richness of salmon, is Chef Kinch's version of a recipe created by Barry Wine at the Quilted Giraffe, whose four-star Manhattan restaurant closed in 1992. It couldn't be simpler, but it wakes up every element on your tongue. And the mirrorlike lacquer finish that results when the sugar in the glaze and the oil are baked on is beautiful, too.

½ cup mustard powder, preferably Colman's
½ cup sugar
2 pounds center-cut salmon fillet,
    about 2 inches thick at its thickest point,
    with skin
2½ tablespoons extra virgin olive oil

1. Heat oven to 250 degrees. In a small bowl whisk together the mustard, sugar and ½ cup water. Set aside.

2. Cut the salmon into 4 uniform portions. Pat dry with a paper towel. Heat 1 tablespoon of oil in a heavy ovenproof skillet over high heat; the skillet should be large enough to hold the salmon without crowding. Add the salmon, skin side up, and sear quickly, about 2 minutes, until it can be lifted

easily with a spatula without sticking. Turn, and sear about 2 minutes, skin side down; the thickest part should still be raw in the center.

3. Brush the top of the salmon with the remaining olive oil and then with the mustard mixture. Bake in the oven about 20 minutes, until medium-rare in center. (An instant-read thermometer inserted in the thickest part should register 100 to 110 degrees.) Remove from the oven and serve.

Yield: 4 servings

Time: 30 minutes

Florence Fabricant

BLUEFISH COOKED IN FOIL

Adapted from *The Best of Craig Claiborne*

You envelope the fish in aluminum foil, bake it in the oven (it can also be cooked over a charcoal grill), and when you unwrap the fish, the skin comes off, attached to the foil. The only seasoning necessary is a little garlic, sliced wafer thin. The recipe may easily be doubled or tripled.

> 1 large, boneless bluefish fillet with skin on,
>   or 2 boneless bluefish fillets with skin on,
>   weighing 1 pound
> 4 tablespoons butter
> 1 small peeled garlic clove, sliced wafer thin

1. Preheat the oven to 500 degrees, or prepare a charcoal grill.

2. Wrap the fillet, or two fillets, in one layer of heavy-duty aluminum foil. The fish must be tightly enclosed and sealed in the foil. Wrap the package neatly and seal the ends, tucking them under.

3. Place the fish on the bottom rack of the oven or on the grill and cook for 10 minutes.

4. When you open the foil and invert the fish onto a plate, the skin will remain stuck to the foil. Heat the butter and garlic and pour over the fish.

Yield: 2 servings

Time: 15 minutes

STEVEN RAICHLEN'S ROSEMARY-GRILLED SCALLOPS

Adapted from *How to Grill*

Sprigs of fresh rosemary make excellent skewers, with stems slender enough to pass through a small item like a scallop, yet stiff enough to hold chunks of chicken or seafood. The heat of the fire releases the rosemary oils, which infuse the kebab with flavor. You can use fresh rosemary sprigs from a greengrocer, but you'll get longer, stiffer skewers if you cut them from a rosemary plant, which will keep growing.

> 1½ pounds sea scallops (about 30)
> About 30 fresh rosemary sprigs
>   (each 3 to 4 inches long)
> 3 ounces prosciutto, sliced paper thin
> 3 tablespoons extra virgin olive oil
> 3 tablespoons fresh lemon juice
> Coarse salt and freshly ground black pepper

1. Pull off and discard the crescent-shaped muscle on the side of each scallop that has one. Strip the leaves off the bottom 2 inches of the rosemary sprigs (slide them off with your thumb and fore-finger). Reserve the leaves, and set the sprigs aside. Cut the prosciutto into strips just large enough to wrap around the scallops (about 1 by 3 inches).

2. Lay a scallop flat on a work surface. Wrap a piece of prosciutto around it. Skewer a rosemary sprig through the prosciutto and scallop to the

other side. Repeat with the remaining scallops. Arrange the scallops in a baking dish. Drizzle the olive oil and lemon juice on both sides, sprinkle with rosemary leaves and season with salt and pepper. (Go easy on the salt, as the prosciutto is fairly salty.) Marinate for 15 minutes, while you light the grill.

3. Set up the grill for direct grilling, and preheat to high. Brush and oil the grate. Arrange the scallops on the grate, and grill until just cooked, about 2 minutes a side. Serve at once.

Yield: 6 appetizer servings or 4 main-course servings

Time: 30 minutes

Steven Raichlen

GRILLED SWORDFISH WITH PESTO-LEMON-CAPER SAUCE

Adapted from the Lansdowne, London

1½ large bunches flat-leaf parsley
¾ cup extra virgin olive oil
Juice of 1 lemon
Grated zest from 2 lemons
1 tablespoon Dijon mustard
1 cup diced red onion
2 tablespoons capers
⅓ cup chopped cornichons
8 anchovy fillets, dried on paper towels
6 swordfish steaks (about 1 inch thick)
Olive oil, for grilling

1. Prepare a charcoal grill or preheat a grill.

2. In the bowl of a food processor, combine all of the ingredients except the swordfish and the olive oil for grilling, and process until coarsely chopped.

3. Rub the swordfish with olive oil, and grill on both sides until cooked, following the Canadian rule: measure at thickest point, and allow 8 to 10 minutes to the inch, turning once. Serve topped with the pesto-lemon-caper sauce.

Yield: 6 servings

Time: 25 minutes

Note: This dish is also delicious with grilled chicken breasts.

Marian Burros

RAINBOW TROUT STUFFED WITH SPINACH, PINE NUTS AND DILL

4 rainbow trout (about 8 ounces each) filleted, butterflied, rinsed and patted dry
Kosher salt or coarse sea salt and freshly ground black pepper
2 tablespoons unsalted butter
¼ cup pine nuts
1 garlic clove, minced
10 ounces baby spinach, cleaned
¼ cup golden raisins, chopped
3 tablespoons chopped fresh dill
2 tablespoons extra virgin olive oil

1. Season each fish inside and out with salt and pepper. In a large pan over medium-high heat, melt the butter. Add the pine nuts and garlic, and sauté until golden and fragrant, about 1 minute. Add the spinach and let wilt, 2 to 3 minutes. Stir in the raisins and dill, and cook 1 minute more. Season with salt and pepper.

2. Divide the spinach mixture into quarters and stuff each fillet with the filling. Secure the fish with metal skewers or tie with kitchen string.

3. Return the pan to medium heat and warm the oil until sizzling. Cook the fish until the skin is golden and the fish opaque, about 5 minutes for the first side and 3 minutes for the second side. Remove the skewer or string before serving.

Yield: 4 servings

Time: 30 minutes

Melissa Clark

ALICE WATERS'S BAKED GOAT CHEESE WITH LETTUCE SALAD

8 rounds of Montrachet or any fresh, very soft, mild goat cheese, about ½-inch thick
1 cup extra virgin olive oil
Freshly ground pepper to taste
Salt, if desired
8 sprigs fresh thyme or any desired herbs such as oregano, rosemary, sage or finely minced garlic
1 cup fresh bread crumbs
8 cups loosely packed assorted salad and herb greens such as chervil, arugula, mâche or field salad or chicory
1 tablespoon red wine vinegar

1. Arrange the goat cheese rounds on a shallow dish. Pour ¾ cup of the olive oil over all. Sprinkle with pepper and salt, if desired. Turn the rounds in the oil. Arrange or sprinkle the fresh herbs over all.

2. When ready to cook, preheat the oven to 450 degrees.

3. Dip the rounds all over in the bread crumbs, patting to make the crumbs adhere. Arrange the rounds on a baking dish. Refrigerate for 15 minutes or longer.

4. Discard the herbs, but reserve the oil.

5. Place the baking dish in the oven and bake 10 to 12 minutes.

6. Meanwhile, put the salad and herb greens in a salad bowl. Blend the vinegar, the reserved oil and the remaining ¼ cup oil, salt and pepper. Pour the dressing over the greens and toss well.

7. Transfer the greens to a flat serving dish. Arrange the cheese rounds around the greens and serve immediately.

Yield: 4 to 8 servings

Time: 30 minutes

Craig Claiborne

FARFALLE, ARUGULA AND TOMATO SALAD

Adapted from *Cooking for the Weekend*

It's always a good idea to have a pasta salad on hand during the weekend. This one keeps well for up to three days in the refrigerator. It can easily be doubled or tripled for a buffet.

½ pound farfalle, cooked, drained and rinsed
3 cups stemmed and torn arugula
½ cup chopped fresh basil
2 large tomatoes, cut in ½-inch pieces
1 teaspoon grated lemon zest
3 tablespoons olive oil
1 tablespoon fresh lemon juice
2 teaspoons salt
Freshly ground pepper to taste

Put the farfalle in a large bowl. Add the arugula, basil, tomatoes, lemon zest, olive oil, lemon juice, salt and pepper. Toss until well combined.

Yield: 8 servings

Time: 25 minutes, using cooked pasta

Molly O'Neill

WILD MUSHROOM QUESADILLAS

Adapted by Traci Des Jardins

The mix of cheeses offers complex flavor and texture, and the wild mushrooms add an earthiness.

- 4 tablespoons vegetable oil
- 1 pound chanterelles, black trumpet or other wild mushrooms (or substitute oyster, cremini or clamshell mushrooms; do not use shiitake), roughly chopped
- Salt
- ½ cup minced yellow onion
- 4 ounces grated Oaxaca or domestic Muenster cheese
- 4 ounces grated panela or aged mozzarella cheese
- 4 ounces grated cotija or Parmesan cheese
- ⅓ cup finely chopped fresh cilantro leaves
- ½ teaspoon dried oregano
- Pinch of ground coriander
- Freshly ground black pepper
- 8 (8-inch) flour or corn tortillas

1. Place a medium sauté pan over medium-high heat and add 2 tablespoons vegetable oil. When the oil shimmers, add the mushrooms and a generous pinch of salt. Sauté until the mushrooms release their liquid, the liquid evaporates and the mushrooms begin to brown, about 10 minutes.

2. Add the onions. Sauté, adjusting the heat as necessary, until the onions are soft and the entire mixture is golden brown but not burned, about 5 minutes. Remove from heat and allow to cool slightly.

3. Using a food processor or a knife, finely chop the mushroom-onion mixture, then transfer to a large bowl. Add the grated cheeses, cilantro, oregano and coriander. Season to taste with salt and pepper.

4. Place a large nonstick or well-seasoned skillet over medium heat, and add the remaining 2 tablespoons vegetable oil. While the pan heats, place a large spoonful of mushroom-cheese mixture into the center of a tortilla, and fold the tortilla in half to make a half-moon. Place the filled tortilla in a preheated skillet and cook, turning once, until the tortilla is nicely browned on both sides and the cheese is melted. Repeat to make 8 filled tortillas. Serve immediately.

Yield: 8 servings

Time: 30 minutes

Kim Severson

BREAKFASTS
AND BRUNCHES
TO START THE DAY

RECIPES FOR
BREAKFASTS AND BRUNCHES

HONEY-ORANGE SMOOTHIE

½ cup milk

1 ripe banana

2 tablespoons honey

½ cup orange juice

½ cup crushed ice

Combine all the ingredients in a blender. Blend until smooth.

Yield: 1 serving

Time: 5 minutes

Molly O'Neill

POWER BERRY SMOOTHIE

½ cup fresh or slightly thawed frozen strawberries

½ cup fresh or slightly thawed frozen raspberries

¼ cup low-fat vanilla yogurt

1½ cups milk

2 tablespoons honey

1 tablespoon soy protein powder

4 ice cubes

Place all the ingredients, except the ice cubes, into the container of an electric blender and blend on high until smooth. With the blender running, add 2 to 3 ice cubes at a time through the center opening in the lid, until all the ice cubes are added. Blend until smooth. Serve immediately.

Yield: 1 serving (about 16 ounces)

Time: 5 minutes

Maura Egan and Christine Muhlke

PLANET PINEAPPLE SMOOTHIE

Adapted from *The Smoothie Deck*

1 cup light, unsweetened coconut milk

2 cups nonfat vanilla frozen yogurt

1 cup diced fresh pineapple, frozen

1 tablespoon fresh lemon juice

Place the ingredients in a blender and blend until smooth. Stir the mixture, and then pour into tall glasses.

Yield: 2 servings

Time: 10 minutes

Florence Fabricant

GREEN TEA SMOOTHIE

Adapted from T Salon, New York City

1½ teaspoons green tea leaves

1½ cups plain low-fat yogurt

2 medium very ripe peaches, pitted and cut in chunks (see Note)

1 to 3 teaspoons honey

6 ice cubes

Place all the ingredients in a blender, and process on purée or frappé speed until the ice cubes are completely blended. Serve immediately in a very tall glass.

Yield: About 2 cups

Time: 5 minutes

Note: One cup ripe honeydew chunks, 1 large or 2 medium ripe nectarines or 1 large ripe mango may be substituted. Adjust the honey depending on the acidity of the fruit and how tart you like your smoothie.

Marian Burros

JIM DODGE'S SIMPLE BLUEBERRY MUFFINS

Adapted from Baking with Jim Dodge

5 tablespoons unsalted butter
1 large egg
6 tablespoons sugar
½ teaspoon salt
1 tablespoon baking powder
½ cup milk
1¾ cups all-purpose flour
2 cups fresh blueberries

1. Preheat the oven to 400 degrees. Line a muffin pan with paper baking cups, or use a nonstick pan.

2. Melt the butter in a small pan. Then put it into a large bowl. Add the egg and sugar, and whisk. Add all the remaining ingredients, and fold gently until they are mixed. Spoon the batter into the baking cups—6 for big muffins, 12 for small ones.

3. Bake in the middle of the oven until the muffins are slightly brown around the edges, about 30 minutes.

4. Let the muffins cool in the pan for 5 minutes before eating.

Yield: **6 big or 12 small muffins**

Time: **45 minutes**

Florence Fabricant

CRAIG CLAIBORNE'S BASIC OMELET AND VARIATIONS

Omelets are conceivably the most versatile of any dish. There is almost no limit to the number of leftovers or raw foods that can be incorporated into an omelet; the filling depends on the imagination and inventiveness of the cook. You can sauté leftover potatoes in a little butter to make a "peasant" omelet. Or use leftover tomato sauce, excess crumbled bacon or almost any raw vegetable to dress it up. Even leftover sandwich fillings, such as chicken or tuna in mayonnaise, make unexpected, tasty additions to the basic omelet. Omelets are easy enough to make, as is clear from the basic omelet recipe outlined here.

3 eggs
Salt, if desired
Freshly ground pepper
1 tablespoon butter

1. Break the eggs into a bowl. Beat lightly with salt, if desired, and pepper to taste.

2. Heat the omelet pan until quite hot. Immediately add the butter and swirl it around to coat the bottom and sides of the pan. Add the beaten eggs. Shake the skillet to and fro, holding it flat on the burner. Simultaneously, stir the eggs rapidly with a fork, holding the tines parallel to the bottom of the skillet. The preparation of the omelet will take only seconds.

3. When the eggs are at the desired degree of doneness, grasp the handle firmly with the hand turned palm up. Sharply and quickly hit the handle near where it joins the pan to make the omelet "jump" to the bottom of the curve of the skillet. Use a fork to "roll" the omelet, seam side down, onto a waiting plate.

Yield: **1 serving**

Time: **10 minutes**

CHEESE AND POTATO OMELET

2 medium potatoes, about ¼ pound

4 tablespoons peanut, vegetable or corn oil

Salt, if desired

Freshly ground pepper

6 eggs

¾ cup finely diced Gruyère or Swiss cheese

2 tablespoons chopped fresh flat-leaf parsley

2 tablespoons chopped fresh chives, optional

2 tablespoons butter

1. Peel the potatoes and cut them into very thin slices.

2. Heat the oil in a skillet and add the potatoes. Add salt and pepper to taste. Cook, shaking the skillet and redistributing the potatoes so that they cook on all sides, about 8 to 10 minutes, or until golden brown on the bottom and top. Drain well.

3. Beat the eggs in a mixing bowl and add salt and pepper to taste, the cheese, potatoes, parsley and chives.

4. Heat the butter in an omelet pan or nonstick skillet and add the egg mixture, stirring. Cook until the omelet is done on the bottom. Invert the omelet onto a hot round platter and serve.

Yield: 2 to 4 servings

Time: 25 minutes

SMOKED SALMON AND SOUR CREAM OMELET

2 thin slices smoked salmon

1 tablespoon plus 1 teaspoon butter

3 eggs

1 tablespoon finely chopped fresh chives

Salt, if desired

Freshly ground pepper

2 tablespoons sour cream

1. Cut the salmon into ¼-inch cubes. Heat 1 teaspoon of the butter in a small saucepan and add the salmon. Heat briefly without cooking. Set aside.

2. Beat the eggs in a mixing bowl and add 2 teaspoons chopped chives, salt, if desired, and pepper to taste.

3. Heat the remaining 1 tablespoon of butter in a small omelet or nonstick pan. Cook according to the recipe for a plain omelet, but before turning the omelet, add ⅓ of the salmon to the center of the omelet. Fold it over and turn it out onto a plate.

4. Using a small knife, make a small incision down the center of the omelet lengthwise. Spoon the sour cream into and on top of this incision. Spoon the remaining salmon on the sour cream and sprinkle with the remaining chives. Serve hot.

Yield: 1 serving

Time: 15 minutes

Craig Claiborne and Pierre Franey

CHORIZO SCRAMBLED EGGS

Adapted from *Country Egg, City Egg*

1½ teaspoons canola or vegetable oil
½ cup crumbled chorizo sausage
⅓ cup diced yellow onion
4 eggs
Coarse sea salt to taste
4 or more corn tortillas, warmed

1. In a medium nonstick pan, heat the oil and cook the chorizo over medium-low heat, stirring frequently to break up the sausage. Remove the sausage from the pan and discard most of the fat, reserving 1 tablespoon.

2. Wipe the pan clean and add the diced onion and the reserved fat to the pan. Cook the onion until tender. Return the chorizo to the pan.

3. Beat the eggs and season lightly with salt. Scramble the sausage and egg together over medium heat until the eggs are just set. Slide the eggs onto warm corn tortillas on warm plates.

Yield: 2 servings

Time: 30 minutes

Note: This is also good with refried beans, sour cream and radishes.

Moira Hodgson

MIGAS EGGS À LA MIKE MARKS

For the Garnish

1 cup shredded Cheddar cheese
2 large tomatoes (about 1 pound), cut into wedges
½ cup chopped fresh cilantro
Extra tortillas (corn or flour), to wrap around the egg mixture

For the Migas

2 corn tortillas (each about 1 ounce)
4 tablespoons corn oil
¾ cup coarsely chopped onion
2 cups sliced fresh mushrooms (a 6-ounce can of drained mushrooms may be substituted)
2 pickled jalapeño peppers (fresh hot peppers can be substituted, with the amount determined by your tolerance for hotness)
12 eggs
¾ teaspoon salt
¾ teaspoon freshly ground black pepper
1 teaspoon cumin powder

1. Cut the 2 corn tortillas into 1-inch pieces (about 1 cup). Place the oil in a 12-inch skillet and fry the tortilla pieces over medium to high heat for about 3 minutes, until the tortillas change color and begin to crisp. Add the chopped onion, the sliced mushrooms and the jalapeño pepper. Cook for about 2 minutes, then lower the heat to medium.

2. Meanwhile, beat the eggs and add to them the salt, pepper and cumin powder. Pour into the skillet and stir until the egg mixture is setting on the bottom and almost ready to set on top but is still quite wet. Remove from the heat. (Remember that it will continue cooking in its own residual heat.)

3. Sprinkle the cheese over the surface of the eggs, arrange wedges of tomato on top and cover with the lid. Set aside for 5 to 10 minutes, then sprinkle with the cilantro and spoon into warm tortillas. To eat, wrap the tortillas around the filling.

Yield: 6 servings

Time: 25 minutes

Jacques Pépin

PIPERADE

3 red or green bell peppers
3 tablespoons extra virgin olive oil
1 medium onion, chopped
1 clove garlic, minced
3 tomatoes, peeled, seeded and chopped
½ teaspoon fresh oregano (or ¼ teaspoon dried)
½ teaspoon fresh thyme (or ¼ teaspoon dried)
6 eggs
Coarse salt and freshly ground pepper to taste
4 tablespoons unsalted butter
Fresh basil leaves for garnish, if available

1. Preheat the broiler.

2. Cut the peppers in quarters, remove the seeds and place the quarters, skin side up, on a rack covered with foil paper. Broil until the skins blister. Place the peppers in a paper bag or wrap them in a dish towel and leave for a couple of minutes. Peel the skin off the peppers and cut them into strips. Set aside.

3. Heat the oil in a heavy skillet and fry the onion and garlic until soft. Add the tomatoes, the oregano and thyme, and peppers and cook over medium heat for 10 minutes, or until soft.

4. Meanwhile, lightly beat the eggs and season them with salt and pepper.

5. In a separate pan, heat the butter over a low flame. Add the eggs and the vegetables and cook

gently until the eggs are soft but not fully set. Sprinkle with basil, torn into strips, and serve.

Yield: 3 to 4 servings

Time: 35 minutes

Moira Hodgson

NIGELLA LAWSON'S OVERNIGHT BACON-AND-EGG BAKE

If you were planning a late breakfast, then you could start frying the bacon and soaking the bread in the egg, cheese and milk in the morning. A few hours' steeping at room temperature will probably do if the bread is slightly stale and therefore more likely to soak up the savory custard. But it is probably easier to get the whole dish assembled before you go to bed, stash it in the refrigerator, and then bake it the next morning. If you can't get the dish to room temperature before putting it in the oven, be sure to give an extra five minutes' cooking. This also can be a supper dish. If you want to make it richer, substitute sour cream for some of the milk. It might be tempting to leave out the ketchup, but try it with it first—it works!

Butter, for baking dish
10 slices (6 ounces) bacon
1½ cups whole milk
¼ teaspoon ground mace
1 cup grated Cheddar cheese
¼ cup ketchup, more if desired
4 large eggs
8 small slices (or 4 large slices, halved) stale or day-old white bakery bread

1. The night before baking, butter a 12 × 8-inch baking dish and set it aside. In a large skillet over medium heat, fry the bacon until crisp; drain on paper towels and allow to cool.

2. In a large bowl whisk together the milk, mace, cheese, ¼ cup ketchup and eggs. Lay the bread, slightly overlapping, in two rows down the length of the dish. Pour the milk mixture evenly over the slices. Crumble the bacon over the top. Cover the dish with plastic wrap and refrigerate overnight.

3. In the morning, remove the dish from the refrigerator and bring to room temperature. Preheat the oven to 350 degrees. Bake the egg mixture until the top is crispy and golden, about 40 minutes. Cut into squares and serve, if desired, with ketchup on the side.

Yield: 4 to 6 servings

Time: About 1 hour, including 40 minutes baking, plus overnight refrigeration

Nigella Lawson

JULIA REED'S MOCK CHEESE SOUFFLÉ

This dish can be made the night before and popped into the oven for a simple, but elegant brunch. Or you might enjoy it at lunch, along with a green salad and a glass of wine.

> Softened butter for greasing dish and
> spreading on bread
> 8 slices white sandwich bread, crusts removed
> 1 pound sharp Cheddar cheese, grated
> 4 large eggs, beaten
> ½ teaspoon salt
> 2 cups whole milk
> 2 teaspoons Worcestershire sauce
> Dash of cayenne pepper

1. Butter an 8-cup soufflé dish that can go from refrigerator to oven.

2. Butter each slice of bread on one side and cut into four squares. Layer half the bread, buttered

side up, in the bottom of the dish. Cover with half the grated cheese. Repeat. Place the remaining ingredients in a bowl and mix well. Pour over the bread and cheese. Cover with plastic wrap and refrigerate overnight.

3. Preheat the oven to 350 degrees. Uncover the soufflé and bake on the center rack until the top is browned and the soufflé is bubbling around the edges, about 45 minutes.

Yield: 6 servings

Time: 1 hour, including 45 minutes baking, plus overnight refrigeration

Julia Reed

OVERNIGHT STRATA WITH SPINACH AND PEPPERS

Adapted from Lula, Chicago

This rich strata is prepared the night before, then popped into the oven the next day and baked. Cheesy and eggy, it is a marriage of quiche and bread pudding.

> 1 large onion, peeled and thinly sliced
> 2 tablespoons extra virgin olive oil, plus
> extra for pan
> 1 each: red, yellow, purple bell peppers, seeded,
> cored and julienned (see Note)
> 1 (36-ounce) loaf brioche
> 2 small bunches spinach, washed, chopped,
> stems removed
> ½ cup pine nuts, toasted
> 1 cup julienne of fresh basil
> Salt and freshly ground black pepper
> 8 eggs
> 1 quart milk
> 2 cloves garlic, chopped
> 1 teaspoon grated nutmeg

1 pound double-crème Brie, sliced

2 cups shredded mozzarella

1. Cook the onion in 1 tablespoon of the oil until caramelized. Set aside. Cook the peppers in the remaining 1 tablespoon oil over high heat until softened. Set aside.

2. Slice the brioche ¾-inch thick, then into triangles. Oil a 13 × 9-inch baking dish. Fit half the bread into the dish to cover the bottom. Distribute half the onions and peppers over it. Arrange the spinach on top, then half the pine nuts and half the basil. Season with salt and pepper.

3. Blend the eggs, milk, garlic and nutmeg in a blender. Pour half the mixture into the dish, pressing in so the bread absorbs it. Distribute half of both cheeses over top. Fit the remaining bread into the dish, then repeat the onion, pepper, pine nut and basil layers. Pour the remaining egg mixture over it, pressing so that the bread soaks it up. Distribute the cheese over the top. Refrigerate overnight.

4. To bake, preheat the oven to 350 degrees. Lay foil on the bottom of the oven rack in case of overflow. Bake 40 to 50 minutes, until set and well browned on top. Cool slightly before cutting.

Yield: 8 to 10 servings

Time: Preparation time: 1 hour, overnight refrigeration; baking time: 40 to 50 minutes

Note: If purple bell peppers are not available, substitute another color (red, green or orange).

Regina Schrambling

HASH BROWN PATTIES

These savory patties, in individual portions, freeze well and are handy to have for breakfasts or at any time.

6 large potatoes, washed but not peeled

2 medium onions, peeled

3 tablespoons vegetable oil

Salt and pepper to taste

Additional oil for the baking sheet

1. Preheat the oven to 400 degrees. Shred the potatoes and onions in a food processor or with a handheld shredder. Place them in a large bowl, add the vegetable oil, salt and pepper and mix well.

2. Oil two 13 × 9-inch nonstick baking sheets and place the potato mixture on the sheets in 12 mounds. Flatten them to a thickness of ½ inch and form them into neat, round cakes. Bake for 30 minutes, or until the undersides of the cakes are browned. It is not necessary to turn the cakes. Remove them from the oven.

3. To serve right away: patties may be served directly from the oven. Or, if desired, brown them further on both sides in butter, bacon fat or oil.

4. To freeze for later use: remove the patties from the oven and allow to cool completely before lifting from the sheet. Wrap them individually, place them on a flat sheet and freeze. When ready to serve, defrost as many cakes as you wish either overnight in the refrigerator or in the microwave, and fry on both sides in butter, bacon fat or oil until nicely browned. Alternatively, put the frozen cakes directly onto the rack of a toaster oven set for dark, and toast until browned but not dry in the center.

Yield: 12 individual portions

Time: Preparation time: 5 minutes; baking time: 30 minutes

Robert Farrar Capon

BROILED MAPLE-GLAZED SAUSAGE

1 pound smoked Polish sausage links
    or other smoked sausage
2 tablespoons top-grade, pure maple
    syrup
Vegetable oil

1. Preheat a broiler with the rack positioned 6 inches from heat. Cut the sausage diagonally into ½-inch-thick slices, and place in a mixing bowl. Add the maple syrup, and stir to coat well.

2. Lightly oil a broiling pan, and add the sausage slices in an even layer. Broil until the sausage is lightly browned, turning once during cooking, 2 to 3 minutes per side. Transfer to a warm platter, and serve.

Yield: 4 servings

Time: 25 minutes

Denise Landis

CRAIG CLAIBORNE'S QUICHE LORRAINE

The quiche is an "egg-thickened" dish, like a mayonnaise or a hollandaise. There is almost no tasty, savory ingredient that cannot be turned into a quiche. The technique for creating your own quiches is simple. You take the basic custard ratio, which is two eggs for one cup of liquid—milk or cream or a blend of both—and add savory seasonings and solids such as the cheese, onion, and bacon mixture.

Pastry for a single-crust, 9-inch pie
4 strips bacon
1 onion, thinly sliced
1 cup Gruyère or Swiss cheese, cubed
¼ cup grated Parmesan cheese
4 eggs, lightly beaten
2 cups heavy cream, or 1 cup each milk and
    cream
¼ teaspoon nutmeg
½ teaspoon salt
¼ teaspoon freshly ground pepper
Tabasco sauce to taste

1. Preheat the oven to 400 degrees.

2. Line a 9-inch pie plate with the pastry. By all means build a rim with the pastry and flute it. This is essential for the amount of custard indicated in this recipe.

3. Cover the bottom of the pastry with a round of wax paper and add enough dried beans or peas to partly fill the shell. Bake 10 minutes.

4. Reduce the oven heat to 375 degrees. Remove and discard the beans and wax paper and set the pastry-lined pie plate aside.

5. Cook the bacon until crisp and remove it from the skillet. Pour off all but 1 tablespoon of the fat remaining in the skillet. Cook the onion in the remaining fat until the onion is transparent.

6. Crumble the bacon and sprinkle the bacon, onion and cheeses over the inside of the partially baked pastry.

7. Combine the eggs, cream, nutmeg, salt, pepper and Tabasco sauce to taste. Strain the mixture over the onion-cheese mixture. Slide the pie plate onto a baking sheet.

8. Bake the pie until a knife inserted 1 inch from the pastry edge comes out clean, about 25 minutes. Remove to a wire rack. Let stand 5 to 10 minutes before serving.

Yield: 6 to 10 servings

Time: 70 minutes

Variations:

Crabmeat Quiche. Follow the recipe for quiche Lorraine but omit the bacon, sliced onion and cheeses. Combine the eggs, cream, and seasonings. Add 2 cups of crabmeat that has been picked over to remove all traces of shell and cartilage. Cook ⅓ cup of finely chopped shallots in 1 tablespoon of butter until wilted and add to the cream mixture. Add 3 tablespoons finely chopped parsley. Pour the mixture into the prepared pie plate or tin and bake as indicated.

Spinach and Cheese Quiche. Cook 1 pound of well-cleaned bulk spinach or one 10-ounce package of spinach in a little boiling water. Cook, covered, about 1 minute. Drain and squeeze to extract most of the excess moisture. Chop the spinach coarsely. Follow the recipe for Quiche Lorraine, but omit the bacon, sliced onion and Gruyère cheese. Combine the eggs, cream, and seasonings. Add the spinach and ½ cup grated Parmesan cheese. Pour the mixture into the prepared pie plate and bake as indicated.

Mushroom Quiche. Melt 2 tablespoons of butter in a skillet and add ¼ cup of finely chopped onion. Cook, stirring briefly. Add ⅓ pound thinly sliced mushrooms. Sprinkle with the juice of half a lemon. Cook until wilted. Continue cooking until the liquid evaporates. Drain on absorbent paper towels. Follow the recipe for Quiche Lorraine, but omit the bacon, sliced onion and Parmesan cheese. Combine the eggs, cream, and seasonings. Add the mushroom mixture and ⅓ cup of grated Gruyère cheese. Pour the mixture into the prepared pie plate and bake as indicated.

Craig Claiborne

ROSE LEVY BERANBAUM'S BUTTERMILK BLUEBERRY PANCAKES

The cookbook author and baking expert Rose Levy Beranbaum suggests dropping frozen blueberries onto buttermilk batter after it has been ladled onto the griddle. This technique will keep the fruit plump and juicy all the way to the table.

> 2 cups sifted unleavened cake flour
> 4 teaspoons baking powder
> ½ teaspoon salt
> 4 large eggs, separated
> 2 cups buttermilk
> ½ teaspoon cream of tartar
> 4 tablespoons unsalted butter, melted and cooled
> 2 full cups frozen blueberries
> Butter, for greasing griddle or skillet

1. In a large bowl, combine the flour, baking powder and salt and whisk to blend. Set aside.

2. In a small bowl, beat the egg yolks and buttermilk to blend slightly. In another bowl, beat the egg whites until foamy, add the cream of tartar and continue beating until stiff peaks form when the beater is raised. Set aside briefly.

3. Add the yolk mixture to the flour mixture and mix lightly with a fork until the flour is moistened. Stir in the cooled melted butter. The batter should be lumpy; overmixing makes tough pancakes. Gently fold in the beaten egg whites.

4. Preheat the griddle or skillet. Lightly butter the hot griddle before each batch of pancakes. Pour out the batter to make 4-inch rounds. Quickly drop 6 to 8 frozen berries onto each pancake. Test for doneness by lifting a corner of a pancake with a metal spatula. When golden brown, turn over and cook about 30 seconds on the other side. Serve with warmed maple syrup, hickory bacon, sausages or scrapple.

Yield: Between 18 and 22 four-inch pancakes

Time: 30 minutes

Note: These pancakes may be frozen and reheated.

Joanna Pruess

LEMON-RICOTTA HOTCAKES

Adapted from the Four Seasons Hotel, New York City

Dorie Greenspan: "Most pancakes recipes are flexible. You can double or triple them, a great idea if you are cooking for a crowd and want to stock your freezer. Pancakes freeze perfectly and can be reheated, without defrosting, in an oven or even a toaster. You can also use any recipe to make cakes of just about any size, from as small as a silver dollar to as large as your favorite DVD. Keep pancakes in a preheated 200-degree oven until a batch is prepared and ready to serve.

6 large eggs, separated
1½ cups whole-milk ricotta cheese
1 stick unsalted butter, melted and cooled
½ teaspoon pure vanilla extract
½ cup all-purpose flour
¼ cup sugar
½ teaspoon salt
2 tablespoons grated lemon zest
Powdered sugar, for dusting
Blackberries for garnish, optional

1. Heat a griddle. Whip the egg whites until they hold firm, glossy peaks, and set aside. Beat the ricotta, butter, egg yolks and vanilla together, and set aside.

2. Whisk together flour, sugar, salt and zest. With a rubber spatula, stir dry ingredients gently into the ricotta mixture. Stir a spoonful of whipped egg whites into the batter; then gently fold in the remainder.

3. Grease the heated griddle, if necessary. Drop 3 tablespoons of batter for each pancake on the griddle, allowing space for spreading. Cook until golden on the bottom and the top shows a bubble or two. Gently flip, and cook until the undersides are light brown. Dust with powdered sugar. Top with berries, if desired.

Yield: About 20 small hotcakes

Time: About 30 minutes

Dorie Greenspan

DAVID EYRE'S FAMOUS PANCAKE

One of the most popular recipes ever to appear in *The New York Times*—and with good reason.

½ cup flour
½ cup milk
2 eggs, lightly beaten
⅛ teaspoon freshly grated nutmeg
4 tablespoons butter
2 tablespoons confectioners' sugar
Juice of ½ lemon
Choice of jams, jellies, marmalade, preserves, maple syrup or honey

1. Preheat the oven to 425 degrees.

2. In a mixing bowl combine the flour, milk, eggs and nutmeg. Beat lightly. Leave the batter a little lumpy.

3. Melt the butter in a 12-inch skillet with a heat-proof handle. When the butter is very hot but not brown, pour in the batter. Bake 15 to 20 minutes or until golden brown.

4. Sprinkle the pancake with confectioners' sugar and place briefly in the oven. Sprinkle with lemon juice and serve with your favorite topping.

Yield: 4 to 6 servings

Time: 30 minutes

Craig Claiborne

MARION CUNNINGHAM'S HEAVENLY HOTS

Marion Cunningham's custardlike "heavenly hots" are kept moist by the novel combination of lots of sour cream and cake flour. "So delicate are they that they must be kept small," cautions their creator, "or they will break as they are turned." Like many griddlecake recipes, the one for heavenly hots is simple and quick, and the batter can be prepared well ahead of time and refrigerated. Keep pancakes warm in a preheated 200-degree oven until a batch is prepared and ready to serve.

4 large eggs

½ teaspoon salt

½ teaspoon baking soda

4 tablespoons cake flour

2 cups sour cream

3 tablespoons sugar

Solid vegetable shortening, for greasing
    griddle or skillet

1. Mix all the ingredients except the vegetable shortening in a large bowl. With a wooden spoon, beat until smooth. This can also be done in a blender.

2. Heat the griddle or skillet until it is very hot. Film with shortening. Drop small spoonfuls of batter onto the griddle, making sure that when they spread out they measure less than 3 inches in diameter. When a few bubbles appear on top of the pancakes, turn and cook the second side briefly. Serve with maple syrup.

Yield: Between 50 and 60 dollar-size pancakes

Time: 20 minutes

Note: The batter will keep, refrigerated, for up to 1 week.

Joanna Pruess

MOLLIE KATZEN'S AMAZING OVERNIGHT WAFFLES

Adapted from *Mollie Katzen's Sunlight Café*

2 cups all-purpose flour

1 teaspoon yeast

1 tablespoon sugar

½ teaspoon salt

2 cups milk

1 large egg, lightly beaten

6 tablespoons unsalted butter, melted

Nonstick spray

Butter for waffle iron

1. Combine the flour, yeast, sugar and salt. Whisk in the milk until blended. Cover the bowl tightly with plastic wrap and let stand overnight at room temperature. (If the room is warmer than 70 degrees, refrigerate.)

2. In the morning, heat the waffle iron. Beat the egg and melted butter into the batter; the batter will be quite thin. Spray the hot waffle iron with nonstick spray, and rub on a little butter with a paper towel or piece of bread. Add just enough batter to cover the cooking surface, about 1⅓ cups for a Belgian waffle, ⅔ cup for a standard waffle.

3. Cook the waffles until crisp and brown but not too dark, 2 to 3 minutes each. Serve hot with toppings of your choice.

Yield: 3 to 4 Belgian waffles, or 6 to 8 standard waffles

Time: 15 minutes, plus overnight resting of batter

Alex Witchel

Mollie Katzen's Amazing Overnight Waffles

BRASSERIE'S ORANGE FRENCH TOAST

Assemble this the night before, to let the bread soak up the delicious liquid.

½ cup milk

1 cup orange juice

5 eggs

6 tablespoons sugar

½ teaspoon vanilla

Zest of 1 large orange

2 medium-size French baguettes, each about
    16 inches long

2 tablespoons butter (approximately)

Confectioners' sugar

1. Beat the milk, orange juice, eggs, sugar and vanilla together until well blended. Strain into a large bowl. Grate the zest of the orange, taking care not to include any of the white pith, and add it to the mixture.

2. Cut baguettes into 1- to 1½-inch-thick slices on an angle. You should have approximately 18 slices. Do not use the ends. Briefly soak the bread slices in the egg mixture, then place them in a single layer on a tray, a large platter, or a shallow baking pan. Pour any of the egg mixture not absorbed by the bread over the slices. Cover and refrigerate at least 5 hours or overnight. If possible, turn the slices once during this time.

3. Peel away all the white pith of the orange and cut the orange into thin slices to use as a garnish. Cover with plastic wrap and refrigerate until ready to use.

4. Melt the butter in 1 or 2 large skillets or on a griddle. Fry the bread slices over medium-low heat until nicely browned, turning once to brown both sides. Depending on the type of skillet, you may need a little more butter.

5. Dust the French toast with confectioners' sugar, garnish with orange slices and serve.

Yield: 6 servings

Time: 30 minutes, and refrigerate 5 plus hours

Florence Fabricant

BREAKFAST CRÊPES

½ cup all-purpose flour
1½ teaspoons baking powder
Pinch of salt
1 egg, lightly beaten
¾ cup skim milk
½ teaspoon peanut or vegetable oil
Unsalted butter
Confectioners' sugar
Fresh fruit, such as berries, diced banana, peach
   or oranges, optional
Maple syrup or fruit syrup

1. Sift the flour and baking powder into a large bowl. Add salt.

2. Add the egg and milk and mix until blended. Do not worry about lumps, they will disappear when the pancakes cook.

3. Heat a small skillet or griddle to medium hot, so that a drop of water will bounce on the surface. Grease the skillet. Spoon out about ¼ cup of batter for each pancake. Cook until bubbles begin to appear. Using a thin spatula, turn the pancakes over and brown the other side. Keep the pancakes warm in a preheated 200-degree oven until ready to serve.

4. When ready to serve them, roll the pancakes over lightly, fill with fruit, if you like, or leave them plain. Dot with pieces of butter and sprinkle with sifted confectioners' sugar. Serve with maple syrup or fruit syrup on the side.

Yield: 6 crêpes

Time: 20 minutes

Moira Hodgson

LUNCHES AT
THE BEACH, NEAR THE LAKE OR ON A COOL AND SHADY BACK PORCH

RECISPES FOR LUNCHES

Leek, Mushroom and Goat Cheese Tart

LEEK, MUSHROOM AND GOAT CHEESE TART

A savory tart built upon a layer of store-bought puff pastry, topped with goat cheese, mushrooms, and leeks.

    1 small fennel bulb
    2 medium leeks, white and light green parts
        only, halved lengthwise and rinsed carefully
        to remove any dirt from inner layers
    16 medium cremini or white mushrooms
        (about 1 pound)
    1 tablespoon plus 1 teaspoon olive oil
    Salt and pepper
    1 (4-ounce) package puff pastry (like Dufour),
        defrosted according to package directions
    3 eggs
    8 ounces goat cheese

1. Preheat the oven to 400 degrees. Trim the fennel of the green top and root end, reserving the fronds, and quarter the bulb from top to bottom. Using a mandoline or very sharp knife, cut the fennel and leeks into paper-thin slices. Clean and slice the mushrooms.

2. Heat 1 tablespoon oil in a skillet over medium heat; add the fennel and leeks and sauté until just tender but not brown, about 6 minutes. Transfer to a bowl and set aside. Heat the remaining teaspoon of oil in a skillet over medium-high heat; add the mushrooms and sauté until they release all their liquid and most of it boils away, about 5 minutes. Combine the fennel mixture with the mushrooms and sauté together briefly; season with salt and pepper. Remove the pan from the heat.

3. Unfold the puff pastry onto a lightly floured surface; cut in half lengthwise to form 2 long rectangles. Gently roll out each rectangle to approximately 5 by 14 inches and place on a cookie sheet (or cut into 2 circles, if desired). Trim the edges by ¼-inch strips all around; set the strips aside. Break 1 egg into a small bowl; beat slightly. Brush the edges of the pastry with some egg. Use the trimmed strips to make a raised border on each. (Or, fold the pastry edges over to form a rim.) Brush the entire surface with the remaining beaten egg. Prick the interior of the pastry all over with a fork. Bake until pale gold, about 10 minutes. If the pastry has puffed up inside the edge, press it down gently. Set aside.

4. Meanwhile, combine the remaining eggs with 6 ounces of the goat cheese and blend until smooth. Spread onto the pastry. Return to the oven and bake just until set, about 4 minutes. Remove from the oven and spread with the mushroom-leek mixture. Crumble the remaining cheese on top. Just before serving, broil the tarts on low heat for 2 to 3 minutes, until the tarts are warm and the cheese softens. Garnish with fennel fronds.

Yield: 10 to 12 servings

Time: 1 hour

Celia Barbour

NIGELLA LAWSON'S BAKED RICOTTA CRUSTLESS TART

Adapted from *Forever Summer*

This light and crustless ricotta tart is bound with the whites of egg. It's a snap to make: you do no more than mix some ricotta with salt, pepper, the zest of a lemon, a little dried oregano (or any herb of your choice) and some egg whites, then bake this mixture in a cake pan for half an hour. It cooks to a creamy, low-rise disk. Nigella Lawson often teams it with roasted cherry tomatoes—which can be made ahead and brought to room temperature before serving—but other seasoned and sautéed garden vegetables would also enhance it. It is an excellent dish for a light supper or for lunch, or as an appetizer.

18 ounces (2 ¼ cups) ricotta cheese
2 large egg whites, lightly beaten
¼ teaspoon dried oregano
Finely grated zest of 1 lemon
Salt and freshly ground black pepper
Vegetable oil for greasing pan

1. Preheat the oven to 350 degrees. In a mixing bowl, combine the ricotta, egg whites, oregano and lemon zest. Season to taste with salt and pepper. Lightly oil an 8-inch springform baking pan. Pour in the ricotta mixture, and smooth the surface.

2. Bake until the ricotta is dry on top but not browned, about 30 minutes; it will have risen slightly but will remain a thin disk. Allow to cool slightly, and release from the pan. Cut into wedges, and serve warm with a plate of roasted tomatoes (recipe follows).

Yield: 4 to 6 servings

Time: 40 minutes, including 30 minutes baking

➤ NIGELLA LAWSON'S ROASTED CHERRY TOMATOES

Adapted from *Forever Summer*

8 ounces cherry tomatoes, halved
Scant teaspoon kosher salt
1 teaspoon olive oil

1. Position an oven rack in the lower third of the oven, and preheat to 350 degrees. Line a jelly-roll pan or a baking sheet with foil. Place the tomatoes on the foil, cut side up.

2. Sprinkle the tomatoes with salt and oil, and bake 30 minutes. Remove from the heat and allow to come to room temperature before serving.

Yield: 4 to 6 servings.

Time: 40 minutes, plus cooling time

Nigella Lawson

E.A.T.'S TARRAGON LOBSTER SALAD

Adapted from E.A.T., New York City

2 pounds cooked fresh lobster meat
2 tablespoons Dijon mustard
3 tablespoons sherry vinegar
½ cup light vegetable oil (not olive oil)
2 tablespoons minced fresh tarragon
Pinch of cayenne or red pepper flakes
    to taste
2 bunches mâche (lamb's lettuce)

1. Cut the cooked lobster meat into chunks.

2. Blend the mustard and vinegar in a food processor. With the machine running, slowly pour the oil in through the feed tube and process until the mixture has thickened and is well blended. This can also be done in a small mixing bowl with a whisk.

3. Fold the dressing and the lobster together and add the tarragon. Season with the cayenne or red pepper flakes. If possible, refrigerate for about 1 hour to allow flavors to mellow. Serve on a bed of mâche.

Yield: 6 servings

Time: 25 minutes, plus about 1 hour refrigeration for flavors to ripen

Florence Fabricant

JASPER WHITE'S OLD-FASHIONED CLAM CHOWDER

Adapted from 50 Chowders

Jasper White, the dean of New England chefs and a noted seafood authority, prefers Ipswich clams for this chowder. In this recipe, a leaner version of traditional chowder, he uses whole milk and evaporated milk or light cream in place of heavy cream. If the clams are clean, you may omit the first step.

2 to 3 pounds soft-shell or steamer clams (30 to 40 clams) in the shell
Brine solution, if necessary: 1 cup salt mixed with 12 cups cold water
2 ounces salt pork, pancetta or blanched bacon (see Note), diced
3 tablespoons unsalted butter
2 medium yellow onions, halved and thinly sliced
2 or 3 medium potatoes, peeled and cubed (about 2½ cups)
Freshly ground black pepper to taste
2 bay leaves
2 cups whole milk
½ cup evaporated milk or light cream
Salt to taste
¼ cup chopped fresh chives or flat-leaf parsley
Common crackers, optional

1. Pick over the clams, discarding any with cracked shells or any that feel heavy, an indication they are full of mud. Rinse them under cold running water to get rid of surface grit. If clams are very gritty, set them in a bowl with brine solution and keep cool, or refrigerate for 2 to 3 hours.

2. Drain the clams and place them in a large, heavy soup kettle; add about ½ inch water to the kettle and set over medium heat. Cook, uncovered, stirring frequently with a wooden spoon, until all the clams have opened. As they open, remove them from the kettle and set aside. (Any clams that fail to open after 10 to 15 minutes should be discarded.) Strain the clam liquor through several layers of cheesecloth into a 2-cup measuring cup, and set aside. Remove the clams from their shells, and set aside.

3. Rinse out the soup kettle and return to the stove top. Add the salt pork, pancetta or bacon dice and 1 tablespoon butter, and cook slowly over medium-low heat until the dice browns a little on the edges. Use a slotted spoon to remove the dice from the fat. Set aside.

4. Add the onions to the fat and cook, stirring frequently, until soft but not brown. Stir in the potatoes, and continue cooking another 5 minutes, until the potatoes begin to soften. Add enough water to the clam liquor in the measuring cup to make 2 cups; pour this over the potatoes. Add black pepper and bay leaves.

5. Simmer gently, partially covered, until the potatoes are tender. Add whole milk and simmer again. Stir in the clams and evaporated milk or cream, stirring gently so as not to break open the clam bellies. Taste, and add salt if necessary. Let come just to a simmer, and remove from the heat. (Do not let the chowder come to a full boil.)

6. Chowder can be set in a cool place for several hours to develop the flavors. Reheat to a simmer (do not let it boil), then stir in chives or parsley and the remaining butter just before serving. Pass common crackers at the table if you wish.

Yield: 6 to 8 servings

Time: About 1 hour plus, if desired, several hours for flavors to develop. Clams that must be cleaned may require an additional 2 to 3 hours of soaking.

Note: Blanched bacon is smoked slab bacon that has been cooked for 3 to 5 minutes in boiling water to remove much of the smoky flavor. If you like the smoky flavor, do not bother blanching the bacon.

Nancy Harmon Jenkins

LOBSTER OR CRAB SALAD ROLL

3 cups lobster or crab salad (recipe follows)
6 frankfurter buns

1. Prepare the salad and set aside.

2. Open the buns and toast them or not, according to taste.

3. Fill each bun with an equal portion of the salad and serve sandwich-fashion.

Yield: 6 servings

Time: 5 minutes

Lobster or Crab Salad Roll

➤ LOBSTER OR CRAB SALAD

2½ cups lobster meat (store bought or the meat from three 1½-pound lobsters), or use the same volume of crabmeat, preferably lump crab
½ cup finely chopped celery
¼ cup finely chopped onion
¾ cup mayonnaise, preferably, homemade
1 tablespoon finely chopped chives
½ teaspoon Worcestershire sauce
Salt to taste, if desired
Freshly ground pepper to taste
Tabasco sauce to taste
1 teaspoon vinegar
2 tablespoons finely chopped fresh flat-leaf parsley

1. Cut the lobster meat into bite-size pieces and put them in a mixing bowl.

2. Add the remaining ingredients and toss to blend well.

Yield: About 3 cups

Time: 30 minutes

Craig Claiborne

ITALIAN LOBSTER SALAD

(Insalata di Astice)

A simple and luxurious summer salad.

2 (2-pound) lobsters
6 ripe red tomatoes, cored and coarsely chopped
1 large red onion, thinly sliced
½ cup olive oil
3 tablespoons white-wine vinegar

Continued

1 tablespoon chopped fresh oregano, or
    ½ teaspoon crumbled dried (see Note)
Salt and freshly ground white pepper to taste
2 tablespoons pinot bianco, or other good-
    quality dry white wine

1. Fill a large pot with 2½ inches of lightly salted water. Bring to a brisk boil and add the lobsters. Steam them for 10 to 15 minutes. (The lobsters are cooked when they turn bright red and you can pull off one of the antennae with a quick jerk.)

2. Drain the lobsters and set aside. When cool enough to handle, remove the shells and cut the tail and claw meat into bite-size pieces.

3. Combine the tomatoes and onions in a large salad bowl. In a small bowl combine the oil and vinegar. Whisk in the oregano and salt and pepper, and pour over the tomatoes and onions. Add the lobster pieces and toss to coat.

4. Sprinkle the wine over the salad and set in a cool place for at least 2 hours before serving. It may be refrigerated, if necessary, but should be brought to room temperature before serving.

Yield: 6 servings

Time: 1 hour, plus 2 or more hours cooling

Note: Other fresh herbs such as thyme, tarragon or dill may be substituted for the fresh oregano.

Nancy Harmon Jenkins

RICK BAYLESS'S MEXICAN CRAB AND GREEN BEAN SALAD

Adapted from Rick Bayless

½ pound green beans, trimmed
¼ cup lime juice
1 tablespoon sherry vinegar

2 tablespoons olive oil
½ teaspoon minced jalapeño pepper
8 ounces lump crabmeat
1 red onion, peeled and thinly sliced
1 large tomato, peeled, cored, seeded, and diced
½ cup minced fresh cilantro leaves
1 tablespoon minced fresh marjoram leaves
½ teaspoon salt, plus more to taste
1 teaspoon freshly ground pepper, plus more
    to taste

1. Blanch the green beans in boiling salted water for 2 minutes. Rinse under cold running water until chilled. Drain. Slice the beans in half lengthwise. Set aside.

2. Combine the lime juice and sherry vinegar in a large glass or ceramic bowl. Whisk in the olive oil. Add the green beans, minced jalapeño, crabmeat, red onion, tomato, cilantro, marjoram, salt and pepper. Toss to combine. Season to taste with additional salt and pepper.

Yield: 4 servings

Time: 30 minutes

Molly O'Neill

CRAB AND CORN SALAD, SOUTHERN STYLE

Adapted from Alexander Smalls

A refreshing combination of crab, corn and cucumber, enhanced by a creamy sherry dressing with a touch of nutmeg and mace. The recipe can easily be halved for 10 servings.

¾ cup half-and-half
2 large hothouse cucumbers, preferably
    seedless, peeled and thinly sliced
½ cup dry sherry

20 ears of corn, shucked with silk removed

4 tablespoons unsalted butter

¼ cup vegetable oil

2 pounds crabmeat, picked over

1½ cups thinly sliced pickled sweet red peppers

2 to 3 teaspoons Worcestershire sauce, to taste

¼ teaspoon ground mace

¼ teaspoon freshly grated nutmeg

Salt and freshly ground pepper to taste

1½ pounds baby spinach

1. In a saucepan, bring the half-and-half to a simmer and poach the cucumbers in it for 3 to 4 minutes, until just cooked. Add the sherry. Set aside.

2. Using a sharp knife, hold each cob vertically in a large dish and strip the kernels from it. In a large pot, heat the butter and oil over medium-high heat. Sauté the corn kernels for 5 minutes, or until heated through. Add the crabmeat, red peppers and the rest of the seasonings. Sauté for another 2 minutes, stirring constantly to blend well.

3. In a large salad bowl, combine the cucumber mixture and half-and-half with the crab mixture and cool to room temperature. Place the spinach leaves on a large platter and arrange the salad over them.

Yield: 20 servings

Time: Preparation time: 45 minutes
(35 minutes if halving the recipe), plus
30 minutes' cooling

Sara Rimer

GERMAINE'S FESTIVE SCALLOP SALAD

Adapted from Germaine Swanson

2½ pounds bay scallops, cleaned and rinsed

1½ cups lemon juice

Freshly ground white pepper to taste

½ cup vegetable oil

6 tablespoons distilled white vinegar

2 cloves garlic, chopped

1 large white onion, chopped

1½ teaspoons sugar

4½ teaspoons Dijon mustard

½ cup chopped fresh dill

6 cups shredded iceberg lettuce

30 snow peas, blanched and halved

5 tablespoons pine nuts

1. Combine the scallops, lemon juice and white pepper in a large glass bowl. Cover and marinate for 2 hours at room temperature, or overnight in the refrigerator.

2. In a blender or food processor, combine the oil, vinegar, garlic, onion, sugar, mustard and ⅓ cup of the dill. Purée until smooth. Refrigerate.

3. To serve, drain the scallops of their marinade and mix them with the dressing. Arrange the shredded lettuce on serving plates and spoon some scallops and dressing over it. Trim with snow peas and sprinkle with remaining dill and pine nuts.

Yield: 12 servings

Time: 30 minutes, plus 2 or more hours' marinating

Marian Burros

COLD PASTA WITH PESTO AND BAY SCALLOPS

Pesto keeps well in the refrigerator and also freezes well.

2 cloves garlic, crushed
$\frac{1}{2}$ teaspoon salt
1 tablespoon pine nuts
1 cup fresh basil leaves
$\frac{1}{3}$ cup olive oil plus 1 tablespoon
$\frac{1}{4}$ cup freshly grated Parmesan cheese
$\frac{1}{2}$ cup dry white wine
Juice of $\frac{1}{2}$ lemon
Coarse salt and freshly ground pepper to taste
1 pound bay scallops
1 pound capellini

1. With a pestle crush the garlic with the salt in a mortar. Add the pine nuts and gradually add the basil and the oil a little at a time. Grind until the ingredients have been reduced to a paste.

2. Add the cheese and grind until blended. (This process can also be done in a blender or food processor.) Scrape the pesto into a large mixing bowl and set aside.

3. In a saucepan bring the wine, lemon juice, salt and pepper to a boil. Add the scallops and simmer briefly, 2 or 3 minutes, until barely cooked. Drain, reserving the juice (there will be about 1 cup), and set aside.

4. Meanwhile, bring a large pot of salted water to a rolling boil. Add the tablespoon olive oil. Add the capellini and cook, separating the strands with a long fork until al dente, 5 to 7 minutes.

5. Drain the capellini and immediately add it to the pesto and toss thoroughly. Add the scallop cooking juice a quarter of a cup at a time. Add the scallops, toss well and adjust the seasoning.

6. Refrigerate in a covered bowl overnight or for up to 2 days.

Yield: 4 servings

Time: 30 minutes and overnight refrigeration

Moira Hodgson

TOBY CECCHINI'S TUNA SALAD

This Mediterranean tuna salad uses lemon, mustard, dill and the mild, crunchy burn of peppers to temper the pungency of the fish, with roasted or smoked almonds to give it added texture and flavor. The crucial element is solid-chunk tuna, preferably in a jar and preferably Italian, and it absolutely has to be preserved in olive oil.

10 to 12 ounces good-quality solid tuna packed in olive oil, well drained
2 scallions, washed, trimmed and chopped fine
6 peperoncini peppers, stems removed and julienned
3 tablespoons chopped fresh dill
$\frac{1}{4}$ cup roasted or smoked almonds, chopped roughly, or a small handful toasted pine nuts
$\frac{1}{4}$ cup good-quality olive oil (or the oil the tuna was packed in)
1 tablespoon smooth Dijon mustard
1 tablespoon whole-grain mustard
1 teaspoon balsamic vinegar
1 teaspoon fresh lemon juice, or more to taste
$\frac{1}{4}$ to $\frac{1}{2}$ teaspoon freshly ground black pepper

Mix all the ingredients well with a fork in a medium-size, nonreactive bowl. Taste and adjust the lemon juice and pepper. The salad can be made up to 3 days in advance and refrigerated.

Yield: About 2 cups

Time: 30 minutes

Toby Cecchini

MOLLY O'NEILL'S NIÇOISE SALAD WITH GRILLED, OLIVE-OIL— MARINATED TUNA

1 (12-ounce) tuna steak, about 1¼ inches thick
Kosher salt and freshly ground black pepper
¾ cup olive oil
4 cloves garlic, thinly sliced
1 pound small Yukon Gold potatoes, scrubbed
½ pound green beans or wax beans, ends trimmed
1 tablespoon lemon juice
1 clove minced garlic
1 large tomato, seeded and chopped
½ cup chopped fresh flat-leaf parsley
⅓ cup Niçoise or other black olives, pitted and sliced

1. Prepare a charcoal grill or preheat a broiler. Season the tuna generously with salt and pepper and grill or broil very close to the heat source until it is seared on the outside but still rosy in the center, 3 to 4 minutes per side. Transfer the tuna to a small bowl and add the olive oil and sliced garlic. Cover and refrigerate for at least 6 hours or overnight.

2. Place the potatoes in a large saucepan and cover with cold, salted water. Bring to a boil, lower the heat and simmer, covered, until tender, about 20 minutes. Drain, cool and slice the potatoes. Set aside.

3. Meanwhile, Bring another large saucepan filled two-thirds full of salted water to a boil and add the beans. Cook until the beans just begin to become tender, about 3 minutes. Drain the beans and immediately plunge them into a large bowl of cold water. When cooled, drain the beans and cut them in half if they are large. Set aside.

4. Drain the tuna, reserving 5 tablespoons of the olive oil and discarding the rest. Place the reserved oil in a large bowl and whisk in the lemon juice, minced garlic, ½ teaspoon of kosher salt, and ¼ teaspoon pepper. Add the potatoes, beans, tomato, parsley, and olives. Toss well and season to taste with more salt and pepper. Using a sharp knife, slice the tuna on the bias into thin slices. Lay the slices carefully over the vegetables and serve.

Yield: 4 servings

Time: 1 hour, plus 6 hours to overnight refrigeration

Molly O'Neill

TUNA PAN BAGNA

The *pan bagna*, typical of the region around Nice, may be an early ancestor of the hero sandwich. Weighting the sandwich down compresses the ingredients and intensifies the flavors.

For each serving

1 small, crusty Italian or French-style roll, approximately 5 inches in diameter
1 garlic clove, peeled and chopped
Pinch of salt
3 tablespoons good-quality olive oil
1 tablespoon red wine vinegar
4 or 5 very thin slices onion
4 or 5 thin slices red, ripe tomatoes
2 or 3 sliced radishes
3 or 4 pitted black Mediterranean-style olives
2 to 3 tablespoons well-drained canned tuna
6 anchovy fillets

1. Cut the roll in half and, using a fork, scrape away some of the bread crumbs from the middle of each half, leaving more room for the sandwich ingredients.

2. With the flat blade of a knife, mash the garlic to a paste with the salt. Mix with the olive oil and

vinegar and coat the open side of each half of the roll with the mixture. Set aside for about 20 minutes to let the bread become impregnated with the oil and vinegar.

3. On the bottom half of the roll, layer the onions, tomatoes, radishes and olives. Sprinkle the flaked tuna over the top and arrange the anchovy fillets in a lattice pattern.

4. Place the top half on the sandwich. Weight the sandwich down to press the ingredients together and set aside for an hour or longer. Just before serving, remove the weights and cut the sandwich in half.

Yield: 1 sandwich

Preparation time: 10 minutes
Weighting time: 1 hour or longer

Nancy Harmon Jenkins

then squeeze the grated pulp to extract 1 teaspoon of juice. Add the ginger juice to the tuna, and blend with the onion, soy sauce, cilantro, garlic, oil, jalapeño, salt and pepper.

4. Shape into 4 patties. Place in the freezer for 10 minutes.

5. To cook, brush the burgers with oil, and place on a well-oiled charcoal grill over high heat. Turn carefully after 2 minutes. Cook for 1 minute more, or until the burgers are seared on the outside and nearly raw inside.

6. Serve open-faced on a toasted burger roll with grilled onions, lettuce and mayonnaise, or with a lemon aioli.

Yield: 4 servings

Time: 40 minutes

Trish Hall

GOTHAM BAR AND GRILL'S TUNA BURGERS

24 ounces fresh tuna
1 (2-inch) piece fresh ginger
3 tablespoons finely minced red onion
1½ teaspoon soy sauce
1 tablespoon chopped fresh cilantro
¼ teaspoon finely minced garlic
1 tablespoon extra virgin olive oil
1 small jalapeño pepper, seeded and minced
Salt and freshly ground pepper to taste
Oil, for rubbing burgers and grill

1. Prepare charcoal grill.

2. Finely chop the tuna, putting the pieces in a bowl.

3. Peel the ginger, and grate it into a small bowl,

FLOUNDER IN SAOR

½ cup golden raisins
3 tablespoons grappa or dry white wine
⅓ cup pine nuts
5 tablespoons extra virgin olive oil
2 cups thinly sliced sweet onions
2 cloves garlic, minced
⅓ cup flour
Salt and freshly ground white pepper
    to taste
4 (6-ounce) flounder or fluke fillets
3 tablespoons white wine vinegar
2 tablespoons chicken stock

1. Place the raisins in a small dish, add the grappa or wine and set aside to soak. Toast the pine nuts in a hot skillet. Set aside.

2. Heat 2 tablespoons of the oil in a large skillet.

Add the onions and garlic and sauté over low heat, stirring frequently, until the onions are soft and golden, about 20 minutes. Remove the onions and garlic from the pan and set aside.

3. Spread the flour on a large plate and season with salt and pepper. Rinse the fillets and pat dry. Dust lightly with the seasoned flour.

4. Place the remaining oil in the skillet and place over high heat. Add the fillets and lightly brown, turning once, about 2 minutes per side.

5. Transfer to a warm serving platter. Return the onions and garlic to the skillet and heat. Stir in the raisins and grappa or wine. Add the vinegar and chicken stock. Quickly bring to a simmer, season to taste with salt and pepper and spread over the flounder. Scatter the pine nuts on top. Best served at room temperature.

Yield: 4 servings

Time: 40 minutes

Florence Fabricant

Caprese-Plus Salad

CAPRESE-PLUS SALAD

This variation on the traditional Italian Caprese salad of fresh tomatoes, mozzarella and basil will keep for several days in the refrigerator. Any leftovers make a terrific filling for a vegetarian sandwich or a zesty addition to sandwiches with cured or cooked meats or cooked poultry.

1½ pounds very ripe tomatoes, preferably vine-ripened (either regular or plum)
1 cucumber (about ½ pound), peeled, cut in half lengthwise, seeded, and cut into ½-inch cubes (about 1½ cups)
1 or 2 Vidalia onions (about 8 ounces total), peeled and cut into ½-inch cubes (about 1½ cups)
½ pound fresh mozzarella cheese, cut into sticks about ½-inch thick × 1½-inches long
½ cup shredded fresh basil
¼ cup chopped fresh chives or parsley
1 teaspoon freshly ground black pepper
1 teaspoon salt
½ jalapeño pepper, optional, seeded and finely chopped (about 1 teaspoon)
3 tablespoons red wine vinegar
½ cup extra virgin olive oil

1. Cut the tomatoes in half crosswise and gently squeeze out the seeds. Cut the seeded tomatoes into 1-inch pieces.

2. In a bowl, combine all the ingredients, stirring well. Serve immediately, or cover and refrigerate until needed. An hour or so before serving, remove the salad from the refrigerator so it is cool, not cold, when eaten. Serve with crusty French bread.

Yield: 6 servings

Time: 15 minutes, plus refrigeration, if desired

Jacques Pépin

PEACH AND TOMATO SALAD WITH CURRY VINAIGRETTE

Adapted from *Cool Kitchen*

¼ cup extra virgin olive oil
· 1 tablespoon lemon juice
¼ teaspoon curry powder
¼ teaspoon salt, or to taste
1 tablespoon chopped fresh flat-leaf parsley
    leaves
2 large ripe tomatoes, each cut into 8 wedges
2 ripe peaches, pitted and each cut into 8
    wedges

1. Whisk together the oil, lemon juice, curry powder, salt and parsley in a small bowl.

2. Arrange the tomatoes and peaches on four salad plates, alternating them pinwheel style.

3. Drizzle the dressing over the peaches and tomatoes; serve immediately.

Yield: 4 servings

Time: 10 minutes

Mark Bittman

A tomato tasting in Northern California

GIGI SALAD WITH SHRIMP AND GREEN BEANS

This salad was invented in 1973 by Gigi Delmaestro when he was at Palm Too, which is located across the street from the original Palm on Second Avenue in Manhattan. It depends on a combination of not only textures but temperatures. The beans and onion should be chilled, the tomato left at room temperature, and the shrimp and crumbled bacon kept slightly warm. Cooked shrimp when stored in the refrigerator become tough and lose their flavor, whereas shrimp cooked and left at room temperature actually taste the way shrimp should taste, assuming they're fresh to begin with.

1 pound green beans

1 large Spanish onion

3/4 pound lean bacon slices

1/2 lemon

1 pound shrimp

1 large ripe tomato, or 2 medium-ripe tomatoes, seeded, cored and diced

3 tablespoons olive oil (see Note)

1 tablespoon red wine vinegar

Salt to taste

Freshly ground black pepper to taste

1. Wash the beans, discard the tops and cut the beans into 1-inch pieces. Boil them in salted water until tender but still crisp, about 5 minutes. Refresh the beans by placing them under cold running water, then dry them in a salad spinner.

2. Chop the onion medium-fine so that it retains some texture. Place the cooked beans and the chopped onion in a large bowl. Cover with plastic wrap and chill for about 1 hour.

3. Chop the bacon slices into 1-inch pieces and fry in a skillet until crisp. Remove them from the pan, drain on paper towels and let cool to room temperature. Crumble slightly and set aside.

4. Place the lemon half and the shrimp in a large saucepan of boiling salted water. When the water returns to a boil, remove the shrimp and let them cool. Peel the shrimp and cut them into a 3/4-inch dice.

5. Remove the onions and beans from the refrigerator. Add the crumbled bacon, chopped shrimp, the tomato and olive oil. Mix thoroughly. Add the vinegar and season with salt and pepper.

Yield: 4 servings

Total time: 45 minutes plus 1 hour refrigeration

Note: To vary the dressing, use 2 tablespoons olive oil and 1 tablespoon hot pepper oil. Hot pepper oil can be bought at most gourmet grocery stores or in any Chinese or Vietnamese market. To make it yourself, add a few dried chilies to a bottle of oil (olive, peanut or other cooking oil) and set aside for a week or so.

Jason Epstein

MARK BITTMAN'S CHICKEN SALAD WITH WALNUT SKORDALIA

Mark Bittman's version of the Greek dip skordalia will bind any cold minced meat or fish (and also makes a good sauce served with hot main dishes). It is an ideal accompaniment for leftover cooked chicken, and assembling a batch takes about five minutes in a food processor. The addition of garlic, paprika or chili powder and cilantro makes it intensely flavorful.

2 ounces French or Italian bread

1 cup milk or chicken stock

4 ounces walnuts, about 1 cup

1 small clove garlic, peeled

Continued

Salt and pepper to taste

¼ cup extra virgin olive oil

Chili powder or paprika to taste

2 to 3 cups shredded cooked chicken

1 cup chopped fresh cilantro leaves

1. Soak the bread in the milk or stock.

2. Put the walnuts, garlic, and salt in a food processor. Pulse to grind coarsely.

3. Squeeze most of the liquid from the bread; reserve the liquid. Add the bread to the processor, along with the oil. Process until combined. Add the reserved milk or stock until the mixture has the consistency of mayonnaise. Add the pepper, along with chili powder or paprika.

4. Bind the chicken with the sauce. Stir in ⅔ cup cilantro. Garnish with the remaining cilantro.

Yield: 4 servings

Time: 30 minutes

Mark Bittman

WARM CHICKEN SALAD WITH ORANGE-TARRAGON DRESSING

On a warm, lazy evening, this chicken salad may be the way to go. The chicken is poached, sliced and laid on lettuces sprinkled with radishes, mint and beans. It is dressed with a tangy yogurt infused with cumin, tarragon and Aleppo pepper.

Kosher salt

1 clove garlic

4 chicken thighs and 2 chicken breasts, skin on

2 teaspoons red wine vinegar

3 tablespoons orange juice

1 tablespoon Dijon mustard

3 teaspoons fresh chopped tarragon

1 teaspoon ground cumin

Pinch of Aleppo pepper

3 tablespoons extra virgin olive oil, plus more for greens

¼ cup whole-milk yogurt

1 romaine heart, in 2-inch pieces

2 handfuls red-leaf lettuce

20 mint leaves

8 radishes, thinly sliced

½ pound green beans, blanched

1. Fill a large pan with water and season with salt. Add the garlic; bring to a boil. Place the chicken in water and simmer gently until cooked through, about 20 minutes. Transfer to a plate.

2. In a small bowl, whisk together the vinegar, orange juice, mustard, tarragon, cumin and pepper. Season with salt. Gradually whisk in the olive oil until smooth, then whisk in the yogurt.

3. In a large shallow bowl, toss the romaine, red leaf lettuce, mint, radishes and beans. Sprinkle with oil and salt, and toss once more. While the chicken is warm, remove the skin; cut the breasts into ⅛-inch slices. Pull the meat from the thighs.

4. Arrange the chicken over the greens and spoon the dressing on top. Serve.

Yield: 4 servings

Time: 1 hour

Amanda Hesser

Nigella Lawson's Roast Chicken Salad with Spinach and Avocado

NIGELLA LAWSON'S ROAST CHICKEN SALAD WITH SPINACH AND AVOCADO

With a prepared roast chicken on hand, you can make this salad in a flash.

10 cups washed baby leaf spinach

5½ cups roast chicken, cooled and roughly shredded

4 scallions, finely sliced into rings

1 cup chopped fresh cilantro

2 ripe Hass avocados

1½ teaspoons Maldon sea salt, or table salt to taste

Finely grated zest of 1 lime

2 tablespoons fresh lime juice

2 tablespoons extra virgin olive oil

Freshly ground black pepper

1. In a large mixing bowl, combine the spinach leaves, chicken, scallions and about ¾ cup of cilantro.

2. Halve the avocados, and discard the pits. Scoop out curls with a spoon, or peel the avocados, and cut into chunks or slices. Add to the salad.

3. In a small bowl, stir together the salt, lime zest and lime juice. Whisk in the oil and pepper to taste. Pour over the salad, tossing gently by hand to mix.

4. Arrange the salad on a large plate or in a salad bowl, and sprinkle with the remaining chopped cilantro. Serve immediately.

Yield: 4 servings

Time: 20 minutes

Nigella Lawson

GRILLED CHICKEN SALAD WITH WARM CURRY DRESSING

Adapted from *The New York Times*

This recipe is ideal for barbecue grills or broilers. The curry dressing can be made in advance. Two whole chicken breasts, boned and skinned to leave four fillets, should cook on a grill or under a broiler in 6 to 7 minutes. While the chicken is cooking, warm the curry dressing over a low flame. When the chicken is ready, lay it over the greens and pour on the dressing.

4 boneless, skinless chicken breast halves (about 1¼ pounds)
2 teaspoons olive oil
2 tablespoons fresh lemon juice
2 tablespoons chopped fresh rosemary or 1 teaspoon dried
2 teaspoons finely chopped garlic
Salt and freshly ground pepper to taste
1 head radicchio, about ¼ pound, core removed, rinsed and dried
2 heads Bibb lettuce, core removed, rinsed and dried
¼ pound arugula, cut into manageable pieces, rinsed and dried
Warm Curry Dressing (recipe follows)
¼ cup coarsely chopped fresh basil or chervil

1. If the chicken breasts are connected, separate the halves and cut away excess membrane or fat.

Place the oil in a mixing bowl with lemon juice, rosemary, garlic, salt and pepper. Stir well. Add the chicken pieces and turn them in the marinade to coat well. Cover and set aside until ready to cook. (If marinating for a long period, refrigerate them.)

2. Preheat a charcoal grill or broiler.

3. Put the chicken pieces on the grill or the broiler rack. Cover the grill or close the broiler. Cook 2 to 3 minutes, turning the pieces. Continue cooking until done, 3 to 5 minutes on the grill, possibly longer under the broiler.

4. Remove the pieces. Slice each breast on the bias about ¼ inch thick.

5. To a large mixing bowl add the radicchio, Bibb lettuce and arugula. Toss well. Add half the warm dressing, and toss again. Place the sliced chicken over the salad and sprinkle with the remaining dressing and basil.

Yield: 4 servings

Time: 30 minutes

➤ WARM CURRY DRESSING

2 teaspoons Dijon-style mustard
1 teaspoon curry powder
2 tablespoons balsamic vinegar
¼ cup chopped scallions
⅓ cup olive or vegetable oil
Salt and freshly ground pepper to taste
¼ cup coarsely chopped fresh basil or chervil

Place the mustard, curry powder, vinegar and scallions in a saucepan. Blend well over low heat with a wire whisk. Add the oil, blending well. Remove from the heat and add the salt, pepper and basil. Keep warm.

Yield: About 1 cup

Time: 10 minutes

Pierre Franey

CHICKEN SALAD WITH GRAPES AND TOASTED NUTS

The hint of both acid and sweetness in the grapes contrasts nicely with the walnuts and chicken. Made with a pre-roasted bird, the salad is a quick and delicious luncheon dish for family or company.

⅓ cup plus 1 tablespoon mayonnaise, preferably homemade
Finely grated zest and juice of 1 lemon
¼ teaspoon salt, or to taste
⅛ teaspoon freshly ground black pepper, or to taste
1½ teaspoons finely chopped fresh chives
1½ teaspoons finely chopped fresh flat-leaf parsley
1 tablespoon finely chopped fresh tarragon
1 (3-pound) roasted chicken, skin removed, meat roughly chopped
⅓ cup finely chopped red onion
½ cup finely chopped celery
1 cup halved red seedless grapes
¾ cup roughly chopped walnuts, lightly toasted
Mesclun, optional
Crusty bread, optional

1. In a small bowl, whisk together the mayonnaise, lemon zest and juice, salt and pepper. Add the chives, parsley and tarragon and mix gently.

2. In a large bowl, combine the chicken, onion, celery, grapes and walnuts. Add the mayonnaise mixture and fold together to combine. Season to taste. If desired, serve over mesclun or with bread.

Yield: 4 to 6 servings

Time: 20 minutes

Jill Santopietro

CHICKEN TONNATO (CHICKEN BREASTS WITH TUNA SAUCE)

Adapted from *The New York Times*

A variation of the traditional Vitello Tonnato, this recipe envelopes poached chicken breasts, instead of veal, in the tuna and mayonnaise sauce. The sauce, given great body and piquancy with the addition of capers and chopped anchovy fillets, is simple to make and produces a dish that's suitable for elegant dining or a buffet table. The turkey variation, below, works equally well with the tonnato sauce. The recipe can easily be doubled or tripled.

½ cup white wine
Juice of 1 lemon
1 celery stalk, sliced crosswise
1 scallion, chopped
3 whole, boned chicken breasts, split and gently pounded
1½ cups Tonnato Sauce (recipe follows)
Seeded thin lemon slices, black olives and fresh parsley, for garnish

1. In a saucepan, combine the wine, lemon juice, celery and scallions. Add enough water to cover the chicken when added (about 3 cups). Bring to a boil, reduce to a low simmer. Add the chicken breasts and poach for 7 to 8 minutes. Let cool in the liquid. Drain.

2. Spoon about half of the sauce into a serving dish and smooth it over. Arrange the chicken breasts, slightly overlapping, over the sauce. Spoon the remaining sauce on top. Garnish the top symmetrically with lemon slices, black olives and parsley. Serve any additional sauce on the side. This dish may be tightly wrapped, refrigerated and served the following day.

Yield: 6 servings

Time: 45 minutes, including sauce

Craig Claiborne and Pierre Franey

➤ TONNATO SAUCE

1 (6½-ounce) can tuna, drained
3 tablespoons drained capers
1½ cups mayonnaise, homemade or good-
    quality commercial
1 teaspoon lemon juice
1 tablespoon finely chopped anchovy fillets,
    or use anchovy paste
2 tablespoons turkey or chicken broth

Put the drained tuna and capers into the container of a food processor or blender and blend. Add the mayonnaise, lemon juice, anchovies and broth. Blend thoroughly.

Yield: About 2 cups

Time: 15 minutes

➤ TURKEY TONNATO

Substitute 1 pound cooked,
    boneless, skinless breast of turkey
    for the chicken.
Seeded thin lemon slices, black olives
    and finely chopped fresh parsley,
    for garnish

1. Cut the breast across the grain into thin slices, each about ⅛-inch thick.

2. Spoon about ¼ cup of the sauce into a serving dish and smooth it over. Arrange ¼ of the turkey slices, slightly overlapping, over the sauce. Spoon another layer of sauce on top. Add another layer of turkey slices and more sauce. Continue making layers until all the turkey slices are used. Finish with a layer of sauce. Garnish the top symmetrically with lemon slices, black olives and parsley or with watercress, capers and lemons. Serve any additional sauce on the side.

Yield: 6 to 8 servings

Craig Claiborne and Pierre Franey

ALICE'S CHINESE BARBECUED CHICKEN

Adapted from Alice Brock

Remember Alice from "Alice's Restaurant Massacree," a song Arlo Guthrie made famous in the '60s? Alice's restaurant did exist (in Stockbridge, Mass.), and Alice Brock did serve wonderful food. This versatile recipe can be made with cut-up whole chickens or with chicken breasts and either baked in the oven or carried to a picnic spot in the marinade and grilled outdoors.

For the Marinade

½ cup reduced-sodium soy sauce
1½ cups dry sherry
2 large cloves garlic, minced
2 tablespoons minced fresh ginger
4 pounds chicken, cut up, or 4 small, whole,
    skinned and boned chicken breasts

For the Sauce

½ cup hoisin sauce
1 cup dry sherry
½ cup ketchup
¼ cup brown sugar, packed
1 clove garlic, minced

1. Combine the marinade ingredients and pour over the chicken pieces in a shallow pan. Marinate for several hours, overnight if desired, turning the pieces occasionally if the marinade does not cover them completely.

2. Combine the sauce ingredients. Remove the chicken pieces from the marinade. Place in a shallow pan and cover with the sauce.

3. Indoors: Bake the chicken pieces at 350 degrees for about 45 to 60 minutes, turning once, or until chicken is done, basting several times with sauce. Bake the breasts for about 30 minutes.

Outdoors: If you are going to grill the chicken, remove it from the marinade and place on the grill. Baste with the marinade, not the sauce. About 7 minutes before the chicken is done, spoon the sauce over both sides of the chicken and continue grilling, basting with the sauce until done. The sauce cannot be used to baste the chicken on the grill throughout the cooking period because the sugar in it will cause it to caramelize and then burn.

Yield: 4 servings

Time: 20 minutes, plus marinating and grilling or baking time

Marian Burros

SPICY DRY-RUBBED TRIANGLE STEAK FOR SALADS AND SANDWICHES

1 tablespoon paprika
1 tablespoon dried oregano
1 teaspoon kosher salt
½ teaspoon garlic powder
½ teaspoon sugar
¼ teaspoon cayenne pepper
¼ teaspoon ground black pepper
1 triangle (tri-tip) steak (about 1¾ to 2 pounds)

1. Preheat the oven to 450 degrees. Combine the paprika, oregano, salt, garlic powder, sugar, cayenne and black pepper, and place the mixture on a plate. Using your hands, make as much of the mixture as possible adhere to all sides of the steak.

2. Place the steak in a roasting pan fitted with a rack. Roast, turning once after about 15 minutes, until the steak reaches the desired state, about 35 minutes total.

3. Remove the steak from the oven and allow it to sit at room temperature for 10 minutes. Carve on the bias against the grain and use, warm or cold, for sandwiches or over salads.

Yield: Steak for 4 to 6 sandwiches

Time: 1 hour

Molly O'Neill

MUSTARD-AND-CHILI-RUBBED ROASTED BEEF TENDERLOIN

The flavors of something cold are usually less pronounced than when they are warm, and since flavors are always muted during storage, the key when preparing something that is to be served chilled is to start with more flavor (a blast of herbs, a rub or a marinade) and to prepare it a day in advance, refrigerate it overnight and bring it to room temperature before serving. In this dish, the primary goal is to serve the tenderloin chilled, and the trick is to swab the meat with flavor—lots of chili powder, oregano, garlic, mustard and olive oil—before sliding it into the oven (roast it rare so it stays tender and juicy). The next day all you need to do is slice and serve, no compensatory condiments necessary. The flavors of mustard and chili, carried by the fat in the olive oil, have penetrated the meat beautifully. The advantages of cooking the meat the evening before serving it can go beyond convenience. Cold meats slice more prettily and easily than their hot counterparts, and turning the oven on at night when it's relatively cool, as compared to the daytime, keeps the kitchen cooler while you work.

1 beef tenderloin (about 2 pounds), trimmed, rinsed and patted dry

Continued

3 tablespoons extra virgin olive oil

1 tablespoon Dijon mustard

1 teaspoon dried oregano

1 teaspoon chipotle chili powder

½ teaspoon chili powder

½ teaspoon ground cumin

½ teaspoon freshly ground black pepper

1 large garlic clove, passed through a garlic press

Kosher salt, to taste

1. Preheat the oven to 450 degrees. Tie the roast with kitchen string in three evenly spaced places to help keep its tubular shape.

2. In a small bowl, whisk together 1 tablespoon oil, the mustard, oregano, chipotle chili, chili powder, cumin, black pepper and garlic.

3. In a large skillet, heat the remaining 2 tablespoons of oil until very hot. Season the beef generously all over with salt. Place it in the pan and sear the bottom, without moving it, until it forms a golden brown crust, 3 to 4 minutes. Turn and repeat with the remaining sides.

4. Transfer the beef to a rimmed baking sheet. Using a pastry brush, smear the mustard-chili rub all over the beef. Roast until an instant-read thermometer registers 115 degrees for rare or 120 for medium rare (beef will continue to cook as it rests), 12 to 15 minutes. Let cool completely, then wrap and refrigerate overnight. Bring to room temperature for at least 2 hours before slicing and serving.

Yield: 4 to 6 servings

Time: 40 minutes, plus overnight chilling

Melissa Clark

GRILLED MARINATED FLANK STEAK

Adapted from *Family Reunion*.

For the Marinade

4 cloves garlic

4 onions, peeled and minced

6 tablespoons peeled and minced fresh ginger

1 tablespoon hot-pepper sauce

1¼ cups soy sauce

1¼ cups honey

½ cup sesame oil

1 cup canola or peanut oil

12 pounds flank steak (about 5 steaks)

1. Emulsify all the marinade ingredients in a blender or a food processor. Put the beef and the marinade in plastic bags, turning occasionally, 24 hours.

2. Make a fire in a grill. Remove the meat from the marinade and pat it dry.

3. Grill the meat 4 minutes on each side for medium-rare consistency. Let the steak sit 5 minutes before slicing into ¼-inch strips, across the grain.

Yield: 25 servings

Time: 30 minutes, plus marinating 8 to 24 hours

Note: For fewer servings, decrease ingredients proportionally.

Molly O'Neill

GRILLED LAMB FILLET WITH TOMATO-ONION CHUTNEY

For an elegant picnic, try this lamb, grilled until medium rare. It is best to not refrigerate it and to slice it just before leaving home, wrapping the slices tightly in heavy-duty aluminum foil for their trip.

1 rack of lamb (about 2 pounds) boned and in a
    solid piece
½ tablespoon extra virgin olive oil
Pinch of kosher salt
½ teaspoon coarsely ground black pepper
Tomato Onion Chutney (recipe follows)

1. Preheat the broiler or barbecue grill.

2. Rub both sides of the meat with the olive oil. Sprinkle with salt and pepper.

3. Broil or grill the lamb to the desired degree of doneness. About 5 minutes on each side should be medium rare.

4. Set the lamb aside to cool to room temperature before slicing. Cut the meat into slices no more than ½-inch thick. When ready to serve, arrange the slices in a fanlike pattern on individual plates and serve with Tomato-Onion Chutney (recipe follows).

Yield: 2 servings

Time: 25 minutes

➤ TOMATO-ONION CHUTNEY

This may be made a day or two in advance and refrigerated until ready to be served.

½ tablespoon extra virgin olive oil
¼ teaspoon cumin seeds
1 small onion, minced
2 medium, ripe tomatoes (about ½ pound),
    peeled, seeded and finely chopped
Salt to taste
Freshly ground pepper to taste
1 teaspoon freshly squeezed lemon juice

1. Heat the olive oil in a small saucepan over high heat. Add the cumin seeds, and when they start to sizzle, stir in the onion. Sauté over medium heat until the onion is tender, about 4 minutes.

2. Add the tomatoes and cook over high heat for about 5 minutes, or until the mixture thickens. Season with salt and pepper, stir in the lemon juice and allow to cool to room temperature.

Yield: ⅓ cup

Time: 15 minutes

Florence Fabricant

GARLIC-AND-HERB-RUBBED BUTTERFLIED LEG OF LAMB

When it is to be served chilled, butterflied leg of lamb should be smeared with a "heavy-on-the-garlic" rub including olive oil, herbs, and citrus, seasoning the meat to the point where any extra sauce would seem gratuitous. The roast is cooked ahead of time, its flavors intensifying as it rests in the refrigerator. Since there's no need for additional condiments, the lamb can be packed up and taken on a picnic without worrying about dripping, leaking containers. A resealable plastic bag or sheet of aluminum foil will work just fine.

1 butterflied leg of lamb (about 7 1/2 pounds), well trimmed
1/4 cup extra virgin olive oil
1/4 cup mixed chopped fresh herbs, such as sage, thyme, basil and parsley
Grated zest and freshly squeezed juice of 1 orange
8 garlic cloves, minced
1 teaspoon kosher salt
1 teaspoon freshly ground black pepper

1. Pat the lamb dry with paper towels and place it on a rimmed baking sheet. In a bowl, combine the oil, herbs, orange zest and juice, garlic, salt and pepper. Rub the mixture all over the lamb. Cover with foil and let marinate at room temperature for 2 hours.

2. Preheat the oven to 500 degrees. Remove the foil and transfer the lamb to the oven. Roast until an instant-read thermometer reads 120 degrees for rare and 130 for medium, 35 to 45 minutes, depending on how you like your meat. Let it cool completely, then wrap and refrigerate for several hours or overnight. Bring to room temperature for at least 2 hours before slicing and serving.

Yield: 12 to 15 servings

Time: 55 minutes, plus 2 hours' marinating and chilling for several hours or overnight

Melissa Clark

CHARLESTON GRILL'S BAKED GRITS WITH SUN-DRIED TOMATOES

2 cups chicken stock
3 1/2 tablespoons unsalted butter
1 cup stone-ground grits
1 cup heavy cream
1 tablespoon chopped garlic
2 teaspoons fresh thyme
1/2 cup diced sun-dried tomatoes
Ground white pepper
1/2 cup goat cheese
Chopped fresh chives, for garnish

1. Bring the chicken stock, butter and 1 cup water to a boil in a saucepan. Stir in the grits and return to a boil. Simmer for 35 minutes, stirring occasionally to keep the grits from sticking, and adding water if the grits become stiff.

2. Preheat the oven to 375 degrees. Add the heavy cream to the pot while stirring; cook at low heat for 25 minutes. The grits should be very thick, but not too stiff. Fold in the garlic, thyme, sun-dried tomatoes and white pepper to taste. Spoon the grits into a lightly greased baking dish or cast-iron skillet. Crumble the goat cheese on top. Bake for 15 minutes. Garnish with chopped chives and serve.

Yield: 4 servings as a side dish

Time: 1 hour 15 minutes

Matt Lee and Ted Lee

PIZZA ON THE GRILL

By Mark Bittman

I'm not sure there is a grilled food that impresses guests more than pizza. The results, once you get the hang of the process, are outstanding.

Yes, grilled pizza presents challenges to the home cook. But if you have a food processor and instant yeast (which can simply be tossed in the food processor with the flour), making the dough is as easy as grating cheese. And you can grill the dough as soon as 1 hour after making it, which is as easy as the recipe makes it appear.

Both rolling out and grilling the dough do require some care. Rolling is much easier if you allow the dough to rest at each stage: when you divide it into three (the recipe makes enough for three small pies, for easier grilling), when you flatten it and then again when you roll it into pies. I usually take a minute to roll the dough initially, then allow it to rest for 5 minutes before proceeding.

The dough can be mixed from an hour to two or three days before you want to cook the pizzas. You can also keep dough for weeks in the freezer.

Like nearly identical bread dough, pizza dough is best when it is moist and a little sticky, so use flour judiciously. The dough should be allowed to rest, especially before and during the final shaping, although you can cut corners.

If you are patient, and stretch the dough a little bit at a time, you can produce a thin crust without tearing it. Small pizzas are easier to handle than large ones, especially if you're grilling. If necessary, grill or bake the pies sequentially, eating one while the second is still cooking. Or serve them at room temperature, as is commonly done in Italy.

Grilling is best done with a covered grill that mimics an oven, and you want part of the grill to be fairly hot. On a gas grill, this means setting one side to high and the other to low, or some similar arrangement. With a charcoal grill, simply build your fire on one side of the fire box. Use the hot side for the initial browning of the dough, the cool side to heat the toppings.

Roll or lightly press a ball of risen pizza dough into a flat round, lightly flouring the work surface and the dough only as necessary. Let the dough sit a few minutes, and then roll or pat it out as thin as you like, turning occasionally, and sprinkling the top with flour as necessary.

Slide the crust directly onto the grill. Cook until brown grill marks appear, 3 to 5 minutes. Flip the dough over with a spatula or tongs, lay on whatever topping you choose, cover the grill and cook until the bottom is crisp and brown and the topping is hot.

Some pies are minimally topped. (Pizza bianco, white pizza, which is topped with olive oil, salt and sometimes rosemary, was, before the American influence, the most popular pizza in Rome.) Others are intuitive: mozzarella, tomato and basil; or caramelized onions and olives; or tomato sauce, Parmesan and anchovies. Still others use less traditional ingredients like fresh goat's milk cheese, sun-dried tomatoes, figs and whatever else you crave.

Fresh toppings should never be too wet or the dough will become soggy. Fresh tomatoes should be seeded and drained; other moist vegetables like zucchini should be thinly sliced and salted and left to drain so they exude some liquid.

Corn kernels, freshly cut off the cob, make a crunchy topping with shredded arugula and diced bacon; the bacon helps the other ingredients adhere to the crust. Black olives add a twist to a typical tomato topping.

One tool makes all of the work easier: a pizza peel with a metal blade (the handles are usually wood). Whereas a wooden peel will char after repeated use, a metal one will not be marred by the heat, and its thinness makes it easier to slide under the pie. I use the peel to roll out the dough, slide it onto the grill, remove it and flip it. Sometimes I use it for serving as well.

PIZZA DOUGH

3 cups all-purpose or bread flour, plus more as needed
2 teaspoons instant yeast
2 tablespoons olive oil
2 teaspoons coarse kosher or sea salt, more for sprinkling

1. Combine the flour, yeast, oil and salt in a food processor. Turn the machine on, and add 1 cup of water through the feed tube. Process for about 30 seconds, adding more water, a little at a time, until the mixture forms a ball and is slightly sticky.

2. Turn the dough onto a floured work surface, and knead to form a smooth, round ball. Put the dough ball in a bowl, and cover with plastic wrap. Let rise until the dough doubles in size, 1 to 2 hours. Use immediately, or wrap tightly in plastic, and freeze for up to a month. Defrost in a covered bowl in the refrigerator or at room temperature.

Yield: Enough dough for 3 pies
Time: 15 minutes, plus at least 1 hour's rising

WHITE PIZZA

Pizza dough (see preceding recipe)
Flour
Extra virgin olive oil
Coarse kosher or sea salt
3 tablespoons or more roughly chopped fresh rosemary leaves, plus sprigs (optional)

1. Divide the dough ball into 3 pieces. Roll each into a ball, and place on a lightly floured surface. Sprinkle with a little more flour, cover with plastic wrap or a towel and let rest while you start a covered grill. The fire should be medium-hot on one side, medium to cool on the other. Set the grill rack about 4 inches from the heat source.

2. Lightly press each dough ball into a flat round, lightly flouring the work surface and dough as necessary. Let the rounds sit for a few minutes. This will relax the dough and make it easier to roll out. Roll out on a cookie sheet, flouring the rolling pin or your hands as necessary.

3. Slide the pie onto the hot side of the grill, and brush the top lightly with olive oil. Grill until lightly browned on the bottom. Remove from the grill with a large spatula. Lightly flour the top, then flip the pie over onto its other side, on the cooler part of the grill. Top the grilled side with salt and a third of the rosemary, and drizzle with a little olive oil. Cover, and grill 6 to 12 minutes, until hot and nicely browned on the bottom. Serve immediately or at room temperature (these will keep for a few hours). Repeat with the remaining dough.

Yield: 3 pies
Time: 30 minutes

Variations:

Margherita Pizza. After flipping the pie, top it with fresh sliced tomatoes, extra virgin olive oil, grated fresh mozzarella and salt to taste. When the pie finishes grilling, top with basil leaves and a little more olive oil.

Fern-Bar Pizza. After flipping the pie, top it with prosciutto, thinly sliced fresh figs, fresh goat's milk cheese and a little extra virgin olive oil. When the pie finishes grilling, drizzle with more oil.

Marinara Pizza. After flipping the pie, top it with fresh sliced tomatoes, thinly sliced garlic, extra virgin olive oil and anchovy fillets.

PIZZA WITH TOMATOES, ONIONS AND OLIVES

4 or 5 ripe tomatoes
Coarse salt
Pizza dough (see recipe, page 100)
1 medium red onion or 4 shallots, peeled and
 chopped
20 black olives like kalamata, pitted and
 chopped
Olive oil as needed

1. Prepare the grill as directed.

2. Core the tomatoes, then cut them in half horizontally. Gently squeeze out the liquid and shake out most of the seeds, then slice the tomatoes as thinly as possible. Salt lightly and let sit at least 10 minutes, then drain off any excess liquid.

3. Slide the crust directly onto the grill. Cook until brown grill marks appear, 3 to 5 minutes. Flip the dough over with a spatula or tongs, lay on the topping. Cover the grill and cook until the bottom is crisp and brown and the topping is hot.

Yield: 1 large, 2 medium, or more smaller pizzas
Time: 30 minutes

ZUCCHINI-SAUSAGE PIZZA

4 small or 2 large zucchini
Coarse salt
Pizza dough (see recipe, page 100)
2 or 3 sweet Italian sausages, meat removed
 from the casing and crumbled
2 teaspoons minced garlic

1. Prepare the grill as directed.

2. Thinly slice the zucchini, salt lightly and let sit at least 20 minutes, then drain off any accumulated liquid.

3. Slide the crust directly onto the grill. Cook until brown grill marks appear, 3 to 5 minutes. Flip the dough over with a spatula or tongs, lay on the topping. Cover the grill and cook until the bottom is crisp and brown and the topping is hot.

Yield: 1 large, 2 medium, or more smaller pizzas
Time: 40 minutes

GREEN TOMATO PIZZA

2 large or 4 small green tomatoes
Coarse salt
Pizza dough (see recipe, page 100)
1 cup freshly grated Parmesan
½ cup coarsely chopped or torn basil

1. Prepare the grill as directed.

2. Thinly slice the tomatoes, salt lightly and let sit at least 20 minutes, then drain off any accumulated liquid.

3. Slide the crust directly onto the grill. Cook until brown grill marks appear, 3 to 5 minutes. Flip the

dough over with a spatula or tongs, lay on the topping. Cover the grill and cook until the bottom is crisp and brown and the topping is hot.

Yield: 1 large, 2 medium, or more smaller pizzas

Time: 40 minutes

FOUR-CHEESE PIZZA WITH BASIL

Pizza dough (see recipe, page 100)
½ cup shredded or cubed mozzarella
½ cup shredded or cubed fontina or taleggio
½ cup freshly grated pecorino Romano
½ cup freshly grated Parmesan
½ cup coarsely chopped or torn basil

1. Prepare the grill as directed.

2. Slide the crust directly onto the grill. Cook until brown grill marks appear, about 3 to 5 minutes. Flip the dough over with a spatula or tongs, lay on the topping. Cover the grill and cook until the bottom is crisp and brown and the topping is hot.

Yield: 1 large, 2 medium, or more smaller pizzas

Time: 30 minutes

PIZZA WITH ARUGULA, CORN AND BACON

Pizza dough (see recipe, page 100)
6 cups loosely packed arugula, measured after washing, drying and shredding
Kernels from 4 ears of corn
½ cup minced bacon

1. Prepare the grill as directed.

2. Slide the crust directly onto the grill. Cook until brown grill marks appear, 3 to 5 minutes. Flip the dough over with a spatula or tongs, lay on the topping. Cover the grill and cook, until the bottom is crisp and brown and the topping is hot.

Yield: 1 large, 2 medium, or more smaller pizzas

Time: 30 minutes

THE TACO JOINT IN YOUR KITCHEN

By Mark Bittman

Just about anything can be called a taco, which essentially means "sandwich." You take a tortilla and you put some stuff in it and you eat it; that's a taco. (If you roll the tortilla, it's a burrito, which appears to have been created in the American Southwest; if you layer food on top of it, it's an enchilada; if you crisp it up and use it as a kind of plate, it's a tostada; if you cut it into pieces and bake or fry it, it's a chip; and so on.) But taco aficionados have a particular taste, a particular feel in mind. It's about the ingredients, as high quality and as fresh as possible.

The best tacos start with corn tortillas; flour is a recent adaptation and, while it is not always inappropriate or scorned, there is nothing like a corn tortilla.

Your best bet is not the supermarket but a Mexican grocery store, or if you're lucky, a bakery. In any case, it should be fresh and have that particular flinty aroma that all corn-lime products have.

A good taco is loaded with several components: something crunchy (lettuce or cabbage usually, but chopped onion or salted radish are also good); the protein; some moisture—crema, sour cream or guacamole will do nicely; and maybe cheese. Many people add salsa for brightness as well.

To make tacos for a crowd, you can't do better than to begin with slow-roasted pork, called *carnitas*. If you start with a piece of shoulder (especially from a well-raised pig), you won't go wrong; the high fat content makes it self-basting, and almost any combination of spices and heat will produce something delicious. Slow, indirect grilling is ideal, but you don't lose much by cooking the pork in the oven, using moderate heat.

Chicken thighs—again, from a good chicken rather than a super-mass-produced one—are another good option, and can be quickly simmered in a flavorful braising liquid that will turn them super-tender and leave them quite moist. Here again, the seasonings can be as varied as you like. I see the spice mixtures here as suggestions rather than ironclad recipes to follow.

Then there is carne asada, which means "grilled meat," which in turn means pretty much anything. But skirt steak is what you most often see made into carne asada. Because of its high fat content, it's perfect here. Rub it with a few spices, grill it for a few minutes and pile it into tortillas with a couple of other ingredients to make a legitimate and near-perfect taco.

Taco Technique, Bottom to Top

Taco building is a free-form exercise; what follows isn't meant to be some unvarying procedure but simply my own preference.

1. Briefly warm the tortilla on both sides in a dry pan. It will take on just a little color.

2. Then, be sure not to overload. If you put too much in there, the stuff will fall right out. Start with the protein, not only because it's the foundation but because as the heaviest component it belongs at the bottom; no more than $1/3$ cup or so for an average 4- or 5-inch taco. I like to put the crunchy stuff, like lettuce, on next, for contrast; a small

handful, as much as you can grab with your fingers, not your fist.

3. Then add the spoonable ingredients, or the sprinkles—salsa or crema, guacamole or crumbled cheese—whatever you like, but we're only talking a tablespoon or two here.

4. At this point you have less than a cup of stuff in your tortilla, which is about all it can handle. Like pizza, pasta or dumplings, the filling is the flavor and the starch the real substance. You're supposed to eat a few of these; if they fall apart in the process, don't worry about it. Use the tortilla to pick up whatever fell out.

SLOW-ROASTED PORK FOR TACOS

10 cloves garlic, peeled

2 pounds pork shoulder, preferably boneless
   and in one piece

1/2 teaspoon black peppercorns

1 teaspoon fresh oregano (or use dried Mexican
   oregano)

1 teaspoon cumin seeds

1 (1-inch) piece cinnamon stick

1 teaspoon coriander seed

1 teaspoon salt

2 tablespoons fresh orange juice

2 tablespoons fresh lemon juice

1. Sliver 4 cloves of the garlic and use a thin-bladed knife to poke holes all over the pork; insert the garlic slivers into the holes.

2. Combine the peppercorns, oregano, cumin, cinnamon and coriander in a small skillet and turn the heat to medium. Toast, shaking the pan occasionally, until the mixture is fragrant, 3 to 5 minutes. Remove from the heat.

3. Combine the toasted spices, salt and remaining garlic in the container of a small food processor or blender. Turn on the machine, and gradually add the orange and lemon juice until you have a smooth purée. Rub all over the pork; let the pork sit at room temperature for up to 2½ hours or in the refrigerator for up to 24 hours.

4. At least 2½ hours before you plan to eat, turn the oven to 300 degrees or prepare a charcoal or gas grill to cook over low indirect heat. Put the pork in a roasting pan in the oven or directly on the grill rack, if you're grilling, and cover the grill.

Cook, checking occasionally and basting with the pan juices if you're roasting (add water to the bottom of the pan if the mixture dries out), until the pork is brown and very, very tender, at least 2 hours. Shred or slice the pork and use hot or at room temperature (pork can be refrigerated for up to 2 days).

Yield: 6 to 8 servings

Time: At least 2½ hours, longer if you have time

Mark Bittman

GRILLED CARNE ASADA FOR TACOS

1 clove garlic

2 pounds skirt steak

2 teaspoons ground cumin

1 teaspoon ground oregano

1/2 teaspoon cayenne

Salt and freshly ground black pepper

1. Start a charcoal or gas grill. Crush the garlic and rub the steak with it. Combine the remaining ingredients and rub into the steak. Let the steak sit until you're ready to grill.

2. Grill the steak 3 to 4 minutes per side for medium rare. Cut into slices and use as soon as possible (hot is best, but warm or room temperature is fine).

Yield: 6 to 8 servings

Time: About 45 minutes

Mark Bittman

SHREDDED CHICKEN FOR TACOS

2 pounds boneless chicken thighs

1 large white onion, peeled and quartered

5 cloves garlic, peeled and lightly crushed

2 bay leaves

1 tablespoon ground cumin

1 ancho or other mild dried chili, optional

Salt and pepper to taste

1. Combine all the ingredients in a saucepan and add water to cover. Turn the heat to high, bring to a boil, and skim any foam that comes to the surface. Partially cover, and adjust the heat so that the mixture simmers steadily. Cook until the meat is very tender, about 30 minutes. Remove from the liquid and cool.

2. Shred the meat with your fingers. Taste and adjust seasonings; use within a couple of days.

Yield: 6 to 8 servings

Time: About 1 hour; this may be prepared 2 days in advance

Mark Bittman

➤ MARK BITTMAN'S SALSA FRESCA

2 large ripe tomatoes, chopped

1/2 large white onion, peeled and minced

1/4 teaspoon minced raw garlic, or to taste

1 habanero or jalapeño pepper, stemmed, seeded and minced, or to taste

1/4 cup chopped fresh cilantro leaves

1 tablespoon fresh lime juice or 1 teaspoon red wine vinegar

Salt and freshly ground pepper

1. Combine all the ingredients, taste and adjust the seasoning as necessary.

2. Let the flavors marry for 15 minutes or so before serving, but serve within a couple of hours.

Yield: About 2 cups

Time: 10 minutes

Mark Bittman

A VISIT TO THE FARM STAND

RECIPES FOR
THE FARM STAND

COCO PAZZO'S PAPPA AL POMODORO

Adapted from Coco Pazzo, New York City

The fragrance of the garlic and olive oil, the gold and red of the bread and the tomatoes set off by the sparkling green of the basil make it a sublime comfort food.

> ½ pound loaf stale Tuscan or other country bread
> 3 pounds very ripe tomatoes
> 6 tablespoons extra virgin olive oil
> 1 large garlic clove, sliced
> 12 large fresh basil leaves
> Freshly ground black pepper to taste
> Freshly grated Parmigiano-Reggiano to taste, optional

1. Cut the bread into large chunks. If any of the center is soft, discard it.

2. Cut the tomatoes in half. Squeeze out the seeds and discard. Cut the tomatoes into large chunks.

3. Heat the oil in a large pot and sauté the garlic until it begins to brown.

4. Stir in the tomatoes and cook for about 5 minutes, until they soften.

5. Add the bread and continue cooking, stirring occasionally, until the bread has absorbed most of the liquid.

6. Shred the basil and stir in along with the pepper. Allow the mixture to stand for about 15 minutes or longer. Serve lukewarm or at room temperature. If desired, serve with grated Parmigiano-Reggiano, about 1 tablespoon per serving.

Yield: 5 to 6 first-course servings, or
3 main-course servings

Time: 30 minutes

Marian Burros

CHILLED YELLOW TOMATO SOUP WITH BLACK-OLIVE CREAM

Adapted from *Cooking for the Weekend*

The black-olive cream garnish topped with chopped tomatoes gives this cold soup a festive look. Warmed and with the addition of minced fresh vegetables and herbs, the soup can be used as a sauce for rice salad. Warmed and with the addition of leftover cooked seafood, the soup makes a pleasing pasta sauce as well.

> 5 tablespoons unsalted butter
> 2 large leeks, white part only, well cleaned and chopped
> 1 tablespoon finely minced fresh thyme, or
>   1 teaspoon dried
> 2 bay leaves
> 2 pounds plum tomatoes, preferably yellow, trimmed and cut in chunks
> 3½ cups chicken broth, homemade or low-sodium canned
> 2 teaspoons sugar
> 1 tablespoon salt
> 1 teaspoon freshly ground black pepper
> ⅓ cup olivada (black olive purée), or
>   ½ cup pitted imported black olives puréed with 1 tablespoon olive oil
> ¼ cup whipping cream
> 2 red plum tomatoes, trimmed and diced, for garnish

1. To make the soup, melt the butter in a large saucepan over low heat. Add the leeks, thyme and bay leaves. Cover, and cook 20 minutes, stirring once or twice. Stir in the tomatoes, chicken broth, sugar, salt and pepper. Bring to a simmer, and cook, uncovered, until the tomatoes are soft and the soup has thickened, about 25 minutes, stirring once or twice.

2. Cool slightly, remove the bay leaves, and purée in a food processor. Place in a bowl, cover, and refrigerate until cold, at least 5 hours. The soup can be prepared to this point up to 2 days ahead.

3. To make the olive cream, put the olivada in a small bowl and whisk in the cream. Taste the soup and adjust the seasoning if needed. Ladle into chilled bowls, and drizzle with the black olive cream. Sprinkle with diced red tomatoes, and serve immediately.

Yield: 8 servings

Time: 1 hour, plus at least 5 hours' chilling

Molly O'Neill

LITTLE SPRING SOUP

1 bunch radishes, cut wafer thin and chilled
2 scallions, sliced wafer thin and chilled completely
½ bunch peppery greens, such as watercress or arugula, minced and chilled
10 leaves lettuce, finely shredded and chilled completely
1 cup minced fresh dill
8 new potatoes, peeled
2 cups whole milk
¾ teaspoon citric acid (also called sour salt) (see Note)
1 tablespoon butter
Salt and pepper

1. Combine the well-chilled radishes, onions, greens and lettuce with half the dill; return to the refrigerator.

2. Boil the potatoes in lightly salted water until tender. Meanwhile, place the milk in a nonreactive bowl, whisk in the citric acid and refrigerate for 10 minutes.

3. Combine the cold vegetables and the soured milk and return to the refrigerator.

4. When the potatoes are tender, toss them with the butter and remaining dill, and season to taste with salt and pepper. Serve the soup cold with the hot potatoes on the side.

Yield: 4 servings

Time: 30 minutes, plus chilling

Note: If you can't find citric acid, omit it and use buttermilk in place of the whole milk.

Molly O'Neill

LEMONGRASS VICHYSSOISE

Adapted from Gerd Knaust

4 tablespoons unsalted butter
3 large cloves garlic, coarsely chopped
1 pound leeks, washed well, trimmed and white parts sliced
¼ pound onions, coarsely chopped
4 stalks lemongrass, trimmed, and bulbs thinly sliced
8 kaffir lime leaves, finely sliced
1 pound potatoes, peeled and coarsely diced
2 bay leaves
Salt and freshly ground black pepper to taste
6 cups water
2 cups heavy cream
1 or 2 bunches fresh chives

1. In a large pot, melt the butter over medium-high heat. Add the garlic, leeks, onions, lemongrass and lime leaves; cover and simmer for 10 minutes. Do not allow to color.

2. Add the potatoes, bay leaves, salt, pepper and water and bring to a boil. Reduce the heat, and simmer 20 minutes, until the potatoes are tender.

Allow to cool a little; strain, reserving broth, and remove the bay leaves.

3. Place some solids with a little broth in a blender, and purée. Spoon into a bowl. Repeat the process until all solids are puréed; you will probably have to use all the broth to do this, but do not allow the mixture to become too thin, because the cream must still be added. Stir in the cream. Adjust the seasoning, and chill completely, at least several hours.

4. To serve, chop the chives, and stir the vichyssoise thoroughly. Spoon 1 cup into a soup bowl, and sprinkle with chives. If the mixture is too thick, add a little milk to thin it out.

Yield: 7 cups (6 or 7 servings)

Time: 40 minutes, plus chilling

Marian Burros

CHILLED CURRIED ZUCCHINI SOUP WITH APPLE GARNISH

1 tablespoon butter
1 cup sliced onion (about 1 medium white onion)
2 cloves garlic, peeled and chopped
2 teaspoons curry powder
Salt
2 medium zucchini, trimmed and cut into
    ⅛-inch rounds (about 3 cups)
3 cups chicken stock, fresh or canned
1 cup plain yogurt
1 Golden Delicious apple
1 bunch fresh mint leaves, cleaned

1. Place the butter and onions in a deep pot over medium heat. Cook, stirring, until the onions are wilted, about 2 minutes. Add the garlic. Cook, stirring, for 1 minute. Add the curry powder. Season with salt to taste. Add the zucchini. Stir for a minute.

2. Add the chicken stock. Bring to a boil, reduce the heat, cover and simmer for 10 minutes.

3. Purée the soup in a blender or food processor. Refrigerate.

4. When the soup is cold, stir in the yogurt, reserving a little for garnish. Peel and core the apple, then cut it into small cubes and stir it into the soup. Garnish the soup with a dollop of yogurt and some mint leaves.

Yield: 4 servings

Time: 30 minutes, plus 30 minutes for chilling

Pierre Franey

ALAN HARDING'S CHILLED CUCUMBER SOUP

Adapted from *The Greenmarket Cookbook*

8 medium cucumbers, peeled
¼ cup fresh lemon juice
2 teaspoons salt, or to taste
¼ teaspoon freshly ground pepper
2 tablespoons white wine vinegar
1 ½ teaspoons curry powder
Pinch of ground cardamom
Pinch of cayenne pepper
1 cup plain yogurt

1. Chop all but one of the cucumbers. Place half of the chopped cucumbers in a blender with the lemon juice, salt, pepper, vinegar, curry powder, cardamom and cayenne. Purée. Transfer to a bowl. Purée the remaining chopped cucumbers, and mix with the first batch. Stir in the yogurt. Chill until ready to serve.

2. Quarter the remaining cucumber lengthwise, remove the seeds and slice thinly. Adjust the

seasoning if necessary, and serve garnished with cucumber slices.

Yield: 4 to 6 servings

Time: 20 minutes, plus chilling

Florence Fabricant

FRENCH LAUNDRY'S GAZPACHO

Thomas Keller: "Gazpacho is the perfect warm-weather soup, and the interpretation I offer here is intense, and easy. The main technique is turning on your blender, and then straining the liquid. The flavor is extraordinary because you're using fresh ingredients—cucumbers, onion, bell pepper, to-matoes—and overnight marinating develops and blends flavors. Serve it in a chilled shot glass. Or serve it hot. Or think of it as gazpacho sauce: it goes perfectly with grilled chicken or fish. I serve it at the restaurant as the sauce for an artichoke salad. (Put a little vodka in your gazpacho sauce and it becomes the world's best Bloody Mary.)"

1 cup chopped peeled tomatoes (see Note)
1 cup chopped peeled red onions
1 cup chopped green bell pepper
1 cup chopped seedless hothouse
    cucumber
1½ teaspoons chopped peeled garlic
1½ teaspoons kosher salt
¼ teaspoon cayenne pepper
¼ cup tomato paste
1 tablespoon white wine vinegar
¼ cup plus 2 tablespoons extra virgin olive
    oil
1 tablespoon fresh lemon juice
3 cups tomato juice
Sprig of thyme

1. In a large nonreactive mixing bowl, combine all the ingredients. Cover and refrigerate overnight.

2. The next day, remove the sprig of thyme. Using a blender, purée the remaining ingredients until smooth. For a smoother texture, the soup may be strained (this will reduce the quantity). Refrigerate the gazpacho until well chilled. Ladle the soup into bowls, and serve cold.

Yield: 2 quarts (8 to 16 servings)

Time: 10 minutes, plus chilling time

Note: To peel fresh tomatoes, cut a shallow "x" on the bottom of each tomato and submerge in boiling water for 5 to 10 seconds to loosen the skin. Remove; chill under cold water. The skins will slip off easily.

Thomas Keller

STEPHAN PYLE'S GOLDEN GAZPACHO WITH CHILIES AND SHRIMP

1½ teaspoons finely chopped fresh chilies,
    preferably serrano although jalapeños could
    be used, stems and seeds removed
¾ cup rich chicken broth
¼ teaspoon saffron threads
2 tablespoons freshly squeezed lime juice
2 pounds (about 6) yellow tomatoes
3 tablespoons finely chopped yellow bell pepper
5 tablespoons peeled, finely chopped
    cantaloupe
5 tablespoons peeled, seeded, chopped papaya
5 tablespoons peeled, seeded, chopped mango
½ cup peeled, seeded, finely diced cucumber
5 tablespoons peeled, finely diced jicama,
    optional (see Note)
2 tablespoons finely chopped scallions
Salt
1 pound cooked, peeled small shrimp
    (see Note)
1 tablespoon finely chopped fresh cilantro

1. Combine the chilies, chicken broth, saffron and lime juice in the container of a food processor or, preferably, an electric blender. Blend thoroughly. Pour the mixture into a small mixing bowl and let stand for a minimum of 10 minutes.

2. Drop the tomatoes into a basin of boiling water and let stand 12 seconds. Drain immediately. Peel the tomatoes and discard the peel and stems. Cut the tomatoes crosswise in half and remove the seeds. Cut the tomato flesh into a very small dice. There should be about 2 cups.

3. Combine the tomatoes, yellow pepper, cantaloupe, papaya, mango, cucumber, jicama and scallions in a mixing bowl. Add the chili and broth mixture and stir to blend. Add salt to taste. There should be about 4 cups. Refrigerate at least 1 hour.

4. Cut each shrimp crosswise in half; there should be about 1¼ cups. Roll the shrimp in chopped coriander.

5. Spoon equal portions of the soup into 4 to 6 chilled soup bowls. Garnish each bowl with equal portions of the shrimp.

Yield: 4 to 6 servings

Time: 1 hour preparation and cooking, plus refrigeration

Note: If you prefer, substitute cooked scallops for the shrimp.

Craig Claiborne

Stephan Pyle's Golden Gazpacho wth Chilies and Shrimp

CORN AND CILANTRO SOUP WITH TOMATO GARNISH

A verdant cold soup tasting richly of corn, served over its diced tomato garnish.

  2 tablespoons extra virgin olive oil
  1 medium onion, chopped
  1 tablespoon minced fresh ginger
  1 hot green chili, seeded and minced, or to taste
  Kernels from 4 ears fresh corn
  1 large bunch cilantro, bottom inch of stems removed
  1½ cups plain fat-free yogurt
  Salt and freshly ground black pepper
  6 ripe plum tomatoes, finely chopped

1. Heat the oil in a 3-quart saucepan. Add the onion, ginger and chili and sauté until softened. Add the corn, sauté 3 minutes, then add the cilantro. When the cilantro starts to wilt, add 1½ cups of water, bring just to a simmer and remove from the heat.

2. Transfer to a blender and process until finely puréed. Transfer to a large stainless steel bowl. Add a cup of ice water. Whisk in the yogurt and season to taste with salt and pepper. If the soup is not cold enough, refrigerate until ready to serve, or set a mixing bowl in a large bowl of ice water and allow to cool about 20 minutes, stirring occasionally.

3. To serve, put a mound of tomato in the center of each soup plate and spoon the soup over it.

Yield: 6 servings

Time: 45 minutes

Florence Fabricant

NIGELLA LAWSON'S RISI E BISI

Adapted from *Forever Summer*

Nigella Lawson: "*Risi e bisi* (rice and peas), the Venetian risotto-cum-soup, is very simple to make. If you cannot find fresh peas that have been recently picked, use frozen young peas. If you use fresh peas, you need to cook the pods to tenderize them before pushing them through a food mill, to make a sweet green purée to thicken and flavor the rice; if using frozen peas, you simply cook a cupful and then blitz them in a processor to add to whatever broth you want to cook the rice in. In a traditional risotto, you have to add broth slowly to the rice, stirring patiently as it is absorbed, ladleful by ladleful. Here, to get the requisite soupy texture you pour in all the broth in one go, clamp on a lid and let it simmer for 15 minutes or so. You need neither skill nor patience, for which, at the end of a long day, I am grateful. To make matters even simpler, you can substitute 3 to 5 sliced scallions for the onion."

  4 tablespoons unsalted butter
  12 ounces (3 cups) frozen young peas, thawed
  5 tablespoons freshly grated Parmesan cheese, plus more for serving
  2 tablespoons olive oil (not extra virgin)
  1 small onion, peeled and very finely chopped
  3 tablespoons chopped fresh flat-leaf parsley
  1 cup plus 2 tablespoons Italian Arborio rice
  6 cups hot chicken or vegetable broth

1. In a small saucepan, melt 1 tablespoon butter over low heat. Add 1 cup peas and sauté until tender, 1 to 2 minutes. Transfer to a blender and add 1 more tablespoon butter and 1 tablespoon Parmesan cheese. Process until puréed; reserve.

Opposite:
Nigella Lawson's Risi e Bisi

2. In a large saucepan, combine the remaining 2 tablespoons butter with the olive oil and place over medium-low heat. When the butter has melted, add the onion and sauté for 1 minute, then add 1 tablespoon parsley. Continue to sauté until onion is tender, another 1 to 2 minutes.

3. Add the remaining 2 cups peas and toss to mix. Add the rice and stir until the grains are well coated with butter. Pour in all the broth at once. Stir well and add the reserved pea purée. Cover, reduce heat to low and allow to simmer until the rice is cooked, about 15 minutes. Remove from heat and allow the mixture to sit covered for 10 minutes before serving.

4. To serve, transfer to a large warmed bowl. Stir in the remaining 4 tablespoons Parmesan and sprinkle with the remaining 2 tablespoons parsley. Serve warm.

Yield: 4 servings

Time: 40 minutes

Nigella Lawson

SQUASH AND APPLE SOUP

Adapted from *Out of the Earth*

The addition of apple gives this soup a sweet richness and complexity that complements the wonderful earth tones of squash, carrots and potatoes. It is as satisfying as anything laced with cream.

> 3 pounds butternut, buttercup,
>   Delicata or Hubbard squash, halved
>   and seeded
> Olive oil
> 3 carrots, peeled
> 2 medium onions, halved but not peeled
> Salt and freshly ground black pepper to taste
> 5 cloves garlic, peeled

> 4 apples, cored but not peeled, cut in ½-inch
>   chunks
> 1 pound red or white potatoes, peeled, cut in
>   ½-inch-thick slices
> 2 large sprigs thyme, plus extra for garnish
> 2 quarts chicken or vegetable stock

1. Preheat the oven to 400 degrees. Place the squash, cut side down, in a baking pan lightly coated with olive oil. Toss the carrots and onions in a little oil and salt. Add to pan with the squash or place in a separate pan. Roast the vegetables until tender: carrots and onions 40 to 50 minutes; squash about an hour.

2. Scoop the flesh from the squash and place in a 6- to 8-quart pot with the carrots. Peel the onions and add to the pot with garlic, apples, potatoes, 2 sprigs thyme and stock. Add water if needed to cover ingredients. Bring to a boil. Lower the heat and simmer until potatoes are falling-apart tender, about 30 minutes.

3. Purée the soup in batches; return to the pot and season with salt and pepper. Reheat very slowly before serving. The soup may be refrigerated or frozen; add a little water or stock when reheating.

Yield: About 10 cups

Time: 1 hour 40 minutes

Marian Burros

HARVEST SOUP

Adapted from Mary Ann Yevuta

> 2 pounds lean pork, cut into 1-inch cubes
> Salt and freshly ground black pepper
> 2½ tablespoons olive oil
> 1 large onion, coarsely chopped
> 6 cloves garlic, finely chopped
> 1 green bell pepper, cored and coarsely
>   chopped

2 Granny Smith apples, peeled, cored and
  coarsely chopped

1 medium butternut squash, peeled, seeded and
  cut into bite-size chunks

1 (15-ounce) can cannellini or other white beans,
  drained

3 tablespoons finely chopped fresh herbs
  (parsley, sage, thyme, tarragon, or as
  desired)

2 quarts (or more as needed) chicken stock or
  canned chicken broth

1. Season the pork with salt and pepper, and set aside. Place a large, wide casserole over medium-low heat, and add 1½ tablespoons oil. Add the onion and sauté until tender, about 3 minutes. Add the garlic and sauté until softened but not browned. Add the bell pepper and sauté for 1 minute. Transfer to a plate and set aside.

2. Add 1 tablespoon oil to the pan and raise the heat to medium-high. Working in batches (do not overcrowd the pan), sauté the pork until browned on all sides. Return the onions, garlic and peppers to the pan with the pork, and add the apples, squash, beans and herbs. Stir well and add stock to cover.

3. Raise the heat to bring the stock to a boil, then reduce the heat to low. Simmer, covered, until the pork is very tender, about 2 hours. Adjust salt and pepper to taste.

Yield: 4 servings

Time: 2 hours 45 minutes

Rebecca Skloot

MAKE-AHEAD SALADS THAT HEAT UP OR COOL DOWN

These side dishes can be prepared in the morning and will hold up nicely without refrigeration for several hours. Make these to taste, adding the seasonings a little at a time, adjusting the quantities as you go.

Sesame Green Bean Salad

Cook green beans until crisp-tender; drain. Toss with sesame oil, soy sauce, rice wine vinegar or lemon juice, olive oil and sliced scallion, and season with salt and pepper. Garnish with sesame seeds if you have them. This can also be made with broccoli or snow peas.

Potato, Parsley and Caper Salad

Cook small red or Yukon Gold potatoes and cut into slices (or use sweet potatoes cut into cubes), and gently toss while still warm with olive oil, red wine vinegar, capers, minced garlic, and plenty of salt and pepper. When cool, add at least one bunch of parsley leaves, coarsely chopped. This salad should be green.

Celery, Blue Cheese and Tabasco Salad

Slice some celery stalks and chop the tender leaves. Toss with plenty of blue cheese, olive oil, salt and pepper and many dashes of Tabasco.

Moroccan-Inspired Carrot-Cilantro Salad

Shred carrots. Toss with olive oil, lemon juice, harissa or a pinch of cayenne and plenty of chopped cilantro. Garnish with golden raisins if you have (and like) them.

Corn-Bread Panzanella

Toss toasted cubes of corn bread with chopped tomato, cucumber, green pepper, red pepper, red onions, olive oil, chopped basil and a sprinkle of balsamic vinegar. Or use toasted country bread or ciabatta.

Shredded Zucchini Salad with Parmesan

Shred tender zucchini. Toss with good olive oil, sea salt and shavings of good Parmesan or young pecorino cheese. Season with pepper.

Cucumber and Tomato Raita

Peel, halve and seed cucumbers, then thinly slice into half-moons. Halve cherry tomatoes and squeeze out their seedy guts. Toss with plain Greek yogurt, chopped mint and toasted cumin seeds. Season with salt.

Melissa Clark

FRESH PEA, ASPARAGUS AND ARUGULA CHOPPED SALAD

Sea salt

½ cup shelled fresh peas

6 spears asparagus, trimmed

1 tablespoon thinly sliced garlic chives, or chives and ½ small garlic clove, crushed

2 teaspoons white wine vinegar

1 teaspoon Dijon mustard

Freshly ground black pepper

3 tablespoons extra virgin olive oil

1 cup roughly chopped baby arugula

2 cups red leaf lettuce

1 tablespoon chopped fresh tarragon

1 (1½-inch) piece daikon radish, sliced into paper-thin rounds with a vegetable peeler (cut rounds in half if larger than 1 inch in diameter)

1. Bring a large pot of generously salted water to a boil. Add the peas, and cook until tender but still slightly firm, about 2 minutes. Using a slotted spoon, remove the peas to a strainer and cool under cold running water. Let dry. Bring the water back to a boil. Add the asparagus, and cook until tender but still slightly crisp, about 4 minutes. Drain, and cool under cold running water. Dry on a dish towel, then slice into ¾-inch pieces; there should be about 1 cup. Set aside.

2. In a small bowl, whisk together the garlic chives, vinegar, mustard and a large pinch of salt and pepper. Slowly whisk in the oil until emulsified. Taste, and adjust seasoning: it should be highly seasoned.

3. In a large serving bowl, combine the arugula, red leaf lettuce, peas, asparagus, tarragon and dai-

kon radish. Pour about half the dressing on top, and toss to coat vegetables, adding more dressing if necessary. Let sit for 15 minutes. Taste, and adjust the seasoning once more before serving.

Yield: 4 serving

Time: 40 minutes, plus standing time

Moira Hodgson

BLACK-EYED PEAS AND ARUGULA SALAD

Adapted from Alexander Smalls

1½ pounds black-eyed peas

6 cups chicken stock, approximately

½ cup olive oil

¼ cup vegetable oil

¼ cup raspberry vinegar

2 cloves garlic, minced

1½ tablespoons Dijon mustard

1 tablespoon honey

¼ teaspoon freshly grated nutmeg

Cayenne pepper to taste

Salt and freshly ground pepper to taste

1 medium red onion, minced

3 bunches arugula, washed and dried

1¼ pounds red cabbage, finely sliced

1. Pick over the peas to remove any stones or dirt. Wash thoroughly and drain. Soak overnight. Drain again.

2. Place the peas in a large pot and add the chicken stock to cover them. Bring to a boil, lower the heat and simmer, covered, for 30 minutes or until done. Drain. Set aside to cool.

3. In a small bowl, combine the remaining ingredients, except the red onion, arugula and cabbage. Whisk to blend.

4. Place the peas, onion, arugula and cabbage in a large serving bowl. Pour the dressing over them, toss well and serve immediately.

Yield: 20 servings

Time: 1 hour, plus overnight soaking of black-eyed peas

Sara Rimer

NIGELLA LAWSON'S BEET AND DANISH BLUE CHEESE SALAD

It's hard to imagine an easier salad than one of chopped cooked beets, vinegar-steeped onion, and crumbled Danish blue cheese. It must surely become one of your summer stalwarts.

½ red onion, finely sliced into half-moons
3 tablespoons red wine vinegar
1 pound (4 large or 8 small) beets, cooked and
    peeled
1 cup crumbled Danish blue cheese

1. In a small bowl, combine the onion and vinegar. Allow to steep 30 minutes or up to 4 hours.

2. Cut the beets into French-fry stick shapes, and arrange on a shallow serving dish. Pour the onion-vinegar mixture on top, and mix gently. Dot with crumbled blue cheese, and serve.

Yield: 10 to 12 servings

Time: 15 minutes, plus 30 minutes to 4 hours for marinating onion

Nigella Lawson

MUSHROOM SALAD WITH VINEGAR AND CORIANDER

1 pound assorted mushrooms, trimmed
½ cup extra virgin olive oil
2 large shallots, thinly sliced
2 garlic cloves, thinly sliced
1 teaspoon toasted coriander seeds
½ teaspoon coarsely cracked pepper
¼ cup raisins or currants
½ cup cider vinegar
Salt
Minced fresh chives

1. Bring a large pot of water to a boil. If the mushrooms are not of uniform size, cut the larger ones up so they are about the same size as the smaller ones. Put them in the boiling water and cook for 2 minutes. Drain, then rinse in cold water; drain again. Put in a serving bowl and set aside.

2. Put the olive oil in a large skillet. Turn the heat to medium-high and add the shallots and garlic. Cook for 2 minutes, then reduce the heat to medium-low. Add the coriander, pepper and raisins or currants. Cook, stirring, for about a minute.

3. Add cider vinegar and salt to taste. Pour the mixture, hot, over the mushrooms, stir and cover with foil. Marinate at room temperature for 3 hours, preferably overnight.

4. Serve at room temperature, garnished with chives.

Yield: 4 servings

Time: 20 minutes hands-on, 3 hours minimum marinating

Moira Hodgson

Opposite:
Nigella Lawson's Beet and Danish Blue Cheese Salad

BABY GREENS WITH BROILED LEMONS

Adapted from Lemon Zest

Lori Longbotham caramelizes lemon slices with salt and a touch of sugar, under the broiler, then tosses them with baby greens for a salad that is fresh, green and low in fat.

- 2 lemons, cut into paper-thin slices and seeded
- 2 tablespoons sugar
- 1 teaspoon salt, more to taste
- 8 cups baby greens, such as arugula or mesclun, washed and spun dry
- 2 tablespoons olive oil
- ¼ teaspoon freshly ground black pepper
- Freshly squeezed lemon juice, to taste, optional

1. Combine the lemons, sugar, and salt in a medium bowl and let stand for 1 hour, stirring occasionally.

2. Heat the broiler. Place the lemons on a rimmed baking sheet in a single layer and spoon any liquid in the bowl over them. Broil about 5 inches from heat until they are lightly browned, about 3 to 4 minutes, turning the pan, if necessary, so that the lemons brown evenly.

3. Meanwhile, place the greens in a serving bowl. Add the hot lemons and their liquid, oil and pepper; toss well. Season with salt and additional lemon juice, if desired. Serve immediately.

Yield: 6 servings

Time: 1¼ hours, including 1 hour marinating

Melissa Clark

NIGELLA LAWSON'S SWEET-AND-SOUR DILLED CUCUMBER SALAD

- 2 medium or 1½ large seedless hothouse cucumbers
- 2 tablespoons sugar
- ¼ cup white wine vinegar
- 1 teaspoon salt, or as needed
- ¼ cup finely chopped dill

1. Peel and finely slice the cucumbers into wafer-thin circles. Place in a large bowl.

2. In a small bowl, whisk together the sugar, vinegar and salt. Pour over the cucumbers, and turn them well to mix. Add the dill, mix again and adjust salt to taste. Spread in a shallow serving dish. Cover with plastic wrap, and refrigerate until chilled, up to 4 hours.

Yield: 10 to 12 servings

Time: 10 minutes, plus chilling

Nigella Lawson

Opposite:
Nigella Lawson's Sweet-and-Sour
Dilled Cucumber Salad

APPLE, CRANBERRY AND GOAT CHEESE SALAD

½ cup *pepitas* (shelled pumpkin seeds)
½ teaspoon olive oil
¼ teaspoon salt
⅓ cup dried cranberries, chopped if desired
¼ cup extra virgin olive oil
1 tablespoon apple cider (or raspberry, pear or other fruity) vinegar
Finely grated zest of half an orange, optional
Salt and freshly ground black pepper
1 apple, cored and quartered
1 head lettuce, cored and torn into pieces, or mesclun mix
1 (6-ounce) log of goat cheese

1. Preheat the oven to 350 degrees. Toss the *pepitas* with olive oil and salt in a bowl. Spread on a baking sheet and toast in the oven until golden and popped, 8 to 10 minutes. Remove and let cool. Place the *pepitas* and cranberries in the bottom of a salad bowl.

2. In another bowl, combine the extra virgin olive oil, vinegar and zest, if using. Season to taste with salt and pepper. Whisk until emulsified.

3. Thinly slice each apple quarter crosswise, and add to the salad bowl. Add the lettuce and dressing, and toss to mix. Crumble the cheese over the salad and serve.

Yield: 4 to 6 servings

Time: 20 minutes

Celia Barbour

Opposite:
Apple, Cranberry and Goat Cheese Salad

ROZANNE GOLD'S WATERMELON AND FETA SALAD

Adapted from *Recipes 1-2-3*

1¼ pounds watermelon
⅓ pound feta cheese, thinly sliced or crumbled
⅓ pound oil-cured black olives, pitted and roughly chopped
2 tablespoons roughly chopped fresh basil
Freshly ground black pepper
2 tablespoons extra virgin olive oil, optional

1. Remove the rind from the watermelon, then pit and thinly slice the flesh. Layer or toss it together with the feta and olives.

2. Top with the basil and pepper, and drizzle with olive oil, if desired. Serve immediately.

Yield: 6 servings

Time: 10 minutes

Mark Bittman

MEZZALUNA'S ARTICHOKE, FENNEL AND ARUGULA SALAD

Adapted from Mezzaluna, New York City

6 marinated artichoke hearts, drained and sliced thin
½ small fennel bulb, chopped medium-fine
1 celery stalk, chopped medium-fine
5 tablespoons olive oil
1 bunch arugula, washed, dried thoroughly and torn into bite-size pieces

Continued

1 small head of radicchio, washed, dried
   thoroughly and torn into bite-size pieces
¼ pound imported Parmesan cheese,
   shaved thin
2 tablespoons balsamic vinegar
Salt and freshly ground pepper to taste

1. In a medium bowl, mix the sliced artichoke hearts with the chopped fennel and celery and 1 table-spoon of the olive oil. Put 1 tablespoon or so of this mixture in the bottom of each of four individual salad bowls. Divide the shredded arugula and ra-dicchio among the bowls. Top each with the shaved Parmesan cheese.

2. Pour the remaining oil over the individual sal-ads, about 1 tablespoon for each bowl. Pour the balsamic vinegar over each individual salad, about ½ tablespoon for each bowl. (The oil-to-vinegar ratio should be approximately 2 to 1.) Season with salt and pepper.

Yield: 4 servings

Time: 30 minutes

Jason Epstein

CARMINE'S CAESAR SALAD

Adapted from Carmine's, New York City

For the Croutons

   1 cup cubed French bread pieces
   Olive oil

For the Dressing

   2 ounces anchovy fillets

   1 egg yolk (see Note)

   1 teaspoon finely chopped fresh flat-leaf
      parsley

   1 tablespoon finely chopped garlic
      (or less to taste)

   1 cup extra virgin olive oil

   ¼ cup grated Parmesan cheese

   ¼ cup red wine vinegar

For the Salad

   1 head romaine lettuce, cut, washed
      and drained

1. Preheat the oven to 300 degrees. Spread the bread on a baking sheet, drizzle with olive oil and bake 4 to 5 minutes, stirring once or twice, until golden. Set aside.

2. In a stainless steel bowl, crush the anchovy fillets with a fork until they are well mashed. Add the egg yolk and stir with a wire whisk for 2 to 3 minutes. Stir in the parsley and garlic. Slowly add the olive oil in a steady stream while whisking to incorporate. Add the vinegar and 2 tablespoons of the Parmesan and stir briskly with the whisk.

3. In a large bowl, toss the lettuce with the dressing and the croutons. Sprinkle the remaining cheese on top.

Yield: 6 to 8 servings

Time: 30 minutes

Note: Because of concern over salmonella contamination in raw eggs, some cooks may choose to substitute 1 tablespoon of Dijon mustard for the egg yolk or to use either a pasteurized egg product or an egg-substitute product.

Alex Ward

ITALIAN TOMATO-POTATO SALAD

(Insalata Pantesca)

   1 pound new potatoes, unpeeled

   1 pound fully ripe tomatoes, preferably
      vine-ripened

   1 large red onion

   2 to 3 tablespoons capers, preferably
      packed in salt

   1½ cups black olives

   1 tablespoon red wine vinegar

   ¼ cup extra virgin olive oil

   2 teaspoons dried oregano

   Sea salt and freshly ground black pepper
      to taste

1. Put the potatoes in a large pot, add water to cover, salt lightly and boil for 20 to 30 minutes, or until tender when pierced with a toothpick. Drain, cool slightly and peel while warm.

2. Cut the tomatoes in half horizontally, and squeeze into a sieve or strainer set over a bowl, pressing the seeds to extract the juice. Discard seeds. Cut the tomatoes into chunks and add to the juice.

3. Peel the onion, cut in half horizontally and then into ¼-inch-thick slices. Slice the potatoes into ½-inch-thick rounds. Rinse the capers to eliminate excess salt or brine.

4. In a large, shallow bowl, toss the potatoes, onions, tomatoes, olives and capers together with the vinegar, olive oil, dried oregano and salt and pepper to taste. Serve at room temperature.

Yield: 6 servings

Time: 50 minutes

Suzanne Hamlin

HOPPIN' JOHN'S SOUTHERN POTATO SALAD

2 pounds boiling potatoes or new potatoes,
    scrubbed and unpeeled
1½ cups minced celery
1 cup scallions, cut in thin slices, including
    some of the green parts
3 hard-boiled eggs, peeled and chopped
½ cup mayonnaise
1 heaping tablespoon prepared mustard
½ cup sweet pickles, diced with some juice
    from the jar
Salt and freshly ground black pepper
Cayenne pepper to taste
1 to 2 tablespoons chopped fresh herbs,
    such as parsley and chives
Paprika to taste

1. Cut the potatoes in half if large, put in a pot and add enough lightly salted water to cover them by 2 inches. Bring to a boil and cook, uncovered, for about 15 minutes, until tender. Drain. Peel, if desired, and cut into 1½-inch wedges.

2. In a large serving bowl, mix the potato pieces with the celery, scallions and eggs.

3. In a small bowl, mix the mayonnaise, mustard, pickle cubes and juice; toss with the potatoes. Season to taste with salt, pepper and cayenne. Sprinkle with chopped herbs and dust with paprika. Serve slightly chilled.

Yield: 6 servings

Time: 40 minutes, plus chilling time

Suzanne Hamlin

SHARON TURNER'S POTATO SALAD WITH GREEN BEAN AND SHELLFISH VARIATIONS

For the Salad Base
¾ cup extra virgin olive oil
3 tablespoons tarragon vinegar
¼ teaspoon salt, or to taste
Several grinds of the pepper mill
4 pounds small new potatoes, steamed until
    barely tender, allowed to cool and cut into
    quarters, about 12 cups prepared
¾ cup thinly sliced scallions

For Variation A, with Beans
⅓ cup finely minced fresh flat-leaf parsley
⅓ cup finely minced fresh tarragon
2 tablespoons minced fresh dill
2 tablespoons minced fresh lovage or
    celery leaves
1 pound green snap beans, steamed until
    barely tender, cooled and cut into
    1-inch lengths, about 4 cups
4 hard-boiled eggs, coarsely chopped

For Variation B, with Shellfish
½ cup finely chopped fresh basil
⅓ cup finely chopped fresh chervil
2 large cloves garlic, finely minced
1 cup finely sliced celery
2 to 3 cups cooked lobster, shrimp, crabmeat or
    mussels, cut if necessary into bite-size
    chunks

1. Whisk the oil with the vinegar, salt and pepper. Transfer a half cup of the dressing to a large bowl and combine with the potatoes, scallions and additions of choice. If the salad seems dry, correct with some or all of the reserved dressing.

ALICE WATERS'S SPICY COLESLAW

A coleslaw made vibrant with tastes of jalapeño, cilantro and lime.

1 medium cabbage (about 3 pounds), outer
    leaves removed
1 large jalapeño pepper
½ small red onion, cut in half through the stem,
    peeled and thinly sliced
1 cup loosely packed fresh cilantro leaves,
    coarsely chopped
3 to 4 tablespoons fresh lime juice
3 to 4 teaspoons red wine vinegar
¼ to ⅓ cup olive oil
1½ teaspoons Maldon or other sea salt,
    or more to taste
½ teaspoon freshly ground pepper, or
    more to taste
Large pinch of sugar, or more to taste

1. Quarter the cabbage through the core; cut out the core. Cut the quarters crosswise in half; finely shred, using a sharp knife. Place the shredded cabbage in a very large bowl or pot (you will have about 5½ quarts). Cut open the jalapeño, discard the seeds and dice it fine. Add the diced jalapeño, onion and cilantro to the cabbage and toss to mix. Sprinkle with the lime juice, vinegar, oil, salt, pepper and sugar, and toss to coat.

2. Let the slaw sit for 1 hour, tossing occasionally. Drain; taste and adjust the seasonings. Wait another hour. Serve at room temperature.

Yield: 8 to 12 servings

Time: 30 minutes, plus 2 hours' resting

Jason Epstein

2. Marinate at room temperature for at least 30 minutes. Taste, adjust seasonings and serve. The salad will keep, refrigerated, for 3 or 4 days.

Yield: 12 to 16 servings

Time: 30 minutes for base, additional for variations A and B

Leslie Land

FESTIVE COLESLAW

This slaw may be made a day in advance of serving. For smaller gatherings, decrease the ingredients proportionally.

For the Dressing

1 cup vegetable oil
1 tablespoon sugar
⅓ cup cider vinegar
2 tablespoons whole-grain mustard
1 tablespoon celery seed
1 tablespoon prepared horseradish
1 teaspoon salt
¼ teaspoon freshly ground white pepper

For the Slaw

2 heads green cabbage (about 3 pounds each)
1 head red cabbage (about 3 pounds)
3 cups red onion (3 large ones), thinly sliced
6 carrots, peeled and shredded
3 large red bell peppers, seeded and cut into thin strips
½ cup chopped fresh dill
¼ cup chopped fresh flat-leaf parsley

1. Combine the dressing ingredients in a blender and emulsify, about 30 seconds. Refrigerate, covered, at least 1 hour and up to 4 days.

2. Cut all the cabbages into quarters, core and shred. Toss all the vegetables in a large bowl with the dill and parsley. Cover and refrigerate. The slaw can be made up to 24 hours ahead. When ready to serve, add the dressing and toss well.

Yield: 25 servings

Time: 30 minutes, plus at least 1 hour refrigeration

Molly O'Neill

TOMATO AND PITA SALAD

(Fattoush)

Adapted from Ramzi Osseiran

For the Salad

1 pita bread
1 large tomato, diced, seeds removed
¼ red onion, diced
2 bell peppers, one red, one yellow, pith and seeds removed, cut into long strips
1 cucumber, peeled and cut in rounds
5 radishes, sliced
2 whole scallions, chopped
1 head of romaine lettuce, purslane or other wild greens, torn in pieces

¼ cup coarsely chopped fresh mint

1 to 3 teaspoons ground sumac (see Sources, page 259)

1 teaspoon dried mint

For the Dressing

2 cloves garlic, peeled and minced (about 2 teaspoons)

⅓ cup extra virgin olive oil

Juice of ½ lemon

4 teaspoons pomegranate syrup

1 teaspoon salt, or to taste

¼ teaspoon ground pepper, or to taste

1. Heat the oven to 350 degrees. Separate the pita into 2 rounds, and bake on a cookie sheet for about 5 minutes, or until very crisp but not browned.

2. Put the tomato, red onion, peppers, cucumber, radishes and scallions into a large salad bowl. Add the romaine or purslane and fresh mint, and sprinkle with sumac and dried mint. Toss.

3. Whisk together the garlic, olive oil, lemon juice, pomegranate syrup and salt and pepper in a small bowl. Just before serving, give the dressing another quick whisk and then pour it over the vegetables and toss.

4. Break the pita into 1-inch pieces and toss with the salad, just before taking the salad to the table. Taste, add seasonings, if needed and serve immediately.

Yield: 6 to 8 servings

Time: 30 minutes

Joan Nathan

FRESH CORN SALAD WITH TOMATOES AND DILL

For fewer servings, decrease ingredients proportionally.

For the Salad

18 ears fresh corn, husk and silk removed
4 scallions, sliced
3 large red bell peppers, cut into 1/2-inch dice
3 large green bell peppers, cut into 1/2-inch dice
3 cucumbers, peeled, seeded and chopped
1/2 cup chopped fresh dill
1 pint cherry tomatoes, sliced in half

For the Dressing

1 1/2 cups extra virgin olive oil
1/2 cup balsamic vinegar
Salt and freshly ground black pepper to taste

1. In a large pot, bring about 2 quarts of water to a boil. Meanwhile, hold each ear of corn upright in a very large bowl and slice off the kernels. Add the corn kernels to the boiling water and cover. Bring to a boil and cook 4 minutes, stirring the corn once every minute. Drain and refresh under cold water.

2. Put the corn in the large serving bowl with the remaining vegetables. Add the oil. Toss well. Add the vinegar and salt and pepper to taste and mix well. Marinate 1 to 2 hours.

Yield: 25 servings

Time: 45 minutes, plus 1 to 2 hours' marinating

Molly O'Neill

SUZANNE HART'S COLD RICE SALAD

This dish is prepared with farm-stand vegetables and ingredients stored in the cupboard. The salad is best if left to sit for 24 hours and can be made the night before. If you are having more guests, simply increase the recipe exponentially.

1 1/2 cups chicken broth
1 cup Texmati or basmati rice
1/4 cup chopped red onions
1/2 cup diced ripe tomatoes
1/3 cup chopped red or yellow bell peppers
1/2 cup chopped celery
6 tablespoons extra virgin olive oil
2 tablespoons sherry vinegar
1/4 cup finely chopped fresh flat-leaf parsley
1/4 cup finely chopped fresh basil
Salt and freshly ground pepper to taste

1. Bring the chicken broth to a boil, add the rice and simmer for 10 to 15 minutes until the rice is cooked but still firm. Remove from the heat and let cool to room temperature, at least 30 minutes.

2. Stir in the onions, tomatoes, peppers and celery and mix thoroughly.

3. In a separate bowl, blend the olive oil and vinegar with a wire whisk, then pour over the salad. Add the parsley, basil and salt and pepper to taste and toss gently. Chill in the refrigerator for at least 1 hour.

Yield: 4 servings

Time: Preparation time: 30 minutes; standing time: 30 minutes; refrigeration time: from 1 to 24 hours

Kathleen Beckett-Young

MOLLY O'NEILL'S SUMMER VEGETABLE SALAD WITH ORZO

The flavor of this colorful salad will improve if the vegetables are prepared a few days in advance and refrigerated. For buffets or larger gatherings, simply increase the ingredients proportionally.

2 medium zucchini, cut into ½-inch dice

6 medium tomatoes, cut into ½-inch dice

2 medium yellow bell peppers, cored and cut into ½-inch dice

4 cups stemmed, coarsely chopped arugula

1 tablespoon grated lemon zest

½ pound orzo

2 tablespoons fresh lemon juice

3 tablespoons extra virgin olive oil

1 tablespoon kosher salt

Freshly ground pepper to taste

1. Blanch the zucchini in salted boiling water for 20 seconds. Drain and refresh under cold running water. Drain well.

2. Put the zucchini in a large bowl and toss with the tomatoes, bell peppers, arugula and lemon zest. Refrigerate until cold.

3. Just before serving, cook the orzo until al dente. Meanwhile, toss the salad with the lemon juice, olive oil, salt and pepper. Drain the orzo, toss with the salad, divide among 4 plates and serve immediately.

Yield: 4 servings

Time: 30 minutes, plus chilling time for vegetables of up to a few days

Molly O'Neill

CLAUDIA RODEN'S BULGUR SALAD WITH POMEGRANATE DRESSING AND TOASTED NUTS

Adapted from *The Book of Jewish Food*

This is one of Claudia Roden's most cherished recipes, handed down in her family for generations. Its origin is Syria, where it is known as *Bazargan* because all of the ingredients can be obtained at a bazaar.

2¾ cups bulgur, preferably coarse-ground

Salt

¾ cup olive oil

6 tablespoons pomegranate molasses (see Sources, page 259)

Juice of 2 lemons

6 tablespoons tomato paste

2 teaspoons ground cumin

2 teaspoons ground coriander

1 teaspoon ground allspice

½ teaspoon cayenne or Aleppo pepper

Freshly ground black pepper

2 cups walnuts, coarsely chopped

¼ cup pine nuts, lightly toasted

1 bunch fresh flat-leaf parsley, finely chopped, about 1 cup

1. Put the bulgur in a large bowl and cover with cold, lightly salted water. Let it soak until tender, from 30 minutes to 2 hours, depending on the coarseness of the bulgur. Drain in a sieve, firmly pressing out excess water, and transfer to a serving bowl.

2. Whisk the olive oil with the pomegranate molasses, lemon juice, tomato paste and spices. Add the salt and peppers and taste; the mixture should be pleasingly tangy. Add more pomegranate molasses and lemon juice as needed.

3. Pour half the dressing over the bulgur and mix well. Set aside to absorb the dressing for about 10 minutes. Taste for salt, adding more if needed. Add half the remaining dressing, all the nuts and parsley and mix well. Before serving, taste again and add more dressing as needed.

Yield: 8 to 10 servings

Time: 20 minutes, plus soaking

Julia Moskin

COUSCOUS SALAD

This salad, with a delightful Middle Eastern touch of saffron, ginger, currants and dates—along with chopped vegetables—is best prepared and set aside to steep in its dressing overnight.

> 6 cups chicken stock
> 9 tablespoons olive oil
> 1/2 teaspoon ground ginger
> 1/4 teaspoon saffron
> 3 cups couscous
> 3/4 cup currants
> 3/4 cup dates, pitted and chopped
> 2 1/4 cups finely diced celery
> 1 1/2 cups finely diced carrots
> 1 cup minced scallions
> 1/2 cup minced fresh parsley
> 2 1/4 tablespoons freshly squeezed lemon juice
> 3/4 teaspoon salt
> 1/2 teaspoon ground cinnamon
> 3/4 cup toasted pine nuts

1. In a saucepan bring the stock, 6 tablespoons of the oil, the ginger and saffron to a boil. Add the couscous and boil until the liquid begins to be absorbed.

2. Remove from the heat and fold in the currants and dates. Cover and let stand for 15 minutes. Add the celery, carrots and scallions. Mix well.

3. In a small bowl combine the parsley, lemon juice, salt, cinnamon and remaining olive oil. Toss well with the couscous, breaking up any clumps. Cover and refrigerate overnight.

4. Bring to room temperature. Adjust the seasonings. Sprinkle with the pine nuts.

Yield: 16 servings

Time: 40 minutes, plus overnight refrigeration and return to room temperature

Nancy Harmon Jenkins

FARM-STAND TABBOULEH

> 3/4 cup bulgur wheat
> 1/2 cup olive oil
> 1/3 cup fresh lemon juice
> 1/2 cup chopped fresh flat-leaf parsley
> 2 tablespoons chopped fresh thyme
> 1 garlic clove, minced
> 2 ears of young corn, husk and silk removed
> 1 medium green bell pepper, seeded and chopped
> 2 medium tomatoes, seeded and coarsely chopped

1. In a large bowl, combine the bulgur wheat with 1 1/4 cups boiling water. Soak for 30 minutes, until the water is absorbed.

2. Whisk together the olive oil, lemon juice, parsley, thyme, and garlic and pour over the wheat.

3. Steam the corn for 5 minutes, or until tender but still firm. Let cool, then scrape off the kernels.

4. Add the corn, green pepper and tomatoes to the wheat mixture and stir gently to combine. Cover and refrigerate until ready to serve.

Yield: 6 servings

Time: 1 hour, including 30 minutes for soaking bulgur

Janet Bukovinsky

MOJITO SALAD

A refreshing salad—with or without the rum.

For the Salad
- ½ cup red onion, halved and thinly sliced crosswise
- Juice of 1 lime
- 1 medium jicama, peeled and cut into matchsticks
- 1 seedless hothouse cucumber, sliced ¼-inch-thick crosswise
- ½ seedless watermelon, cut into 1-inch cubes
- 1 pound strawberries, hulled and halved lengthwise
- ⅓ cup packed fresh mint leaves, thinly sliced

For the Dressing
- ½ cup vegetable oil
- ⅓ cup honey
- ½ cup fresh lime juice (about 2½ limes)
- 1½ teaspoons sea salt
- 3 teaspoons light rum, optional

1. To make the salad: marinate the onion in the juice of 1 lime for at least 2 hours or overnight. Combine all salad ingredients in a large bowl.

2. To make the dressing: Whisk together the dressing ingredients and pour over the salad. Toss. Serve or transport to a picnic.

Yield: 12 servings

Time: 20 minutes, plus marinating onion for at least 2 hours

Madhu Puri

BROCCOLI RABE WITH RAISINS AND GARLIC

Adapted from *Cucina Simpatica*

- 2 pounds broccoli rabe, washed, trimmed and chopped
- 4 tablespoons extra virgin olive oil
- 2 cloves garlic, minced
- ½ cup raisins
- ¾ teaspoon kosher salt
- ½ teaspoon red pepper flakes

1. Bring a gallon of water to a boil in a large pot. Blanch the broccoli rabe for 7 minutes and cool under cold running water. Drain.

2. Heat 2 tablespoons of the olive oil in a large skillet over medium heat. Add the garlic and toss, cooking for about 2 minutes, until golden. Add the cooked broccoli rabe, raisins, salt and pepper flakes. Shake the skillet and cook until hot, about 7 minutes.

3. Pour the remaining oil over the vegetables and adjust seasoning. Serve hot or at room temperature.

Yield: 6 servings

Time: About 30 minutes

Molly O'Neill

FAITH WILLINGER'S ASPARAGUS WITH A CITRUS SPLASH

Adapted from Red, White & Greens

This is an excellent buffet dish and can easily be increased for larger gatherings.

> 1 pound fresh asparagus, trimmed, preferably uniform pencil-thin or medium stalks
> 2 to 3 tablespoons extra virgin olive oil
> Fine sea salt and freshly ground black pepper to taste
> 2 tablespoons fresh lemon juice
> 1 tablespoon orange juice

1. Place the asparagus in a single layer in a large nonstick skillet and drizzle with 1 tablespoon of olive oil. Shake the pan to coat the asparagus with oil and place over medium heat. Cook the asparagus, shaking the pan every few minutes to brown evenly.

2. Lower the heat and continue cooking until the asparagus is tender (cooking time may vary widely), 10 to 15 minutes. Test by poking the asparagus stems with a toothpick or knife. Transfer to a serving dish. Season with salt and pepper to taste. Drizzle with 1 to 2 tablespoons of olive oil. Combine the lemon juice and orange juice and sprinkle over the asparagus. Serve immediately or at room temperature.

Yield: 3 to 4 appetizer or side-dish servings

Time: 30 minutes

Molly O'Neill

Opposite:
Faith Willinger's Asparagus with a Citrus Splash

MARIO BATALI'S ROASTED CAULIFLOWER WITH LEMON, CAPERS AND OLIVES

Adapted from Zach Allen

The cauliflower is roasted and then coated with lemon, capers, olives and garlic. Served at room temperature, it makes a splendid side dish, appetizer or addition to an antipasto. The roasted cauliflower is so tasty that you can omit the embellishments and serve it plain.

> 1 large head cauliflower, cut into florets the size of a small plum
> Kosher salt and freshly ground black pepper
> About 2 cups best-quality olive oil, or as needed
> Grated zest of 2 lemons
> 3 cloves garlic, peeled and green germ removed
> 2 tablespoons fresh thyme leaves
> 2 tablespoons salt-cured capers, rinsed well and drained
> ¼ cup pitted kalamata olives
> Lemon olive oil or freshly squeezed lemon juice, for sprinkling

1. Heat the oven to 375 degrees. Place the cauliflower in a large bowl, and season to taste with salt and pepper. Toss by hand to distribute the seasonings. Pour about ⅓ cup olive oil over the cauliflower and toss to coat. Spread on a baking sheet, and roast until browned and tender, 30 to 35 minutes, rotating the sheet halfway through. Remove from the oven and allow to cool.

2. While the cauliflower roasts, in a small saucepan, combine the lemon zest, garlic, thyme and 1 cup olive oil. Place the pan over medium-low heat until bubbles form; do not boil. Cook until the garlic is soft, about 20 minutes, then remove from the heat and allow to cool. Pour the cooled mixture in a blender, and blend on lowest speed to purée.

3. In a separate small saucepan, combine the capers, olives and ½ cup olive oil. Warm over medium-low heat for 5 minutes.

4. Transfer the cauliflower to a large serving bowl. Pour over about half the lemon-garlic oil, and toss gently to coat. (Reserve remainder for another use.) Spoon over the caper–olive oil mixture and toss once more. Adjust salt and pepper to taste. Just before serving, sprinkle with lemon olive oil or fresh lemon juice to taste.

Yield: 6 appetizer servings or 3 to 4 side-dish servings

Time: 45 minutes, plus cooling to room temperature

Amanda Hesser

CHRISTOPHER IDONE'S POACHED BABY LEEKS

Adapted from *The New Glorious American Food*

12 baby leeks, about ¾-inch-thick in diameter at base
1 cup champagne vinegar or good white wine vinegar
1 long strip lemon zest
2 to 3 peperoncini or other small, whole, very hot red peppers (see Note)
1 bay leaf
8 black peppercorns
1 tablespoon sea or kosher salt

1. Two or three days before serving, trim the roots and dark green tops from the leeks, leaving the leeks about 6 inches long. Peel away any wilted leaves. Quarter lengthwise from top to beginning of white part. Wash in cold running water, spreading the leaves to rinse off any sand. If the leeks are gritty, soak in a bowl of cold water for 20 minutes, then rinse again.

2. In a large shallow pan that will fit the leeks side by side, combine the vinegar, lemon zest, peppers, bay leaf, peppercorns and salt. Add 3 cups cold water. Place over medium heat and bring to a simmer. Arrange the leeks in the pan, adding more water to cover, if necessary. Simmer, partially covered, until the whites of the leeks can be pierced easily with the tip of a knife, 10 to 15 minutes.

3. Using a spatula or tongs, transfer the leeks from the cooking liquid to a shallow pan or baking dish and set aside. Continue simmering the liquid until it is reduced by half. Pour over the leeks and allow to cool. Cover and refrigerate for 2 or 3 days to allow the leeks to marinate. Allow to rest at room temperature for 1 hour before serving. Serve 2 to 3 leeks per person.

Yield: 4 to 6 servings

Time: 45 minutes, plus 2 to 3 days for marinating and 1 hour resting to room temperature

Note: The peppers' heat will increase with marinating.

Christopher Idone

Opposite:
Christopher Idone's Poached Baby Leeks

POTATOES BAKED WITH GRUYÈRE

Adapted from *The Best of Craig Claiborne*

A rich and delicious potato dish.

> 2½ pounds potatoes
> Butter
> 2 garlic cloves, peeled
> 2 cups whole milk
> 1 cup heavy cream
> Salt and freshly ground pepper to taste
> Grated nutmeg to taste
> 1 cup grated Gruyère or Swiss cheese

1. Preheat the oven to 375 degrees.

2. Peel the potatoes and cut them into very thin slices. As they are sliced, drop them into cold water to prevent discoloration. Drain when all are sliced. There should be 6 or 7 cups.

3. Rub a baking dish (an oval one measuring about 14 × 8 × 2 inches is convenient) with butter and a peeled clove of garlic. Crush both cloves of garlic lightly and put them in a saucepan.

4. Add the milk, cream, salt, pepper, and nutmeg to the garlic cloves and bring to a boil. Strain this mixture over the potatoes. Discard the garlic. Sprinkle the top with grated cheese. Place in the oven over a baking sheet to catch any drippings. Bake for about 1 hour, or until the potatoes are tender and the cheese is golden.

Yield: 12 servings

Time: 1½ hours, including 1 hour baking

SAVOY'S SMASHED POTATOES

Adapted from Peter Hoffman, New York City

Smashing—roughly mushing a baked or boiled potato with a fork or wire masher—generally leaves potato skin, flakes and lumps intact and deploys olive oil or cooking juices as often as it does butter or cream. "Basically, you give the potato a good kick in the pants and send it to the plate," said Peter Hoffman, the chef and owner of Savoy in Manhattan. The result? An innocent, "warts-and-all" potato, nothing gussied up or airbrushed.

> 12 ounces fingerling, Russian Banana, or other
>   waxy, rich-flavored potatoes, washed
> Kosher salt
> 4 teaspoons butter
> Freshly ground black pepper
> Chopped fresh herbs, optional

1. Place the potatoes in a large pot, and add enough cool water to cover by 1 inch. Add 1 teaspoon of salt for each quart of water. Cover, bring to a boil, and cook until tender when pierced with a knife tip, 20 to 25 minutes.

2. Drain the potatoes and remove them from the pot. Cool slightly, about 5 minutes. On a flat work surface, whack each potato once or twice with the flat side of a large knife or the back of a plate; the potatoes should pretty much retain their original shape. Divide the potatoes among four plates, and top with butter, salt, a few grinds of pepper and, if desired, herbs. Serve hot.

Yield: 4 servings

Time: 30 minutes

Molly O'Neill

PICHOLINE'S TRUFFLED SMASHED POTATOES

Adapted from Terrance Brennan

The starchy Idaho, Russet Burbank or large Yukon Gold potatoes are great in mashed and smashed potatoes alike, but smashing allows the use of waxier varieties like the tiny fingerling and also heirloom varieties, which become gluey when subjected to a ricer or handheld mixer. Baking most varieties is the simplest way to get a good texture and a toasty flavor. The fingerlings or heirloom varieties can be baked, boiled or steamed in their skins.

    12 ounces fingerling potatoes
    1 tablespoon olive oil
    4 tablespoons finely chopped black truffle,
        plus 12 paper-thin slices (about 2½ ounces
        in all)
    5 tablespoons unsalted butter, room
        temperature, cut into pieces
    Coarse sea salt and freshly ground black pepper
        to taste

1. Preheat the oven to 375 degrees. Toss the fingerlings with olive oil, place them on a baking sheet and bake until they can be easily pierced with a fork, about 22 minutes. Remove from the oven, and cool.

2. When the potatoes are cool enough to handle, remove the skins with a paring knife. Transfer the potatoes to a bowl, and add the chopped truffle and butter. Roughly crush the potatoes, using a serpentine-style masher. Switch to a fork or a slotted spoon, and continue to smash and fluff the potatoes until the butter and chopped truffle are all incorporated, but the potatoes retain a rough texture. Add salt and pepper to taste.

3. Divide the potatoes among four plates, garnish with three truffle slices each, and serve hot.

Yield: 4 servings

Time: 40 minutes

Molly O'Neill

STEPHAN PYLES'S DRUNKEN BEANS

Adapted from *The New Texas Cuisine*

    2 slices bacon, diced
    1 onion, peeled and diced
    2 cloves garlic, peeled and minced
    2 cups pinto beans, soaked overnight and
        drained
    1 quart chicken broth, homemade or low-
        sodium canned, or water
    2 cups beer
    2 to 4 jalapeño peppers, thinly sliced, with seeds
    Salt and freshly ground pepper
    2 tablespoons chopped fresh cilantro

1. Place the bacon in a large pot over medium heat until the fat is rendered. Remove the bacon with a slotted spoon and discard. Add the onion and garlic and cook until soft, about 5 minutes. Add the beans, the broth or water and the beer. Bring to a boil, reduce the heat to a simmer and cook for 30 minutes.

2. Stir in the jalapeño slices. Cook until the beans are tender, about 30 minutes more, adding water if necessary to keep beans covered. Season with salt and pepper to taste. Stir in cilantro and serve immediately.

Yield: 6 to 8 servings

Time: 1 hour 15 minutes

Molly O'Neill

CREAMED CORN

6 ears fresh corn
2 tablespoons butter
Sliver of garlic
Sea salt
¾ cup milk
¼ cup heavy cream

1. Scrape corn kernels from the cobs, running the knife edge along the cobs to squeeze out the juices. (If the corn is not very fresh, then blanch in boiling water for 2 to 3 minutes before scraping the kernels from the cobs.)

2. Place a medium saucepan over medium heat. Drop in the butter and melt until foamy. Add the corn, garlic and juices. Season with salt, and cook until the kernels become tender. Pour in the milk and simmer until the milk is almost gone. Pour in the cream and simmer for 5 minutes. Taste and adjust seasoning. Serve.

Yield: 4 servings

Time: 20 minutes

Amanda Hesser

MOLLY O'NEILL'S GRILLED CORN WITH FLAVORED BUTTERS

The butters may be frozen and may be used to flavor other vegetables.

20 ears fresh corn
½ cup unsalted flavored or plain butter (recipes
   follow), at room temperature
Kosher salt and freshly ground pepper to taste

Preheat a charcoal grill. Pull back the corn husks and remove the silk. Spread the ears with the butter and re-cover the corn with the husks. Soak in water for 10 minutes. Grill until tender, turning from time to time, 15 to 20 minutes. Remove the husks and season with salt and pepper.

Yield: 20 servings

Time: 30 minutes

➤ ANCHO CHILI BUTTER

2 small ancho chilies
½ cup unsalted butter, softened
½ teaspoon kosher salt, plus more to taste

Stem the chilies, break them open and shake out all the seeds. Bring a small saucepan of water to a boil. Lower the heat, add the chilies and simmer until softened, about 5 minutes. Drain and let cool. Use a small knife to scrape the flesh of the chilies from the skin. Chop the chilies into a paste, and cream together with the butter in a small bowl. Stir in the salt.

Yield: ½ cup

Time: 25 minutes

➤ LIME BUTTER

½ cup unsalted butter, softened
4 teaspoons grated lime zest
1 teaspoon kosher salt
2 tablespoons fresh lime juice

Cream the butter with the lime zest and salt in a small bowl. Gradually stir in the lime juice.

Yield: ½ cup

Time: 10 minutes

Molly O'Neill

SQUASH AND SWEET CORN WITH CILANTRO

2 pounds small (4- to 7-inch × 1-inch) yellow
    squash, cut in thin rounds, about 5 cups
    prepared
4 or 5 ears tender corn, or enough to make at
    least 3½ cups prepared
¼ cup heavy cream or crème fraîche, not
    ultrapasteurized
¼ cup coarsely chopped fresh cilantro
Tiny pinch of salt

1. Put a half cup of water in a large, heavy, nonre-active saucepan and bring to a boil. Add the squash, cover the pan, lower the heat to medium-low and cook, stirring occasionally, until the squash is more or less falling apart and all the water has cooked away, about 20 minutes. If necessary, uncover the pan and raise the heat near the end of the cooking so there is no free water.

2. While the squash is cooking, cut the corn ker-nels from the cobs, keeping the knife perpendicu-lar so only the tips are removed. Then scrape the cobs with the back of the knife to get all the juice and kernel hearts.

3. When the squash is ready, stir in the corn and cream. Cook, stirring often, for about 3 minutes, just long enough to heat everything through. Add the cilantro, taste and add the merest smidgen of salt if you think it's necessary. Serve at once.

Yield: 2 main-course servings;
4 to 6 side-dish servings

Time: 30 minutes

Leslie Land

MARK BITTMAN'S PEACH-CHIPOTLE SALSA

2 cups peaches, cut in ¼-inch dice
½ cup red bell pepper, stemmed, seeded and cut
    into ¼-inch dice
1 chili in adobo, puréed or minced
    (or 1 dried chipotle, soaked until soft
    and puréed or minced)
2 tablespoons freshly squeezed lime juice
¼ cup minced fresh cilantro
1 tablespoon sugar

Combine all the ingredients, and let them sit for up to an hour before serving.

Yield: About 2 cups

Time: 15 minutes

Mark Bittman

RICE-STUFFED TOMATOES WITH PINE NUTS AND RAISINS

Adapted from *The Best Book of Greek Cookery*

Rice flecked with currants and nuts and a whiff of mint enriches the sweetness of the tomatoes in this dish, which can be served either as an appe-tizer, as a side dish or as part of a buffet. It goes particularly well with grilled lamb or poached fish. The tomatoes are best prepared in advance. They may be refrigerated, but they should be served at room temperature.

12 medium ripe tomatoes
4 tablespoons sugar
1 cup extra virgin olive oil, preferably Greek
1 large onion, finely chopped

1 cup uncooked long-grain rice

½ cup dried currants

2 tablespoons pine nuts, lightly toasted

2 tablespoons chopped fresh mint leaves

Salt and freshly ground black pepper

¼ cup dry bread crumbs

1. Cut a thin slice off the tops of tomatoes and reserve. Scoop out the tomato pulp, chop, drain and reserve. Sprinkle the sugar inside tomatoes.

2. Heat ¼ cup olive oil in a 10-inch skillet. Add the onion. Cook over medium heat until soft. Add the rice, stir and cook for a few minutes. Add the currants, pine nuts, mint, half the tomato pulp and ½ cup water. Season with salt and pepper. Cover and simmer 10 minutes.

3. Heat the oven to 300 degrees. Purée the remaining tomato pulp, and spread in the bottom of a shallow baking dish that will hold all the tomatoes without much room to spare.

4. Spoon the rice mixture into the tomatoes; it will not fill them. Replace the tops, spoon a tablespoon of oil over each tomato and sprinkle with bread crumbs. Bake 1½ hours.

5. Allow to cool to room temperature before serving.

Yield: 6 servings

Time: About 2 hours, including 1½ hours of baking, plus cooling to room temperature.

Florence Fabricant

LE BERNARDIN'S TOMATO PROVENÇAL

Adapted from Le Bernardin, New York City

2 small to medium ripe tomatoes

Salt and freshly ground pepper to taste

1 shallot, peeled

½ garlic clove, peeled

2 tablespoons fresh thyme

1 tablespoon fresh rosemary

½ bunch fresh parsley

½ cup bread crumbs

2 tablespoons olive oil

1. Preheat the oven to 375 degrees.

2. Cut the tomatoes in half and cut off the ends so they can stand. Season with salt and pepper.

3. Place the shallot, garlic, thyme, rosemary and parsley in the bowl of a food processor and chop with a steel blade. Combine with the bread crumbs and 1 tablespoon of the olive oil. Adjust the seasoning.

4. Spoon the bread-crumb mixture generously on top of each tomato half.

5. Oil the bottom of a casserole dish with the remaining olive oil. Put the tomatoes in the casserole and bake 20 minutes.

Yield: 4 servings

Time: Preparation time: 20 minutes; Cooking time: 20 minutes

Dena Kleiman

FRESH TOMATO TART

Adapted from Marie Martin

2 cups flour, plus more for dusting

1 egg yolk

Salt and pepper to taste

1 stick butter, at room temperature

Extra virgin olive oil, as needed

4 to 5 tablespoons Dijon mustard

4 medium to large ripe tomatoes

1 teaspoon dried herbes de Provence or dried
    thyme, or 1 tablespoon fresh thyme leaves

1. Combine the flour and egg yolk in a bowl with a pinch of salt; quickly mix in the butter with your hands, then add enough cold water to gather the dough into a ball. If time allows, refrigerate it for 30 minutes or longer (you can leave it in the refrigerator, well wrapped, for up to a day, or freeze it for up to a month).

2. Preheat the oven to 450 degrees. Use olive oil to lightly grease a 10- to 12-inch round pizza pan, preferably nonstick. Roll out the dough on a lightly floured surface or simply press it into the pan, right up to the edges. Bake about 10 minutes, or until it is just beginning to color. Remove and set on a rack.

3. Turn the oven to 400 degrees. Spread the crust with mustard. Core the tomatoes; if they are very juicy, cut in half through the equator and squeeze out some juice, shaking out most of the seeds as well. Cut into slices about ¼-inch thick and place in a single layer on the crust. Sprinkle with salt, pepper and herbs, then drizzle with olive oil. Bake the tart about 30 minutes, or until the tomatoes

are shriveled and hot, and the crust is browned. Serve hot or warm; this does not keep very well.

Yield: 4 to 8 servings

Time: 45 minutes plus 30 minutes' chilling

Mark Bittman

ALICE WATERS'S ROASTED TOMATO SAUCE

Adapted from *Chez Panisse Vegetables*

Roasting the tomatoes intensifies their flavor. This versatile sauce can be refrigerated and also frozen.

> 2 pounds ripe tomatoes
> 1/4 cup olive oil
> 1 large yellow onion, peeled and sliced
> 1 medium leek, washed, trimmed and diced
> 1 small carrot, peeled and diced
> 1 head garlic, cut in half crosswise
> 1 bay leaf
> 1 sprig thyme
> 1 small bunch basil (about 1/4 pound)
> Salt and freshly ground black pepper to taste

1. Preheat the oven to 350 degrees. Cut out a cone at the stem end of each tomato to remove the core. Cut the tomatoes into quarters. Spread them in a baking dish. Toss the tomatoes with half the olive oil, and roast them, uncovered, for 30 minutes, stirring them several times. The tomatoes are cooked when the flesh is very soft and the skin separates easily from the flesh.

2. Heat the remaining olive oil in a stainless steel or other nonreactive pot. Add the onion, leek, carrot and garlic, and cook over medium heat until completely soft, about 10 minutes. Add the roasted tomatoes and herbs. Simmer, stirring frequently, to prevent scorching, until the flavors come together,

30 to 45 minutes. Pass the sauce through a food mill, and season with salt and pepper.

3. Heat gently to use as a sauce for pasta, grains or vegetables. If refrigerated in a covered container, the sauce will keep for a week; if frozen, for several months.

Yield: 1 quart

Time: 1 1/2 hours

Suzanne Hamlin

EASY FRESH TOMATO SAUCE WITH OLIVES AND BASIL

> 2 teaspoons extra virgin olive oil
> 3 cloves garlic, peeled and minced
> 1 medium onion, peeled and finely chopped
> 4 medium ripe tomatoes, diced
> 1 cup fresh basil leaves, coarsely chopped
> 3 tablespoons pitted and chopped green olives
> 3 tablespoons pitted and chopped imported black olives
> 1/2 teaspoon kosher salt, plus more to taste
> Freshly ground black pepper to taste

1. Heat 1 teaspoon of the olive oil in a medium nonstick skillet over medium heat. Add the garlic and onion and cook, stirring often, for 5 minutes. Stir in the tomatoes and cook for 5 minutes.

2. Meanwhile, combine the basil and olives in a medium mixing bowl. Stir the tomato mixture into the basil and olives and let cool to room temperature. Stir in the remaining olive oil and season with salt and pepper.

Yield: 3 cups

Time: 25 minutes, plus cooling

Molly O'Neill

TUSCAN GRILLED SUMMER VEGETABLES

1 eggplant (about 1 pound) sliced into
    2-inch-thick rounds

1 white eggplant (about ½ pound) sliced into
    2-inch-thick rounds

2 summer squash, cut into 2-inch-thick slices,
    lengthwise

2 zucchini, cut into 2-inch-thick slices,
    lengthwise

2 pattypan squash, cut into 2-inch-thick slices

1 tablespoon kosher salt

3 large, ripe tomatoes, cut into 2-inch-thick
    slices

1 yellow bell pepper, seeded, deveined, cut into
    2-inch-wide slices, lengthwise

1 red bell pepper, seeded, deveined, cut into
    2-inch-wide slices, lengthwise

1 medium red onion, peeled, sliced into
    ½-inch-thick rounds

1 cup coarsely chopped fresh basil

2 cups Tuscan marinade (recipe follows)

1. Put the eggplant, zucchini and squash in a colander. Add salt. Toss and set aside to drain for 30 minutes. Rinse, pat dry and place in a large, shallow glass or ceramic dish. Add the remaining vegetables and basil. Cover with the Tuscan marinade. Refrigerate for 8 hours, turning once.

2. Grill over hot coals until tender, about 5 to 10 minutes per side.

Yield: 4 to 6 servings

Time: 1½ hours, plus 8 hours' marinating

➤ TUSCAN MARINADE

This marinade is particularly good with grilled vegetables or with chicken paillards or flank steak. For chicken, pound four 6- to 8-ounce chicken breasts until they are ¼ inch thick. Marinate in the refrigerator for 4 hours. Grill over hot coals until tender, about 2 to 3 minutes per side. For flank steak, marinate a 1½- to 2-pound piece in the refrigerator for 8 hours. Grill over hot coals until medium rare, about 3 to 4 minutes per side.

⅓ cup red wine

⅓ cup olive oil

2 cloves garlic, peeled and minced

1 tablespoon grated orange zest

½ cup minced fresh sage leaves

¼ cup minced fresh rosemary leaves

1 tablespoon black peppercorns,
    crushed

Combine all ingredients in a glass or ceramic bowl. Refrigerate in an airtight container for up to 3 days.

Yield: 1 cup

Time: 15 minutes

Molly O'Neill

FLORENCE FABRICANT'S LEMON-GARLIC SAUCE

Florence Fabricant: "I came up with a smooth, lemony, garlic-scented version that borrows some of its personality from avgolemono, the Greek sauce. This sauce is extremely tolerant. A little cornstarch stabilizes and helps thicken it, so fewer egg yolks are needed. In place of butter, I whisked in olive oil and thinned it with stock. This sauce can be served over cold poached salmon or lobster, without any coagulated fat to worry about. It can dress a salad. Minced chives, a spoonful of pesto, a little anchovy paste or tapenade are seasonings that come to mind. It can be refrigerated for a few days and then reheated to nap steamed vegetables or grilled chicken or fish. Add fresh trout roe or California caviar and you have an elegant topping for lightly baked oysters, which will sit up and beg for that glass of sauvignon blanc."

2 cloves garlic, minced
1 tablespoon minced shallot
$2/3$ cup dry white wine
$1/2$ cup lemon juice (about 2 lemons)
3 large egg yolks, lightly beaten
2 teaspoons cornstarch
$1/4$ cup extra virgin olive oil
$1/2$ cup chicken, fish, or vegetable stock, approximately
Salt and freshly ground white pepper
Minced fresh herbs, pesto, or other seasoning to taste, optional

1. Place the garlic and shallots in a small, heavy saucepan. Add the wine and simmer slowly until reduced by half and the shallots and garlic are soft, about 10 minutes. Remove from the heat and stir in the lemon juice.

2. Gradually whisk in the egg yolks, return to the stove and cook, whisking constantly over medium heat, until the mixture thickens to the consistency of heavy cream. Do not allow it to boil or the eggs will curdle.

3. Dissolve the cornstarch in 1 tablespoon cold water. Whisk into the pan and cook until the sauce thickens. Slowly but vigorously whisk in the olive oil. Add the stock, adjusting the quantity to make the sauce thicker or thinner as desired. Strain the sauce into a clean saucepan, pressing on the solids. Season with salt and pepper and add additional seasonings to taste, if desired.

4. To serve hot, reheat, but do not boil. The sauce may also be served at room temperature or chilled.

Yield: $1\frac{1}{2}$ cups

Time: 30 minutes

Florence Fabricant

ANNE WILLAN'S GRATIN OF SUMMER VEGETABLES IN HERB PESTO

Adapted from *From My Chateau Kitchen*

2 medium zucchini, about $3/4$ pound
2 medium yellow or pattypan squash (about $3/4$ pound)
3 medium onions, thinly sliced
1 pound ripe, firm, meaty tomatoes
Salt and freshly ground black pepper to taste
$3/4$ cup extra virgin olive oil
1 medium bunch basil, flat-leaf parsley, cilantro or mint
3 cloves garlic, peeled
$1/3$ cup freshly grated Parmesan cheese
2 tablespoons pine nuts

1. Preheat the oven to 350 degrees. Wipe the zucchini and squash with a damp paper towel. Cut into $3/4$-inch chunks and place in a large bowl along with the onions. Core the tomatoes, cut into chunks, and add. Season with salt and pepper.

2. Brush an 8- by 11-inch, 9-inch square, or 10-inch round baking dish with a little oil.

3. Reserve a couple of herb sprigs for garnish and tear remaining leaves from the stems (you should have $1\frac{1}{2}$ ounces). Place the leaves in a food processor with garlic, cheese, pine nuts and 2 to 3 tablespoons oil, and purée. With the machine running, gradually add the remaining oil through the feed

tube. Season the pesto with salt and pepper, then toss with the vegetables to coat.

4. Spread in a baking dish and bake until very tender and lightly browned, about 45 minutes. Serve warm or at room temperature, decorated with herb sprigs.

Yield: 4 to 6 servings

Time: 1 hour 10 minutes

Florence Fabricant

JACQUES PÉPIN'S RATATOUILLE

Aside from the basic ingredients—tomatoes, onions, peppers, zucchini, eggplant, garlic, herbs and olive oil—there is no standard method for making ratatouille. You can simmer all the ingredients together for a short period or for hours, or bake them, or sauté them separately and then combine them. In this recipe, Jacques Pépin creates a splendid version in about an hour. In addition to serving it hot or cold, as a side dish or a first course, ratatouille is extraordinarily versatile: Use it to fill an omelet or a quiche for a light supper or an elegant brunch. You can bake eggs on a bed of ratatouille, stuff a chicken with it, cook it with sautéed chicken parts, spoon it over pasta or use it as a stuffing for ravioli. If you have just a little left over, fold it into pilafs of rice or bulgur, or chop it fine into a "caviar," seasoned with a dash of red pepper flakes or cayenne pepper, and served as a dip with potato chips, corn chips or crackers.

$\frac{1}{4}$ cup virgin or extra virgin olive oil, plus extra
    for garnish
3 onions, peeled and cut into 1-inch pieces
    (about 3 cups)
1 large green bell pepper, cut in half, seeded
    and cut into $\frac{1}{2}$-inch pieces
1 large eggplant, trimmed at both ends, and
    cut into 1-inch pieces (about 6 cups)

4 small zucchini, trimmed at both ends, and
    cut into 1-inch pieces (about 4 cups)
$\frac{1}{4}$ teaspoon red pepper flakes
$1\frac{1}{2}$ teaspoons salt
6 to 8 cloves garlic, peeled and sliced
    (about 3 tablespoons)
4 very ripe tomatoes, cut into 1-inch cubes
    (about 4 cups)
1 cup shredded fresh basil (see Note)
Freshly ground black pepper for garnish

1. Heat the oil in a large saucepan. When hot, add the onions and green pepper and sauté for about 5 minutes over high heat. Then add the eggplant, zucchini, pepper flakes and salt, reduce the heat to medium, cover and cook 25 minutes, stirring occasionally to prevent the mixture from sticking. (There is enough moisture in the vegetables to keep the mixture from burning.) Add the garlic and tomatoes and continue cooking, covered, for 6 to 8 minutes.

2. Remove from the heat, transfer to a serving bowl and cool to room temperature. Just before serving, stir in half the basil, sprinkle the remaining basil on top, and garnish with a few tablespoons of olive oil and ground black pepper.

Yield: 6 servings

Time: Preparation time: 20 to 25 minutes; cooking time: 40 minutes

Note: If serving the ratatouille cold, garnish it with additional fresh basil. Leftover ratatouille can be refrigerated for a few days or packed into plastic containers and frozen for up to 8 months. Be sure to leave at least $\frac{1}{2}$ inch of space at the top of the container for expansion. The flavor will be better if the garlic is omitted and the mixture is underseasoned. Thawed ratatouille can be reseasoned with minced garlic briefly sautéed in a little olive oil and with salt, pepper and fresh parsley.

Jacques Pépin

BAKED GARLIC, TOMATO, AND ZUCCHINI CASSEROLE

Adapted from *The Buffet Book*

4 tablespoons extra virgin olive oil
8 large or 16 medium tomatoes, cored and
    cut in ½-inch slices
6 medium zucchini, stems removed, cut on the
    diagonal in ½-inch slices
12 cloves garlic, peeled and sliced
10 sprigs fresh basil, leaves only,
    shredded
½ cup grated aged goat cheese, Parmesan or
    Asiago cheese
Coarse salt and freshly ground black pepper
    to taste

1. Preheat the oven to 400 degrees. Use 1 tablespoon of oil to coat a large, shallow casserole.

2. Layer the tomato and zucchini slices alternately, overlapping slightly. Sprinkle with the garlic, basil and cheese. Add salt and pepper to taste. Drizzle with the remaining oil.

3. Bake about 30 minutes, until the vegetables are tender. Serve hot or at room temperature.

Yield: 20 servings

Total time: 45 minutes

Florence Fabricant

MARINATED GRILLED PORTOBELLOS

Adapted from *Portobello Cookbook*

4 large portobello mushroom caps,
    4 to 6 inches in diameter
1 cup good-quality olive oil
1 cup red or white wine vinegar
2 tablespoons soy sauce
1 tablespoon sugar
1 tablespoon dried herbs—thyme,
    rosemary, sage—or ⅓ cup finely
    chopped fresh herbs

1. Cut the stems from the caps. Slice each stem lengthwise.

2. Mix the remaining ingredients together and set aside for 1 hour so the herbs can soften.

3. Preheat a grill.

4. Place the caps and sliced stems in a shallow dish and pour the marinade over them. Marinate for 10 minutes, turning the mushrooms once.

5. Remove the mushrooms and discard the marinade. Grill the mushrooms on each side for 2 to 3 minutes. Remove from the grill, slice and serve at once.

Yield: 4 servings

Time: 1 hour 30 minutes, including 1 hour for the herbs to soften

Florence Fabricant

MARK BITTMAN'S COLD EGGPLANT WITH SESAME DRESSING

A classic Japanese eggplant salad, unusual for its cooking method. Though the eggplant should be salted, as usual, if it is not extremely firm (small ones are almost always better than the common globular variety), it is cooked swiftly thereafter with a quick immersion in boiling water. Once the eggplant is tender, it is chilled, then tossed with a soy sesame dressing.

>   4 to 6 small to medium eggplants, or
>   1 large one (about 1½ pounds)
>   Salt
>   1 tablespoon sesame seeds
>   2 tablespoons soy sauce, or to taste
>   2 tablespoons lemon juice
>   ½ teaspoon sugar

1. Trim the eggplant, and cut into ½- to 1-inch cubes. If using large eggplant, sprinkle with salt, put in a colander, and let sit at least 30 minutes, preferably an hour. Rinse.

2. Boil a large pot of water. Blanch the eggplant in the boiling water 2 minutes, no more; it will become just tender. Drain in colander as you would pasta.

3. Toast the sesame seeds in a small dry skillet over medium heat, shaking frequently until they color slightly. Dry the eggplant with paper towels. Combine the remaining ingredients, and toss with the eggplant and sesame seeds in a bowl. Serve at room temperature, or refrigerate until ready to serve. Covered well, the salad will remain flavorful for a day.

Yield: 4 servings

Time: 20 to 40 minutes, plus cooling

Mark Bittman

QUILTY'S SMOKY EGGPLANT

Charred puréed eggplant makes a tasty base for spreads of many flavors. Simply place the eggplant on a charcoal grill or under the broiler. Turn it slowly until the skin chars and the flesh softens, which gives it a smoky flavor. Then, peel it and drain the excess moisture—and any bitter juices—and purée it with a combination of flavorings, such as olive oil and salt, or yogurt, cumin and cilantro or tahini and garlic. Or stir tomatoes, garlic, lemon juice, olive oil and oregano into the charred pulp, thin and lighten it with a little sparkling water, if necessary. Serve as a spread or under grilled meats or seafood.

>   2 medium eggplants
>   Vegetable oil, for coating
>   2 tablespoons tahini
>   ¼ teaspoon freshly ground cumin
>   seed
>   Juice of ½ lemon
>   ¼ cup extra virgin olive oil
>   Kosher salt and freshly ground black
>   pepper

1. Rub the eggplants with vegetable oil. Place directly on a hot grill or under a broiler. Char the skin well on all sides, turning the eggplant with tongs. Continue until the eggplant is blackened and collapsed, about 20 minutes. (Eggplant may leak a small amount of liquid.) Transfer to a platter and allow to cool slightly.

2. When the eggplants are cool enough to touch, peel them, removing as many seeds as possible. Place the pulp in a fine sieve, and drain, pressing it lightly to remove the juices.

3. Transfer the pulp to a blender, and add tahini, cumin and lemon juice. Purée, adding olive oil in a steady stream while the blender is running. Season to taste with salt and pepper. Serve at room temperature as a spread or on a plate under grilled meat or seafood.

Yield: About 1½ cups

Time: 30 minutes

Amanda Hesser

ZUCCHINI WITH CRÈME FRAÎCHE PESTO

Adapted from *The Crème Fraîche Cookbook*

For a change of pace, blanched fresh beans—green beans, lima beans or cranberry beans—may be substituted for the zucchini.

> 1½ cups packed fresh basil leaves
> 1½ tablespoons toasted pine nuts
> 1½ cloves garlic, peeled and smashed
> 4 tablespoons extra virgin olive oil
> Coarse sea salt or kosher salt
> ¼ cup crème fraîche
> ⅓ cup freshly grated Parmesan cheese
> 1½ pounds small zucchini, trimmed and cut
>   into ½-inch dice
> Freshly ground black pepper

1. For the pesto: In a blender or food processor, combine the basil, pine nuts, garlic, 2 tablespoons of the olive oil and a pinch of salt. Purée, scraping the sides once or twice with a spatula, until a coarse mixture develops. Add the crème fraîche, and continue to purée until the mixture is a smooth paste the color of a fresh pea. Add the Parmesan cheese, and pulse until combined. Adjust the seasoning, transfer to a jar or other container and refrigerate. (Makes about 1½ cups.)

2. In a large sauté pan, heat the remaining 2 tablespoons of olive oil over medium heat. When it shimmers, add the zucchini and stir to coat it with oil.

Season generously with salt and pepper. Sauté until the zucchini brightens and turns soft on the edges, but is still fairly firm. Add 2 heaping tablespoons of pesto, and stir to coat the zucchini. Add more if needed. Adjust seasonings to taste, and serve hot.

Yield: 4 servings

Time: 30 minutes

Amanda Hesser

ZUCCHINI BOATS WITH HERB STUFFING

Stuffed zucchini can be served cold or hot. When cold, sharpen the flavor by garnishing it with additional oil or a little vinaigrette and fresh herbs just before serving; fresh basil, tarragon, parsley or chives are good choices in summer. Zucchini boats can also be stuffed with a meat mixture. Leftover cooked meat or cold cuts can be chopped and added to the vegetable stuffing to extend it and make it heartier.

> 6 zucchini of equal size (about 3 pounds)
> 2 tablespoons extra virgin olive oil, plus 2 to 3
>   tablespoons for garnish
> 1½ cups coarsely chopped onions
> 1 tablespoon chopped garlic
> ½ cup minced scallions
> 5 cups 1-inch cubes leftover bread
> 1 cup milk
> ½ cup chopped, fresh herbs (chives, parsley or
>   basil or a mixture of these), plus extra for
>   garnish
> ½ cup grated Parmesan cheese
> ⅛ to ¼ teaspoon cayenne pepper
> 2 eggs
> 1 teaspoon salt
> ½ teaspoon freshly ground black pepper
> Red wine vinegar for garnish, optional

1. Wash the zucchini, trim the ends and cut in half lengthwise. Using a metal measuring tablespoon with sharp edges, hollow out the inside of the zucchini; remove most of the seeds and a little of the flesh so that the remaining hollows have a shell about ¼ inch thick. There should be about 4 cups of flesh and seeds. Chop coarsely into ½-inch pieces and set aside.

2. Heat 2 tablespoons oil in a skillet. When hot, add the onions and sauté for 4 to 5 minutes over medium to high heat. Add the garlic, scallions and reserved zucchini flesh and sauté for 10 to 15 seconds. Then cover and cook for 5 minutes over medium to high heat, until the mixture is soft. Set aside.

3. Preheat the oven to 375 degrees.

4. Add the bread to the milk and mix until most of the milk has been absorbed by the bread. Crush the mixture to create a paste and add to it the chopped herbs, Parmesan cheese, cayenne, eggs, ½ teaspoon of the salt and pepper. Mix well and add the reserved zucchini mixture.

5. Arrange the zucchini boats in a large roasting pan and sprinkle with the remaining ½ teaspoon of salt. Mound equal portions of the stuffing into the boats and place in the oven. Cook for 30 to 35 minutes, then place under a hot broiler for 4 to 5 minutes to brown the stuffing on top.

6. Serve hot, sprinkled with the remaining 2 to 3 tablespoons olive oil, or serve at room temperature, sprinkled with olive oil and additional herbs. If you prefer a more pungent taste, sprinkle a little vinegar on top before serving.

Yield: 6 servings

Time: Preparation time: 45 minutes;
Cooking time: 1 hour 15 minutes

Jacques Pépin

RICK BAYLESS'S RED-CHILI RICE

1 large dried ancho chili, stemmed, seeded, and deveined
2½ teaspoons vegetable oil
1 small onion, diced
2 small cloves garlic, peeled and minced
1½ cups chicken broth, homemade or low-sodium canned
1 teaspoon salt, plus more to taste
1 cup medium-grain rice

1. Tear the chili into flat pieces and toast in a heavy skillet over medium heat, pressing firmly with a spatula until it cracks, blisters and changes color, about 45 seconds per side. Place in a bowl and cover with boiling water. Weight with a plate to keep the pieces submerged, and let stand for 30 minutes. Drain and place in a blender jar.

2. Heat 1 teaspoon of oil in a small skillet over medium heat. Add the onion and cook, stirring frequently, until browned, about 7 minutes. Add the garlic and cook 2 minutes. Scrape into the blender and add ½ cup of the broth. Blend to a smooth purée and strain through a medium-mesh sieve into a small saucepan. Stir in the salt and remaining broth. Set over low heat.

3. Combine 1½ teaspoons of oil and the rice in a deep pot over medium heat. Stir frequently until the rice is light brown, about 7 to 10 minutes. Carefully add the broth mixture—it will spatter—stir well, scrape down the sides of the pan, cover and simmer over medium-low heat for 15 minutes. (More broth may be required to make the rice tender, add ¼ cup at a time and continue cooking.) Remove from the heat and let stand, covered, 5 to 10 minutes, until the grains are tender but still quite firm. Season with additional salt if needed.

Yield: 4 servings

Time: 1 hour, plus 30 minutes standing

Molly O'Neill

PIERRE FRANEY'S INDIAN RICE WITH SAFFRON AND GOLDEN RAISINS

2 tablespoons butter
¼ cup finely chopped onions
1 cup converted rice
1½ cups fresh or canned chicken broth
¼ cup golden raisins
1 teaspoon grated lemon zest
1 bay leaf
½ teaspoon stem saffron
¼ teaspoon Tabasco sauce
Salt and freshly ground pepper

1. In a heavy saucepan with a tight-fitting lid, melt 1 tablespoon of the butter and add the onions. Cook, stirring, until wilted.

2. Add the rice and cook, stirring, about 30 seconds. Add the broth, raisins, lemon zest, bay leaf, saffron, Tabasco, salt and pepper. Bring to a boil.

3. Simmer over low heat for 17 minutes. Uncover and remove the bay leaf. Add the remaining butter and stir to fluff the rice well.

Yield: 4 servings

Time: 30 minutes

Pierre Franey

ANNIE WAYTE'S PAN-GRILLED ONION AND CHIVE RELISH

Adapted from Nicole's, New York City

As a condiment, the relish enhances grilled meats or fish. Or toss it with arugula for an unusually tasty salad.

⅓ cup golden raisins
Freshly grated zest and freshly squeezed juice
    of 1 small orange
1 garlic clove, minced
¼ teaspoon (or more to taste) fresh hot chili
    pepper, with seeds, finely chopped
2 yellow or red onions (or a combination),
    sliced ¼ inch thick
2 tablespoons extra virgin olive oil
Coarse sea salt or kosher salt
Freshly ground black pepper
⅓ cup pine nuts
1 tablespoon sliced chives

1. In a large bowl, combine the raisins, orange zest and orange juice. Let it soak until the raisins have plumped, 10 to 15 minutes. Using a mortar and pestle, mash together the garlic and chili pepper, and add to the raisins.

2. Place a seasoned ridged grill pan over medium heat until well heated. Add the onion slices and cook, turning once, until golden brown and softened, 5 to 6 minutes on each side. Transfer the hot onions to the bowl of raisins. Working quickly, add 1 tablespoon olive oil and season with salt and pepper to taste. Cover the bowl with a tightly fitting lid or large plate, and set aside to steam.

3. Place a small skillet over medium heat, and add the remaining tablespoon oil and the pine nuts. Stir until golden and fragrant, about 5 minutes. Add the nuts and their oil to the bowl of onions. Add the chives, and adjust salt and pepper to taste. Serve with grilled fish, meat or vegetable dishes.

Yield: 4 servings

Time: 40 minutes

Melissa Clark

OSTERIA DEL CIRCO'S WATERMELON SOUP WITH RED SUMMER BERRIES AND LIME

Adapted from Patrice Caillot

> 4 pounds watermelon
> ½ cup sugar
> ½ cup lime juice
> 1 cup blackberries
> 1 cup raspberries
> 1 cup cherries
> 1 cup strawberries

1. Remove the rind and seeds from the watermelon. Cut the flesh into chunks, and purée in a blender. Strain into a bowl (there should be about 4 cups).

2. Mix the purée with the sugar and lime juice. Chill 2 hours.

3. To serve, cut the blackberries and raspberries in half. Pit the cherries, and cut in half. Slice the strawberries.

4. Divide the fruits into six chilled soup bowls. Pour the watermelon mixture over them, and serve immediately.

Yield: 6 servings

Time: 20 minutes, plus 2 hours' maceration

Karen Baar

TOM COLICCHIO'S ROASTED SUMMER FRUIT

Almost any fruit except berries or citrus can be roasted, and roasting does wonders for fruit that is not dead ripe. Tom Colicchio: "With roasted fruits, you can go in lots of directions. They're delicious on their own for dessert, just touched with some ice cream or crème fraîche and maybe a shortbread cookie on the side. And, since the excess moisture is baked off, the fruit can become part of a more elaborate dessert, as a filling or a topping."

> ½ cup sugar
> 1 tablespoon light corn syrup
> 4 ripe but firm large yellow peaches, halved and pitted (8 firm apricots, 8 firm Italian prune plums, 4 firm nectarines or 4 large, firm pluots (plums may be substituted)
> 4 sprigs fresh lavender, basil, lemon verbena, or mint
> 1 tablespoon unsalted butter
> ⅓ tablespoon heavy cream
> Vanilla ice cream for serving, optional

1. Preheat the oven to 375 degrees. Place the sugar in a 10-inch nonstick, ovenproof skillet. Drizzle with syrup. Cook over medium heat, stirring, until the mixture liquefies. Continue cooking until the mixture is a light caramel color.

2. Place the fruit in the pan, cut side down. Top with herbs. Place in the oven and bake 5 minutes, until the caramel has darkened and the fruit is tender but still holds its shape. Use a spatula to turn the fruit cut side up, return to the oven and roast another 3 to 5 minutes, until the edges of the fruit have browned. Do not cook long enough for the fruit to collapse.

3. Remove from the oven. Discard the herbs. Transfer the fruit to a serving dish or to individual plates.

Lift off the skins, if desired, especially from the peaches, if thick.

4. Place the pan on top of the stove, and swirl in the butter. Cook a few seconds over low heat. Whisk in the cream to make a caramel sauce. Pour the sauce over and around the fruit, and serve warm, with ice cream on the side, if desired.

Yield: **4 servings**

Time: **30 minutes**

Tom Colicchio and Florence Fabricant

MARK BITTMAN'S FREE-FORM FRUIT TART

Mark Bittman: "The most basic tart, and a favorite of mine—and of many other busy cooks who will sacrifice a bit of form, as long as the substance is intact—resembles a pizza: an open, somewhat crudely shaped affair with a dead simple topping. You start by making a slightly sweet, very short (note to beginners: this is a code word for "loaded-with-butter") crust, enriched with an egg yolk. You're already ahead of the game because this crust is essentially a cookie. It can be refrigerated for a day or two or frozen for a week. When ready, you roll the dough as crudely or as finely as you like, then top it with fruit and bake. A little powdered sugar, some whipped cream or ice cream, and you're set. If your fruit is really great, you might use crème fraîche, which you can mimic by adding a little sour cream to your fresh cream. If your fruit is a little tart, serve it with ice cream. The result is a delicious free-form tart, commonly described as 'rustic' in appearance."

1 ⅛ cups (about 5 ounces) all-purpose flour, plus some to dust work surface

½ teaspoon salt

2 tablespoons sugar

10 tablespoons cold unsalted butter

1 egg yolk

2 cups pitted, peeled and sliced ripe stone fruit, such as peaches, plums or nectarines (or use apples, pears or berries)

Confectioners' sugar, whipped cream, ice cream or crème fraîche

1. Combine the flour, salt, and sugar in a food processor; pulse once or twice. Add 8 tablespoons of butter and turn on the machine; process until the butter and flour are blended and the mixture looks like cornmeal, about 10 seconds. Add the egg yolk and 2 tablespoons ice water and pulse the machine on and off a couple of times. Remove the dough and gather the mixture into a ball, adding a little more water if necessary. Wrap in plastic, flatten into a small disk and freeze the dough for about 15 minutes (or refrigerate for 30 minutes or more) to ease rolling. (You can also refrigerate it for a day or two, or freeze it for a week or so.)

2. Preheat the oven to 425 degrees. Roll the crust out on a board sprinkled with flour, or sprinkle it lightly with flour and roll it between two sheets of plastic until about ¼ inch thick; it need not be perfectly round. Put it directly on a baking sheet. Melt the remaining butter.

3. Cover the round with fruit, leaving about a 1½-inch border all around. Fold up the edges of the crust around the fruit, pinching them together. Cover just the outer rim of the fruit. Brush the exposed dough with most of the butter, and brush a little onto the fruit as well. Bake until the crust is golden brown and the fruit bubbly, 20 to 30 minutes.

4. Remove from the oven and cool on a rack; serve warm or at room temperature, dusted with confectioners' sugar, or topped with ice cream, whipped cream or crème fraîche.

Yield: 8 servings

Time: About 1½ hours

Note: Use perfectly ripe fruit. Anything less will mean too much acidity in the finished product, something for which you can compensate by adding more sugar or pastry cream, which ultimately will make it not only too acidic but too sweet, not a happy balance and one that might remind you of a less-than-brilliant pie.

Mark Bittman

Opposite:
Tom Colicchio's Roasted Summer Fruit

PEACH ICE CREAM

2 cups whole milk

¾ cup sugar

1 (1-inch) piece vanilla bean

3 egg yolks

1½ pounds ripe peaches

2 tablespoons lemon juice

1. In a small, noncorrosive, heavy saucepan, warm the milk with the sugar and the vanilla bean. Whisk the eggs slightly and add a little of the hot milk to them. Mix them and add the remaining milk. Cook over low heat, stirring constantly, until the custard is thick enough to coat the spoon. Do not cook too fast or the mixture will curdle. Remove from heat and cool.

2. Meanwhile, peel the peaches and remove the pits. Coarsely purée the peaches with the lemon juice in a food processor. Set aside.

3. Remove the vanilla bean from the custard. Mix the custard with the peach purée and freeze in an ice cream maker according to the manufacturer's directions.

Yield: 1 quart

Total time: 45 minutes, plus freezing

Moira Hodgson

Opposite, in foreground: Mark Bittman's Free-Form Fruit Tart

FROZEN BANANA ICE CREAM

The cut-up bananas are frozen and then combined with sour cream, sugar and a little dark rum in a food processor to create a dense, rich ice cream. If the banana pieces are frozen hard, let them soften briefly at room temperature so they can be puréed smoothly in the food processor with the other ingredients. After hardening a little in the freezer, the ice cream can be served as is or with a little more rum. For dessert lovers who are counting calories, yogurt can be substituted for the sour cream with good results.

> 5 medium ripe bananas (about 2 pounds)
> ³/₄ cup sour cream
> ¹/₃ cup sugar
> 2 tablespoons dark rum, plus 2 tablespoons, optional, to sprinkle on top at serving time
> 6 sprigs mint, optional

1. Peel the bananas and cut them crosswise into 1-inch slices. Arrange the slices in a single layer on a tray and put the tray in the freezer for at least 2 hours, until the bananas are frozen.

2. Put half the frozen bananas in a food processor with half the sour cream, half the sugar and 1 tablespoon of the rum. Pulse the machine a few times, and then process the mixture for about 20 seconds, until smooth. Transfer to a cold bowl, and process the rest of the bananas, sour cream, sugar and a second tablespoon of rum. Return the ice cream to the freezer until serving time, at least 1 hour.

3. To serve, scoop the ice cream into six chilled glasses. Garnish each, if desired, with 1 teaspoon of rum and a sprig of mint.

Yield: 6 servings

Time: 15 minutes, plus 3 hours for freezing

Jacques Pépin

HOT FUDGE SAUCE

> 2 cups heavy cream
> 4 tablespoons unsalted butter
> ¹/₂ cup light brown sugar, well packed
> ³/₄ cup granulated sugar
> ¹/₄ teaspoon fine sea salt
> 2 ounces bittersweet chocolate in small pieces
> 1¹/₄ cups sifted high-fat, Dutch-process cocoa such as Valrhona, Pernigotti or Droste (sifted, then measured)
> ¹/₂ teaspoon vanilla extract

1. In a medium saucepan, combine the cream, butter, sugars and salt. Bring to a simmer over medium-low heat. Simmer 45 seconds. Add the chocolate, and whisk to dissolve. Remove from the heat, add the cocoa and whisk until no lumps remain.

2. Return the pan to low heat, and simmer the sauce until glossy, whisking constantly, about 20 seconds. Remove from the heat, and stir in the vanilla. Serve warm. To reheat the sauce, warm in a saucepan over low heat, stirring constantly. Do not boil.

Yield: 3 cups

Time: 10 minutes

Kay Rentschler

STRAWBERRY SAUCE

2 pounds ripe strawberries, hulled
½ to ⅔ cup granulated sugar (depending on berries' sweetness)
2 teaspoons cornstarch
Juice of ½ lemon
Pinch of salt

Combine the ingredients in a medium saucepan over medium-low heat. Stir gently until the sugar dissolves and the berries are soft, about 10 minutes. Remove from heat and cool.

Yield: 3 cups

Time: 10 minutes

Kay Rentschler

SUMMER BERRIES WITH RASPBERRY SAUCE

2 pints raspberries
⅓ cup confectioners' sugar
2 tablespoons fresh orange juice
1 tablespoon fresh lemon juice
3 pints strawberries (reserve 6 berries for garnish)
2 pints blueberries
¼ pint heavy cream, whipped

1. Put the raspberries in the container of a blender or food processor and purée. Add the sugar, orange and lemon juices and blend until smooth. Correct the sweetness, adding a little more sugar, if necessary. Strain the purée through a fine sieve to remove the seeds and chill for at least 2 hours.

2. When ready to serve the dessert, pile the strawberries and blueberries in six dishes or sundae glasses and pour the sauce on top. Top with whipped cream and top each serving with a strawberry.

Yield: 6 servings

Time: 2 hours' chilling, 15 minutes' preparing

Note: Serve the berries at room temperature with the whipped cream and chilled sauce.

Moira Hodgson

LONDON RIVER CAFÉ'S STRAWBERRY SORBET

Adapted from *London River Café Cook Book*

The brilliance of this sorbet lies in its proportions: a whole lemon (rind and all) is ground up, sweetened with crushed strawberries and then kept in check with some fresh lemon juice. You let the machine do the work.

1 lemon, seeded and roughly chopped
2 cups sugar
2 pounds strawberries, hulled
Juice of 1 to 2 lemons

1. Place the chopped lemon and sugar in a food processor, and pulse until combined. Transfer to a bowl.

2. Purée the strawberries in a food processor, and add to the lemon mixture, along with the juice of 1 lemon. Taste and add more juice as desired. The lemon flavor should be intense but should not overpower the strawberries.

3. Pour the mixture into an ice cream machine and churn until frozen.

Yield: 1½ quarts

Time: 20 minutes, plus freezing time

Amanda Hesser

LE CIRQUE'S
FRUIT SALAD IN
VANILLA-MINT
SYRUP

Adapted from Le Cirque, New York City

Zest from 1 orange, in strips

1 strip lemon zest

1 vanilla bean, split

½ cup sugar

6 sprigs mint; plus 3 leaves, cut crosswise into
    thin strips

2 cups water

½ fresh pineapple, peeled, quartered
    lengthwise, cored and thinly sliced
    crosswise

½ ripe papaya, peeled, seeded and thinly
    sliced crosswise

½ ripe mango, peeled and thinly sliced
    lengthwise

1 banana, peeled and sliced

1. Combine the orange and lemon zests, vanilla bean, sugar, 5 sprigs of mint and the water in a saucepan. Bring to a boil. Remove from the heat and let stand at least 2 hours. Strain.

2. Stir the fruit into the syrup and refrigerate for 2 hours. Stir in the sliced mint and garnish with a mint sprig.

Yield: 4 servings

Time: 25 minutes, plus 4 hours' standing

Molly O'Neill

MIXED FRUITS
À LA MARGARITA

1½ cups seedless grapes

1½ cups halved strawberries

1½ cups peeled, sliced navel oranges

1½ cups peeled, sliced kiwis

1½ cups peeled, pitted peaches, cut into wedges

5 tablespoons confectioners' sugar

3 tablespoons Cointreau or Triple Sec liqueur

3 tablespoons tequila

1½ tablespoons lime juice

1. Combine all the fruits and berries in a large bowl.

2. In a small jar, combine the confectioners' sugar, Cointreau or Triple Sec liqueur, tequila and lime juice. Stir or shake until blended into a syrup. Pour this over the fruit and stir to blend. This dessert can be served with raspberry sherbet, if desired.

Yield: 4 to 6 servings

Time: 30 minutes

Craig Claiborne

ALFRED PORTALE'S
POACHED PEACH AND
RASPBERRY COUPE

Adapted from Gotham Bar and Grill, New York City

1½ cups red wine

½ cup orange juice

¼ cup sugar

1 (3-inch) piece cinnamon stick

1 vanilla bean, split lengthwise

1 thin slice lemon

2 large ripe but firm peaches

6 ounces (1 small box) raspberries

1 quart vanilla ice cream

2 tablespoons sliced almonds, toasted

4 sprigs fresh mint

1. Place the wine, juice, sugar, cinnamon, vanilla bean and lemon in a 1½- to 2-quart nonreactive saucepan; stir to mix the ingredients, and bring to a boil over medium heat.

2. Cut the peaches in half (do not peel) and add to the pan. Reduce the heat so that the liquid simmers, and poach the peaches for 5 to 10 minutes, or until they can be pierced easily by the point of a sharp knife. (If the liquid does not cover the peaches, turn them frequently.)

3. Remove the pan from the heat and add the raspberries. Allow the fruit to cool in the liquid for 5 minutes. Remove the fruit from the liquid with a slotted spoon and, when cool enough to handle, peel the peaches; chill the peaches and berries. Meanwhile, return the poaching liquid to the heat and boil to reduce by half; a scant cup will remain. Strain the syrup and place in the refrigerator until well chilled, about 3 hours.

4. Place 2 scoops of vanilla ice cream in the center of each of four rimmed soup plates. Arrange a peach half and some raspberries around the ice cream, pour on the chilled sauce and garnish with toasted almonds and a mint sprig.

Yield: 4 coupes

Time: 30 minutes plus 3 hours' refrigeration

Dorie Greenspan

HUBERT KELLER'S FIGS AND BLUEBERRIES IN CITRUS BROTH

Adapted from Fleur de Lys, San Francisco

1½ cups fresh orange juice
1 cup fresh grapefruit juice
3 tablespoons fresh lemon juice
½ teaspoon grated fresh ginger
2 tablespoons honey
1 tablespoon rum
16 ripe black figs, pricked a few times with a fork
4 tablespoons fresh blueberries
1 banana, peeled and cut into ¼-inch slices
8 fresh mint leaves

1. Combine the juices in a nonreactive saucepan. Add the ginger, honey and rum and bring to a boil. Gently place the figs, blueberries and banana in the liquid. Cover, remove from heat and set aside to cool. Refrigerate until cold.

2. Take the figs out of the liquid, cut them in half lengthwise and return them to the liquid. Divide among four shallow rimmed soup plates, garnish with the mint leaves and serve.

Yield: 4 servings

Time: 20 minutes plus chilling

Molly O'Neill

JAMES BEARD'S DRUNKEN MELON

1 watermelon
Light rum, Cognac, champagne or gin

1. Cut a 2-inch-square plug in a watermelon deep enough to go into the cavity.

2. Deeply prick the flesh with an ice pick, and fill to near the top with light rum, Cognac, champagne or gin. Replace the plug, and seal with heavy tape.

3. Refrigerate the melon for 24 hours, turning it over four or five times. Serve sliced.

Yield: 8 or more servings

Time: Preparation Time: 10 minutes; 1 day refrigeration

Marian Burros

FRENCH LAUNDRY'S VANILLA ROASTED FIGS WITH WILDFLOWER HONEY ICE CREAM

Thomas Keller: "This is one of those great recipes, because it's so easy and so satisfying. Hot figs and cold ice cream with honey—that's virtually all there is to it. You don't even have to make the ice cream: buy some, let it sit until it's pliable and fold in the honey. To make it even simpler, drizzle the honey on top of the ice cream, or add it to the pan when you cook the figs. However you want to incorporate the honey is fine. But it's important to use a honey of good quality, so taste a variety. In the Napa Valley, there are a lot of wildflowers, so wildflower is the kind I like to use. Any fig will work, as long as it's ripe. The baking turns the fig into a sauce within its own skin. The vanilla bean is a separate element, and it's fun to scrape the seeds out of the pod and eat them with the ice cream and buttery sauce. I love the hot and cold combination in this dessert. It reminds me of hot fudge sundaes."

For the Figs

18 ripe figs (Mission, Brown Turkey,
    Adriatic Green or a combination),
    washed and dried
4 vanilla beans, split lengthwise
3 tablespoons unsalted butter
1½ teaspoons sugar

For the Ice Cream

2 cups whole milk
2 cups heavy cream
½ cup wildflower honey
12 large egg yolks
¼ cup sugar

1. To prepare the figs: Slice off and discard the tops of the figs. Cut the split vanilla beans into 2-inch pieces. Make a small slit in the top of each fig, and insert a section of vanilla bean.

2. Preheat the oven to 400 degrees. In an ovenproof pan large enough to hold all the figs standing upright, melt the butter over medium heat. Add the sugar, and stir to dissolve. Stand the figs in the butter, and add any remaining vanilla bean pieces to the pan. Place the pan in the oven until the figs are thoroughly heated, about 10 minutes. Serve the figs warm or at room temperature.

3. To serve: place a scoop of ice cream into each of six bowls. Arrange 3 of the figs (with vanilla bean) around each scoop. Serve immediately.

4. To prepare the ice cream: In a large saucepan, combine the milk, cream and honey. Place over medium heat, and stir. When the honey is completely dissolved, remove the pan from the heat and allow to cool.

5. With an electric mixer, or by hand in a metal bowl, whisk the egg yolks and sugar until they have thickened and lightened in color. Gradually whisk in the warm milk mixture. Return the mixture to the saucepan and place over medium-low heat. Stir until the mixture coats the back of a wooden spoon and reaches 175 degrees; do not overheat. Immediately remove from the heat and transfer to a mixing bowl. Chill the bowl by placing it in ice water, and allow the mixture to cool to room temperature.

6. Strain the mixture into a container. Cover, and refrigerate for at least 5 hours, or overnight. Freeze in an ice cream maker according to the manufacturer's instructions; then, transfer to a covered container. Freeze for several hours, or until hardened.

Yield: 6 servings

Time: 30 minutes, plus chilling and freezing for the ice cream; 20 minutes for the figs

Thomas Keller

BING CHERRY CLAFOUTIS

Adapted from Marie Martin

This cakelike dessert that is made with what amounts to pancake batter and is popular throughout France, is a little different from most. For one thing, it is creamier, more flanlike. For another, Ms. Martin leaves the pits in about half of the cherries because, she says, "The pits have a huge amount of flavor." Just be sure to tell everyone about the pits before they dig in. Or, if you prefer, pit all the cherries.

> Butter
> About 30 large Bing cherries
> 1 cup flour
> 2 tablespoons cornstarch
> ¼ cup sugar, more for sprinkling
> 3 eggs
> 1 cup milk
> 2 teaspoons vanilla extract

1. Heat the oven to 400 degrees. Butter a 9-inch round glass dish or an 8- to 10-inch ovenproof skillet, preferably nonstick. Pit about half the cherries, and arrange them, with the unpitted cherries, in the dish.

2. Combine the flour, cornstarch and sugar in a bowl. Whisk in the eggs, milk and vanilla extract until smooth, but do not overbeat. Pour over the cherries. Sprinkle with a little more sugar and dot with butter; put in the oven.

3. Bake until puffy and firm, about 25 to 35 minutes. When done, let rest on a rack for a few minutes, then invert onto a plate. Sprinkle with a little more sugar and serve warm.

Yield: 6 to 8 servings

Time: 45 minutes

Mark Bittman

NIGELLA LAWSON'S JUMBLEBERRY GRUNT

The name borrows from two cooking traditions. In old-fashioned country kitchens in Britain, jams that were made with a mixture of berries at the end of the summer used to be known as jumbleberry jam. In American homesteads, the grunt was the precursor to the cobbler. They seemed to belong together. It feels like a pie but requires no skillful blending or rolling out of crust. You simply pile berries, sugar and cornstarch in a dish; mix together flour, sugar and heavy cream; and place clumps on top of the fruit before baking. If it helps, you can lightly flour your hands before putting a dollop of the thick batter on top, but don't worry about coverage: it isn't meant to be a factory-made sheet of crust, but a biscuity berry-bubbling roof.

For the Filling

4 cups blueberries

2 cups raspberries

2 cups blackberries (or a total of 8 cups mixed berries of your choice)

¾ cup sugar

3 tablespoons cornstarch

For the Topping

1 cup heavy cream

1 teaspoon vanilla extract

1 cup flour

Pinch of salt

1 teaspoon baking powder

¼ cup plus 2 tablespoons sugar

1. For the filling: Preheat oven to 375 degrees. Mix berries in a baking dish measuring about 12 × 8 inches with a 3-inch depth. Sprinkle with sugar and cornstarch; toss to coat the berries.

2. For the topping: In a mixing bowl, combine the cream and vanilla extract. Whip until the cream is thick enough to hold medium-soft peaks. Add the flour, salt, baking powder and ¼ cup sugar. Using a rubber spatula, fold everything together just until blended.

3. Pat dollops of the mixture over the berries, flattening the topping as much as possible; do not worry if there are gaps. Sprinkle with the remaining 2 tablespoons sugar. Bake until the topping is lightly colored and the fruit is soft and pulpy, about 45 minutes. Serve warm or cool.

Yield: 8 servings

Time: 1 hour, including 45 minutes' baking

Nigella Lawson

HOT BLUEBERRIES

Adapted from Jimmy Steinmeyer

4 tablespoons sweet, unsalted butter

1 quart blueberries

4 tablespoons sugar

Vanilla ice cream

In a large skillet, over low heat, melt the butter. Add the berries, sprinkle with the sugar and cook until they give off their liquid and collapse, about 8 minutes. Remove from the heat. Serve hot over the vanilla ice cream, or over pound cake, or lemon or orange cake.

Yield: 6 servings

Time: 15 minutes

Linda Wells

NIGELLA LAWSON'S SUMMER BERRY CREAM CAKE

The spongecake is light and not too sweet, and the cream and berries make it seem almost more of an unmolded trifle than a cake. Although the cake is moistened with a strawberry purée, you can use any fruit. The purée can be made ahead and refrigerated.

For the Cake

Vegetable oil or nonstick vegetable oil spray
4 large eggs
1 cup sugar
1 teaspoon vanilla extract
Finely grated zest of 1 lemon
1 cup flour

For the Sauce

2 cups strawberries, hulled
2 tablespoons confectioners' sugar
1 tablespoon lemon juice

For the Filling and Topping

$3/4$ cup blueberries
$3/4$ cup blackberries
$3/4$ cup red raspberries
$1/2$ cup red currants or golden raspberries
2 cups heavy cream
1 teaspoon vanilla extract
1 cup strawberries, hulled
$1/2$ teaspoon confectioners' sugar

1. To prepare the cake: First preheat the oven to 350 degrees. Oil or spray a 10-inch springform pan, and line the bottom with parchment paper.

2. Using an electric mixer at high speed, whisk the eggs and sugar together until they triple in volume, becoming thick and airy. Add the vanilla and lemon zest, and whisk to combine. Reduce the speed to medium-low, and gradually add the flour. Remove the bowl from the mixer, give a final fold with a spatula and pour into the prepared cake pan. Bake until risen and light golden brown, 25 to 30 minutes. Cool on a wire rack 10 minutes, and remove the sides from the pan.

3. When the cake is cool, use a long, thin knife to split it into 2 thin disks. Place the bottom half, cut side up, on a serving platter; place the other half, cut side up, on a large piece of foil. In a blender, combine the 2 cups strawberries, confectioners' sugar and lemon juice. Purée until smooth. Set aside $1/4$ cup of the purée, and divide the remaining purée between the two cake layers, pouring it over the cut sides and spreading it with a rubber spatula.

4. In a large bowl, combine the reserved $1/4$ cup purée with $1/2$ cup blueberries, $1/2$ cup blackberries, $1/2$ cup red raspberries and currants or golden raspberries. Fold gently to mix.

5. Whisk the heavy cream with the vanilla until thick but still soft. Spread half over the cake sitting on the serving dish. Top with the fruit mixture, and place the remaining cake half on top, cut side down. Spread the remaining cream on top. Cut the strawberries into halves or quarters, and place in a bowl. Add the remaining $1/4$ cup each of blueberries, blackberries and raspberries, and toss to mix. Arrange the berry mixture on top of the cake, and dust with confectioners' sugar.

Yield: 12 servings

Time: 1 hour 30 minutes

Nigella Lawson

Opposite:
Nigella Lawson's Summer Berry Cake

LARRY FORGIONE'S OLD-FASHIONED STRAWBERRY SHORTCAKE

Adapted from An American Place

6 cups strawberries, washed, hulled, and
    halved or quartered
1/4 cup plus 3 tablespoons sugar
1 3/4 cups heavy cream

2 cups all-purpose flour
1 tablespoon plus 1/2 teaspoon
    baking powder
6 tablespoons unsalted butter, chilled and cut
    into small pieces, plus additional for
    baking sheet
2 hard-boiled large egg yolks, mashed until
    smooth
2 tablespoons unsalted butter,
    melted

1. In a medium bowl, combine the strawberries and 2 tablespoons of the sugar. Cover and refrigerate. Whip 1 cup of the cream until soft peaks form, cover and refrigerate.

2. Heat the oven to 375 degrees. Into a large bowl, sift the flour, baking powder and the remaining 1/4 cup sugar. Add the 6 tablespoons of chilled butter pieces. Using your fingertips, quickly work the butter into the flour until it has the texture of very fine crumbs. Add the remaining 3/4 cup cream and egg yolks, and stir with a fork until the dough just holds together.

3. Lightly butter a baking sheet. On a lightly floured surface, pat or roll the dough to a thickness of 3/4 inch. Using a floured 2 1/2- or 3-inch cookie cutter, cut out 6 rounds of dough, rerolling the scraps as necessary. Place on a baking sheet, brush with melted butter, and sprinkle with the remaining 1 tablespoon sugar. Bake until golden brown and firm, about 15 minutes. Transfer to a rack and allow to cool 2 to 3 minutes.

4. Split the biscuits in half and set the tops aside. Place the bottoms on six dessert plates, and heap strawberries onto each one. Generously spoon the whipped cream on top, and replace the biscuit tops. Serve immediately, offering any remaining whipped cream separately.

Yield: 6 servings

Time: 1 hour

Regina Schrambling

BLUEBERRY CRUMB CAKE

Adapted from *Cooking for the Weekend*

This versatile cake can be made several days ahead and can be served as either a dessert or at a breakfast or brunch. As a dessert, slices of the cake can be garnished with whipped cream, a compote of fresh berries or ice cream. For breakfast, slices can be toasted and served with butter, fresh ricotta, or mascarpone, or warmed in the oven and served with fresh fruit.

For the Topping

> ¾ cup all-purpose flour
>
> ½ cup sugar
>
> ½ teaspoon ground cinnamon
>
> ½ teaspoon salt
>
> 4 tablespoons cold unsalted butter,
>   cut in pieces

For the Cake

> ½ cup unsalted butter at room temperature,
>   plus additional for greasing pan
>
> 1 cup sugar
>
> 2 eggs
>
> ½ cup milk
>
> 1 teaspoon vanilla extract
>
> 2 cups plus 3 tablespoons all-purpose flour
>
> 2 teaspoons baking powder
>
> ½ teaspoon salt
>
> 2 cups blueberries

1. Preheat the oven to 350 degrees. To make the topping, combine the flour, sugar, cinnamon and salt in a bowl. Add the butter, and rub it in with your fingers until the mixture resembles coarse meal. Set aside.

2. To make the cake: Butter a 9-inch springform pan and set it aside. Using an electric mixer, cream the butter and sugar until it is very light and fluffy. Add the eggs one at a time, and beat well, stop-ping to scrape down the sides of the bowl. Add the vanilla to the milk.

3. Sift 2 cups of the flour with the baking powder and salt. Add the flour mixture to the egg mixture alternately with the milk, beginning and ending with flour. Mix just until combined. Toss the blueberries with the remaining 3 tablespoons flour, and stir into the batter.

4. Scrape the batter into the prepared pan and smooth the top. Sprinkle with the topping. Bake until the cake springs back when touched in the center, about 1 hour. Put on a rack to cool for a few minutes. Run a small knife around the edge of the pan to loosen, and remove the sides of the pan. Let cool.

Yield: 8 to 10 servings

Time: 1 hour 40 minutes, including 1 hour baking

Molly O'Neill

"FORGET-IT" MERINGUE TORTE WITH RASPBERRIES

Adapted from Molly Chappellet

This is an elegant, easy-to-make dessert for a festive occasion. The preparation is simple, and the great part of the recipe is the effortless baking. The night before serving, you plop the meringue into the tube pan, slip it into a 425-degree oven and turn off the heat. Then you promise yourself not to peek until morning, at which point it's done, earning its name: Forget-It Meringue Torte. When it comes from the oven, it looks like a disaster, but what you bring to the table is a plump meringue cake with crunchy edges and a marshmallow-like center, slathered in a layer of whipped cream and garnished with raspberries. Or, for a Fourth-of-July effect, alternate rows of blueberries and strawberries on the whipped cream topping to create a snazzy red, white and blue finish to the holiday meal.

Butter
1½ cups egg whites (9 to 11 eggs)
¼ teaspoon cream of tartar
2½ cups, plus 1 tablespoon sugar
1 teaspoon vanilla extract
½ teaspoon almond extract
1 cup heavy cream
Fresh raspberries or raspberry sauce (see Note)

1. Preheat the oven to 425 degrees. Butter an angel-food-cake pan. In a mixer on medium speed, beat the egg whites until frothy. Add the cream of tartar. With the mixer on high speed, gradually add 2½ cups of sugar. Add the vanilla and almond extracts, and beat to stiff, glossy peaks.

2. Spoon the meringue into the pan. Level the top. Place in the oven, and turn off the heat. Do not open the door until the oven is cool, 4 hours or overnight.

3. Push up the removable bottom of the pan. Cut away the top crust; reserve the crust and the crumbs. Unmold the cake onto a plate. Just before serving, whip the cream with 1 tablespoon sugar, then ice the cake with it. Chop the reserved crust to make crumbs, then sprinkle them around the sides and top of the cake, pressing gently.

4. Serve the cake sliced with the raspberries on the side.

Yield: 12 servings

Time: 30 minutes, plus overnight resting

Note: If you prefer a raspberry sauce to the fresh berries: in a bowl, combine three 10-ounce packages frozen raspberries, defrosted, with ½ cup sugar and, if desired, 2 tablespoons kirsch or framboise liqueur. Stir until the sugar is dissolved. Serve the cake sliced with the sauce spooned on the side.

Craig Claiborne and Pierre Franey

SARABETH'S LEMON ROULADE

Adapted from Sarabeth's Kitchen, New York City

For the Lemon Curd Filling
10 egg yolks
1 cup, plus 1 tablespoon sugar
Zest of 2 lemons
6 tablespoons lemon juice
¼ pound unsalted butter

For the Sponge
4 eggs, separated
¾ cup sugar
½ teaspoon vanilla
¾ cup cake flour
¼ teaspoon salt
1 teaspoon baking powder
Confectioners' sugar for dusting
Whipped cream for garnish

1. To make the lemon curd: combine the egg yolks, sugar, lemon zest and juice in a double boiler over hot water. Stir, without aerating, until the mixture thickens.

2. Remove from the heat. Gradually add the butter. Chill.

3. To make the sponge: separate the eggs. Set aside the egg whites, beat the egg yolks until thick and lemon-colored. Gradually beat in ¼ cup sugar and the vanilla.

4. Beat the whites until almost stiff. Gradually add the remaining sugar. Beat until stiff.

5. Fold the whites into the yolks. Sift the flour, salt and baking powder and fold into the eggs.

6. Butter and line a 10 × 15-inch baking pan with buttered paper. Spread the batter evenly in the pan.

7. Bake at 375 degrees for approximately 12 minutes. Do not overbake. Turn out onto paper or a

towel that has been lightly coated with confectioners' sugar. Remove the wax paper and roll quickly with a new sheet of wax paper. Wrap in the sugared towel; cool.

8. Unroll the sponge and spread with lemon curd filling. Reroll it without paper. Refrigerate for several hours.

9. Garnish with whipped cream.

Yield: 8 to 10 servings

Time: 1 hour, plus several hours' refrigeration

Note: This cake may be frozen. If frozen, sprinkle with additional confectioners' sugar after defrosting and garnish with whipped cream.

Marian Burros

LEMON CREAM CUPCAKES

Adapted from *Instant Gratification*

The tender yellow cake encloses creamy, tart lemon filling that is made with just cream cheese, lemon and sugar—no need to fuss with frosting.

    Nonstick cooking spray
    1½ cups sugar
    ¾ cup (1½ sticks) unsalted butter
    6 large eggs
    ¼ cup fresh lemon juice
    2¼ cups cake or all-purpose flour
    3 teaspoons grated lemon zest
    1½ teaspoons baking powder
    ½ teaspoon salt
    ¾ cup cream cheese, softened
    Confectioners' sugar, optional

1. Preheat the oven to 350 degrees. Coat a muffin tin with nonstick cooking spray.

2. In the bowl of an electric mixer, beat 1¼ cups sugar and the butter at medium speed until light and fluffy. Add the eggs and 3 tablespoons lemon juice, and beat until well combined, scraping down bowl once or twice as necessary. Mix in the flour, 2 teaspoons lemon zest, the baking powder and salt.

3. In a small bowl, mash together cream cheese and remaining sugar, lemon juice and zest.

4. Spoon about 3 tablespoons batter into each muffin cup. Place about 1 tablespoon cream cheese mixture on top, and cover cheese with some remaining batter (batter should reach three-quarters of the way to the top of each cup). Bake until golden, about 20 minutes.

5. Let cupcakes cool in the pan for 10 minutes before turning over onto a wire rack to cool completely. Dust with confectioners' sugar before serving, if desired.

Yield: 12 servings

Time: 50 minutes

Melissa Clark

ZUCCHINI CAKE WITH GINGER AND HAZELNUTS

Grated ginger and chopped hazelnuts give character to this moist cake.

2 cups flour
1 teaspoon baking soda
¾ teaspoon baking powder
¼ teaspoon salt
1¼ cups sugar
2 large eggs
½ cup vegetable oil
⅓ cup orange juice
2 teaspoons orange zest
2 teaspoons peeled, grated fresh ginger
1 teaspoon vanilla extract
1½ cups grated zucchini
½ cup finely chopped hazelnuts

1. Preheat the oven to 350 degrees. Sift the flour, baking soda, baking powder and salt into a large bowl. Stir in the sugar.

2. In another bowl, whisk together the eggs, oil, orange juice, zest, ginger and vanilla. Pour the wet ingredients into the bowl with the flour and stir until just combined. Fold in the zucchini and hazelnuts.

3. Butter and flour a tube pan. Scrape the batter into the pan and bake until a toothpick inserted into the center of the cake comes out clean, about 45 minutes. Cool the cake in the pan for 10 minutes. Remove from the pan and cool completely on a wire rack. Slice and serve.

Yield: 12 servings

Time: 1 hour 20 minutes

Molly O'Neill

DINNER:
THE MAIN EVENT

RECIPES FOR
DINNER

HALIBUT WITH INDIAN RUB AND CORN SALSA

2 teaspoons ground cumin

1½ teaspoons ground turmeric

1 teaspoon ground coriander

½ teaspoon ground fennel seeds

Salt and freshly ground black pepper

4 halibut steaks (1 inch thick, 2 to 2½ pounds total) (Pacific salmon, wild striped bass, hake steaks or fillets of these fish can be substituted)

2 lemons

4 tablespoons ghee (sold in Indian stores and fancy food shops) or clarified butter; vegetable oil can be substituted

1 tablespoon minced fresh ginger

½ cup finely chopped onion

1 cup cooked fresh corn kernels (about 1 ear corn)

Oil for the grill

1 tablespoon chopped fresh cilantro leaves

1. Combine the cumin, turmeric, coriander, fennel, ½ teaspoon black pepper and ½ teaspoon salt or to taste. Rub the fish steaks on both sides with the juice of ½ lemon, then rub with all but 2 teaspoons of the spice mixture. Refrigerate 3 hours.

2. While the fish marinates, heat 2 tablespoons ghee in a skillet, add the ginger and onion and sauté until the onion just starts to brown. Stir in the remaining spices and sauté, stirring, until the spices smell toasty, then add the corn and the juice of ½ lemon. Cook briefly and set aside.

3. Remove the fish from the refrigerator and brush on both sides with remaining ghee or butter. Preheat the grill and oil the grates. When hot, place the fish on the grill over medium-hot coals or a gas fire and cook about 5 minutes. Use a spatula to turn the fish and grill 3 to 4 minutes, until a little

liquid just begins to pool on the surface of the fish and a paring knife inserted just at the bone can move the flesh away from it easily. Salmon should be cooked about 3 minutes on each side. Remove the fish to a warm platter or individual plates.

4. Reheat the corn mixture, adding the cilantro and a couple tablespoons of water to moisten it. Spoon the corn on the fish, garnish with wedges cut from the remaining lemon and serve.

Yield: 4 servings

Time: 25 minutes, plus 3 hours' marinating

Florence Fabricant

CHARRED STRIPED BASS NIÇOISE

3 tablespoons extra virgin olive oil, plus more for grill

2 cloves garlic, sliced

1 (2-pound) fillet of wild striped bass, with skin (Pacific salmon, mahi-mahi or barramundi may be substituted)

Juice of ½ lemon

Salt and freshly ground black pepper

2 medium ripe tomatoes, in ¼-inch-thick slices

12 pitted oil-cured black olives, coarsely chopped

1 tablespoon finely slivered fresh basil leaves

1. Prepare a charcoal grill.

2. Heat 1 tablespoon of the oil in a small pan, add the garlic and cook over medium heat until golden. Remove from the heat, drain the garlic and chop.

3. Brush the fish with half the oil on both sides. Brush the flesh side with lemon and season with salt and pepper. You will need two large spatulas to turn the fish; if you do not have them, cut the fillet in half or in 4 portions. Brush the tomato slices with the remaining oil.

4. Preheat the grill to very hot and oil the grates. Briefly sear the tomato slices, turning once. Remove to a platter and tent with foil to keep warm. Use the edge of the spatula to scrape the grates clean. Re-oil. Place the fish, skin side up, on the grill. Cook about 5 minutes. Use spatulas to turn. Cook 3 to 4 minutes on the skin side, until a skewer inserted horizontally in the middle feels just warm. Salmon needs less time.

5. Transfer the fish to a warm platter and pave the flesh side with overlapping tomato slices. Scatter with the olives, chopped garlic and basil.

Yield: 4 servings

Time: 30 minutes

Florence Fabricant

CRAIG CLAIBORNE'S "POACHED" BAKED SALMON

Although the salmon is not technically poached or steamed, the result of foil baking is similar enough to seem almost interchangeable with that of the more proper method. Any leftover salmon can be flaked with either mayonnaise or olive oil, and minced red onion and/or dill, if desired, for sandwiches or tossed with minced dill in a lemon vinaigrette over fresh-cooked pasta.

> 1 whole salmon, cleaned, (about 6 to 8 pounds) preferably with head left on (see Note)
> 1 cup thinly sliced carrot
> 1 cup thinly sliced onion
> ¼ cup thinly sliced shallots
> 1 cup thinly sliced celery
> ½ teaspoon dried thyme
> Salt
> 8 black peppercorns, crushed
> 1 clove garlic, unpeeled and crushed

> 1 bay leaf
> 2 cups dry white wine

1. Preheat the oven to 400 degrees.

2. Select a baking sheet large enough to accommodate the fish.

3. Lay out a long double length of heavy-duty aluminum foil on top of the baking sheet. Place the cleaned salmon in the center of the foil and add the carrot, onion, shallots, celery, thyme, salt to taste, peppercorns, garlic, bay leaf and wine. Bring up the edges of the foil and seal as compactly and tightly as possible.

4. Place the fish in the oven and bake 50 minutes to 1 hour. At the end of 50 minutes, loosen the foil and test for doneness. The fish is cooked when the back center fin can be easily removed when pulled with your fingers. Remove from the oven. Serve hot or cold with Dill-and-Cucumber Mayonnaise (recipe follows); serve hot, if desired, with Lemon-Chive Beurre Blanc (see page 197).

Yield: 8 to 12 servings

Time: 15 minutes, plus 1 hour baking and refrigeration, if desired

Note: Before baking the fish, measure it to make certain it will fit in the oven. It may be baked when placed diagonally to obtain more space. If the fish will not fit with the head left on, it will be necessary to cut it off. The head may be used for soup or discarded. The meat from a poached fish head also may be used cold in salads.

➤ DILL-AND-CUCUMBER MAYONNAISE

1 cup peeled, seeded and diced cucumbers

Salt

2 egg yolks

Freshly ground black pepper

2 teaspoons imported mustard, such as
    Dijon or Dusseldorf

2 teaspoons vinegar or lemon juice

2 cups peanut, vegetable or olive oil

¼ cup finely chopped fresh dill

1. Put the cucumbers in a bowl and sprinkle with salt to taste. Refrigerate 30 minutes.

2. Meanwhile, place the yolks in a mixing bowl and add salt and pepper to taste, mustard and vinegar or lemon juice. Beat vigorously for a second or two with a wire whisk or electric beater.

3. Start adding the oil gradually, beating continuously with the whisk or electric beater. Continue beating and adding oil until all of it is used.

4. Drain the cucumbers. Add the cucumbers and dill to the mayonnaise and blend well.

Yield: 3 cups

Time: 10 minutes, plus 30 minutes refrigeration

Craig Claiborne and Pierre Franey

Craig Claiborne's "Poached" Baked Salmon with
Dill-and-Cucumber Mayonnaise

TANDOORI-SPICED SALMON WITH YOGURT-MANGO SAUCE

Adapted from Christer Larsson

6 salmon steaks (with bone)
  (8 to 10 ounces each)
2 tablespoons olive oil
2 cloves garlic, minced
1 tablespoon garam masala (see Note)
1 tablespoon sugar
3 tablespoons grated fresh ginger
¼ cup rice vinegar
2 ripe mangoes, peeled, pitted and diced
1 tablespoon honey
½ teaspoon tamarind concentrate, optional
2 tablespoons finely minced fresh mint leaves
Pinch of ground cumin
Pinch of ground turmeric
1 pint plain low-fat yogurt
Salt and freshly ground black pepper to taste

1. About 3 hours in advance, rub the salmon steaks with the oil, garlic and garam masala. Cover and refrigerate.

2. While the fish is marinating, melt the sugar in a saucepan; then, add 2 tablespoons of the ginger and the vinegar. Bring to a simmer, and cook for a minute; then, add the mangoes. Simmer over low heat about 15 minutes, stirring occasionally, so the mangoes don't stick. The mangoes should hold their shape. Remove from the heat, and refrigerate.

3. Whisk the honey with the tamarind concentrate (if using), the remaining ginger, the mint leaves, cumin and turmeric. Fold into the yogurt, and season to taste with salt and pepper. Refrigerate.

4. Preheat the grill. Remove the salmon from the marinade, and grill 4 to 5 minutes on each side, or until cooked to taste. Serve accompanied by the cooked mango and the yogurt sauce.

Yield: 6 servings

Time: 40 minutes, plus about 3 hours for marinating

Note: Garam masala is an Indian spice blend available in some food shops. It can be made by combining a tablespoon each of ground spices: coriander, cumin, black pepper, cayenne, fennel seeds, ginger, cinnamon and cardamom, plus a teaspoon each of ground cloves and nutmeg.

Florence Fabricant

RICK BAYLESS'S SKILLET-SEARED SNAPPER WITH TOASTED GARLIC, PRUNES AND PECANS

1 large head garlic, broken into cloves and
  peeled
1 small ancho chili, stemmed, seeded and cut
  into ⅛-inch strips
½ cup olive oil
¼ cup red wine
½ teaspoon salt, plus more to taste
4 scallions, coarsely chopped
⅔ cup pitted prunes, cut into ⅛-inch pieces
½ cup pecans, broken
4 boneless red snapper fillets (about 6 ounces
  each)
Freshly ground pepper to taste

1. Chop the garlic into small bits; do not mince. Place in a 9-inch nonstick skillet with the ancho chili and olive oil. Set over low heat and cook, stirring often, until the garlic is very tender and just beginning to brown, about 25 minutes.

2. Add the wine, ½ teaspoon of salt, scallions and half of the prunes. Raise the heat to medium and simmer until the wine has evaporated and the mixture starts to sizzle, approximately 7 to 10 minutes. Add the pecans and the remaining prunes, and stir until the pecans smell toasted, about 5 minutes.

3. Scrape the garlic mixture into a bowl, and wash and dry the skillet. Set over medium-high heat and spoon in a couple of tablespoons of the oil from the garlic mixture. Season the fish with salt and pep-per to taste and place in the skillet. Let it brown on one side for 2 to 3 minutes; turn and finish cooking on the other side, about 3 minutes longer.

4. Add the garlic mixture to the pan and let it heat through. Place a fillet on each of four plates. With a slotted spoon, spoon the garlic mixture over the fish and serve immediately.

Yield: 4 servings

Time: 1 hour

Molly O'Neill

TUNA STEAKS WITH RED-ONION COMPOTE

4 center-cut tuna steaks (about 6 ounces each)
4 tablespoons olive oil
Salt to taste
4 sprigs fresh thyme or 1 teaspoon dried
¼ teaspoon red pepper flakes
2 teaspoons coarsely cracked black peppercorns
2 tablespoons chopped fresh basil

1. Preheat a charcoal grill or broiler.

2. Place the tuna steaks on a flat surface, and cut out the dark streak of meat, if any. Brush with olive oil on both sides, and sprinkle with salt, thyme and pepper flakes. Cover with plastic wrap, and let stand for 15 minutes before broiling.

3. Meanwhile, prepare the Red-Onion Compote (recipe follows).

4. Sprinkle the tuna on both sides with the cracked peppercorns.

5. If you are using a grill, rub the rack lightly with oil. Place the fish on the grill. If you are using a broiler, place the fish on a rack about 4 inches from the heat. Cook for 3 minutes, and turn. For rare, cook for another 3 minutes or to desired doneness.

6. To serve, place equal portions of onion compote on the side of four warmed plates. Place a tuna steak on each plate, and sprinkle with basil.

Yield: 4 servings

Time: 1 hour, including preparation of compote

➤ RED-ONION COMPOTE

Remaining olive oil (see previous recipe)
4 red onions, chopped
2 tablespoons red wine vinegar
1 whole clove
¼ teaspoon Tabasco sauce
Salt to taste
2 tablespoons drained capers
2 tablespoons honey

1. Heat the remaining olive oil in a heavy casserole, and add the onions. Cover. Cook over medium-high heat for 15 minutes, stirring occasionally.

2. When the onions start to brown, uncover and add the vinegar, clove and Tabasco. Add salt to taste. Cook briefly, stirring, until the vinegar has almost evaporated.

3. Stir in the capers and honey. Cover tightly, and simmer for 15 minutes more.

Yield: 2 cups compote

Time: 45 minutes

Note: This compote is also a tasty accompaniment for grilled or roasted meats.

Pierre Franey

UNION SQUARE CAFÉ'S FILET MIGNON OF TUNA

Adapted from Michael Romano

The tuna filet mignon marinated in a ginger-teriyaki sauce is a signature dish at one of Manhattan's most popular restaurants.

For the Marinade

2 cups teriyaki sauce
½ cup dry sherry

4 tablespoons finely chopped fresh ginger

½ cup chopped scallions

2 cloves garlic, peeled and thinly sliced

½ teaspoon cayenne pepper

2 teaspoons freshly ground black pepper

Juice of 2 lemons

For the Tuna

4 yellowfin tuna steaks (8 to 10 ounces each)

2 tablespoons olive oil

¼ cup pickled ginger, for garnish

1. Combine all the marinade ingredients in a bowl and place the tuna steaks in it. Refrigerate for 3 hours, turning the tuna every hour.

2. About half an hour before cooking, remove the tuna from the marinade to a plate, and let it reach room temperature. Preheat a grill, barbecue or pan to very hot.

3. Brush the tuna steaks with olive oil. Grill for 1 to 2 minutes on each side. The outside should be well seared, and the center should be just warm and very rare.

4. Garnish each tuna steak with pickled ginger, and serve.

Yield: 4 servings

Time: 10 minutes, plus 3½ hours for marinating and bringing to room temperature

Bryan Miller

GRILLED TROUT WITH ZESTY CUCUMBER-TOMATO RELISH

Adapted from David Page, Home, New York City

1 large cucumber, seeded and diced

2 cups seeded, chopped tomatoes

¼ cup diced red onion

2 tablespoons fresh mint, cut into ribbons

½ teaspoon red pepper flakes

2 tablespoons fresh lemon juice

Salt and freshly ground black pepper to taste

1 cup plain yogurt

Grated zest of 1 lemon

1 teaspoon toasted cumin seeds

1 teaspoon toasted coriander seeds

4 whole brook trout (about 10 ounces each)

Olive oil for basting the trout

1. To make the cucumber-tomato relish, combine in a bowl the cucumber, tomatoes, onion, mint, red pepper flakes, 1 tablespoon lemon juice, salt and pepper. Refrigerate until served.

2. To make the yogurt sauce, combine in a bowl the yogurt, the remaining lemon juice, lemon zest, cumin seeds, coriander seeds, salt and pepper. Refrigerate until served.

3. Brush the trout with olive oil. Season with salt and pepper. Grill the trout over charcoal (or broil) for 4 minutes per side. Serve each trout with some relish on the side and the yogurt sauce.

Yield: 4 servings

Time: 40 minutes

Bryan Miller

WOOD-GRILLED BLACK SEA BASS WITH MINT VINAIGRETTE

Adapted from Peasant, New York City

At Peasant, the fish is grilled over wood, which imparts a richer-tasting flavor than charcoal. The wood imparts a smoke. Many hardware stores sell bags of mesquite or hickory wood chunks. They can be lit in a chimney starter, exactly like charcoal, and produce a bed of embers in 20 minutes. When grilling for one or two people, a single chimney starter full of chunks will be enough. For larger crowds, use several starters.

For the Bass

    4 black sea bass (each about 1½ pounds), cleaned and trimmed
    4 tablespoons extra virgin olive oil
    Coarse salt and freshly ground black pepper
    1 lemon, thinly sliced
    3 bunches fresh mint

For the Vinaigrette

    3 tablespoons red wine vinegar
    ¾ cup extra virgin olive oil
    1 clove garlic, minced
    ¼ cup chopped fresh mint leaves

1. Wash the fish inside and out, and blot dry. Make 3 slashes in the thick part of the sides of each fish. Generously rub the fish inside and out with olive oil, and generously season with salt and pepper. Place a few lemon slices and mint sprigs in the cavity of each fish. Save the remaining mint for the sauce and grilling. Arrange the fish in a baking dish, and let it marinate while you make the vinaigrette and build the fire.

2. Not more than 30 minutes before serving, place the vinegar in a mixing bowl and add salt and pepper (about ½ teaspoon each). Whisk until the salt crystals are dissolved. Whisk in the oil in a thin stream, followed by the garlic and mint.

3. Light a grill, and rake out the embers into a single-zone fire with an ember-free safety zone. (In a gas grill, place the wood chips in a smoker box or pouch, and preheat until you see smoke.)

4. Arrange the fish on a grate, and grill over a medium fire until just cooked, 10 to 14 minutes per side. You may need to add fresh wood chunks to the fire. Baste the fish with olive oil as it grills, using a bunch of mint as a basting brush. (To check for doneness use a slender paring knife to cut into the fish at the backbone; the flesh should come away easily.) Using a long spatula, move the fish to the side of the grill. Lay the remaining mint on the grill over the hottest part of the fire (stems perpendicular to the grate). Place the fish on the mint for a few minutes to absorb the flavor.

5. Transfer the fish and mint to a platter. Stir the vinaigrette with a fork, removing and discarding the garlic cloves. Serve the fish with the vinaigrette spooned over it.

Yield: 4 servings

Time: 40 minutes

Note: The Barbecue Industry Association says mesquite is the most popular grilling wood in the United States, followed closely by hickory. Mesquite is best for grilling beef because it burns the hottest and has the most pronounced flavor. It also has a tendency to pop and shoot sparks, which can be disconcerting. Almost all wood produces leaping flames when lighted, so be sure there are no overhanging plants, trees, umbrellas or canopies. Never light a grill under a carport. Softwoods like pine and spruce should be avoided—they send up too much soot and resinous smoke. And never use processed wood like plywood or pressure-treated lumber, which can give off toxic chemicals.

Steven Raichlen

BLACK COD (SABLE) WITH MISO

Adapted from Ruby Foo's, New York City

1 cup miso
1 cup sake
1 cup mirin
1 cup brown sugar, packed
4 (6-ounce) black cod fillets
1 tablespoon soy sauce
1½ teaspoons Asian sesame oil
2 chopped scallions, green part only

1. Combine the miso, sake, mirin and sugar; set aside ½ cup. Marinate the fish in the mixture in the refrigerator for 24 hours.

2. Preheat the broiler; cover the broiler pan with foil. Place the fish on the pan, skin side up, 4 to 6 inches from the heat. Broil until the fish is caramelized, 8 to 10 minutes.

3. Meanwhile, whisk the soy sauce and sesame oil together. When the fish is cooked, spoon the ½ cup reserved marinade over the fish and then the soy-sesame mixture. Garnish with chopped scallion.

Yield: 4 servings

Time: 20 minutes, plus one day's marinating

Marian Burros

EASTERN SHORE CRAB CAKES

The crab cake is the hamburger of the Chesapeake. On the Eastern Shore, it is eaten on a soft bun slathered with tartar sauce and a squeeze of lemon. What makes the best crab cake is the subject of great debate, often conducted at blind taste tests. Should a bit of onion be added? Should the crab be held together with bread crumbs, mayonnaise or mashed potatoes? Everyone agrees that lump crabmeat is essential to a respectable crab cake, and that no more filler should be added than necessary to bind the meat together. Vegetable oil may be used in place of butter.

1 pound lump crabmeat (picked and any cartilage removed)
1 egg, lightly mixed
2 tablespoons mayonnaise, preferably homemade
1 teaspoon dry mustard
¼ teaspoon Spicy Seafood Seasoning (recipe follows) or cayenne pepper
4 tablespoons chopped fresh parsley
1 tablespoon minced onion
2 to 4 tablespoons dry bread crumbs
Zest of 1 lemon, grated
3 tablespoons butter

1. Place the crabmeat in a mixing bowl. Pick it with a fork and check to see that all the cartilage is removed. Add the egg, mayonnaise and mustard. Toss lightly together, using the fork so as not to shred the crabmeat too much.

2. Add the seafood seasoning, parsley, minced onion, bread crumbs and grated lemon zest. Toss together lightly.

3. Melt the butter in a skillet over medium-high heat. Scoop up enough crab mixture to make a plump patty about 5 inches in diameter. Place the crab cakes in the skillet and fry for 3 minutes or until a golden brown crust forms on the bottom. Flip the crab cakes over and continue to fry on the other side for another 3 or 4 minutes.

4. Serve the crab cakes on soft hamburger buns or simply with a spoonful of tartar sauce.

Yield: 6 crab cakes

Time: 30 minutes

Rena Coyle

SPICY SEAFOOD SEASONING

½ cup kosher salt

3 tablespoons coarsely ground black pepper

3 tablespoons dry mustard

1½ tablespoons cayenne pepper

1 tablespoon mustard seeds

1 teaspoon paprika

Combine all the ingredients in a bowl and mix thoroughly. Place the spices in a jar and cover until ready to use.

Yield: 1½ to 2 cups

Time: 5 minutes

Rena Coyle

SHRIMP STEAMED IN BEER WITH DILL

Adapted from *The Best of Craig Claiborne*

At an informal gathering, bring the shrimp to the table and have your guests peel their own. The shrimp are flavorful on their own but may be enhanced with a dip or a condiment of your choice.

1 pound small shrimp (about 30)

1 bay leaf

6 fresh dill sprigs

1 garlic clove

9 whole peppercorns, crushed

1 teaspoon ground allspice

1 whole dried, hot red pepper

½ to 1 cup beer

Salt to taste

2 small celery stalks with leaves

Melted butter, salsa verde, basil mayonnaise, or sauce of your choice for dipping, optional

1. Do not peel the shrimp. Put them in a saucepan or deep small skillet and add the remaining ingredients.

2. Cover and bring to a rolling boil. Remove from the heat and serve. For elegance, you can peel and devein the shrimp before bringing them to the table. But for informal occasions, that is not necessary.

Yield: 2 to 4 servings

Time: 25 minutes

SPICY GRILLED SHRIMP FOR A CROWD

Marinating the shrimp in their shells with plenty of hot pepper before grilling them intensifies their flavor. The recipe can be reduced for smaller gatherings.

1½ cups olive oil

¾ cup fresh lemon juice

9 large cloves garlic, peeled and minced

1½ teaspoons freshly ground black pepper

¼ cup Tabasco sauce

10 pounds jumbo shrimp, in the shell

Kosher salt to taste

1. Whisk the oil, lemon juice, garlic, pepper, and Tabasco. Divide between 2 large bowls. Place half of the shrimp in each bowl and toss with the marinade. Refrigerate overnight.

2. Preheat a grill or broiler. Grill or broil the shrimp until just cooked through, about 1½ minutes on each side. Season with salt.

Yield: 20 servings

Time: 15 minutes and overnight refrigeration

Molly O'Neill

MUSSELS STEAMED WITH WHITE WINE AND CURRY LEAVES

Adapted from Raji Jallepalli, Restaurant Raji, Memphis

2 tablespoons extra virgin olive oil

½ cup finely chopped onion

1 cup finely chopped, seeded plum tomatoes

¼ cup fresh curry leaves (sold in some Indian markets) or fresh cilantro leaves

1½ teaspoons cumin seeds, crushed in a mortar

Salt to taste

2 pounds scrubbed, debearded mussels

¾ cup dry white wine

1. Heat the oil in a large saucepan with a lid. Add the onion, tomatoes and curry leaves or cilantro, and cook, stirring, over medium heat until the vegetables soften.

2. Stir in the cumin, and cook a few minutes longer, until the onion starts to brown. Season with salt.

3. Add the mussels and wine, cover and cook over medium heat until the mussels open, about 8 minutes. Serve at once.

Yield: 2 main-course servings, or 4 appetizers

Time: 30 minutes

Florence Fabricant

OLD STONE FISH STEW

1¼ pounds skinless tilefish, monkfish or cod
1 pound halibut or red snapper
¼ cup olive oil
1½ cups finely chopped onions
1 cup finely chopped celery
1 cup finely chopped green bell pepper
1 teaspoon finely chopped garlic
1 cup dry white wine
1 bay leaf
5 sprigs fresh thyme, chopped, or 1 teaspoon
    dried thyme
4 cups canned tomatoes, peeled and crushed
¼ teaspoon red pepper flakes
Salt to taste, if desired
Freshly ground black pepper to taste
1 pound mussels, scrubbed and cleaned
½ pound shrimp, shelled and deveined
¼ cup chopped fresh flat-leaf parsley leaves

1. Cut the fish into 1½-inch cubes. Set them aside.

2. Heat the oil in a large saucepan or kettle over medium heat and add the onions, celery, green pepper and garlic. Cook, stirring, for 5 minutes. Add the wine, bay leaf and thyme. Cook for 1 minute. Stir in the tomatoes, pepper flakes, salt and pepper. Simmer for 10 minutes.

3. Add the fish and mussels, stir and cook over high heat for about 3 minutes. Add the shrimp and parsley and cook for 3 minutes more. Remove the bay leaf and serve immediately.

Yield: 6 servings

Time: 1 hour

Bryan Miller and Pierre Franey

ERIC RIPERT'S SOFT-SHELL CRABS WITH GARLIC VINAIGRETTE

For the Vinaigrette
    ¼ teaspoon kosher salt
    Freshly ground pepper to taste
    1 tablespoon Dijon mustard
    2 tablespoons sherry vinegar
    ¼ cup corn oil
    ¼ cup olive oil
    1 clove garlic, peeled and minced
    2 tablespoons chopped fresh tarragon
    2 tablespoons chopped fresh chives
    2 tablespoons chopped fresh chervil

For the Crabs
    4 medium soft-shell crabs, cleaned
    1 tablespoon all-purpose flour
    Kosher salt and freshly ground pepper to taste
    1 tablespoon corn oil

1. To make the vinaigrette: In a mixing bowl, whisk together the salt, pepper, mustard and vinegar. Whisking constantly, slowly drizzle in the corn oil and then the olive oil. Stir in the garlic and herbs. Set aside.

2. Coat the crabs lightly with the flour. Season on both sides with salt and pepper. Heat the corn oil in a large nonstick skillet over high heat until the oil smokes. Add the crabs, top side down, and sauté for 1½ minutes. Turn the crabs over, lower the heat to medium and sauté until browned on the bottom and cooked through, about 3½ minutes.

3. Spoon a pool of the vinaigrette into the center of 4 plates. Pat the crabs dry and place in the vinaigrette. Serve immediately.

Yield: 2 to 4 servings

Time: 30 minutes

Molly O'Neill

PEARL OYSTER BAR'S LOBSTER MIXED GRILL

Adapted from Rebecca Charles

You never want to turn the lobsters on the grill because all the juices in the shell would run out, and that's what makes them taste so good. When the shell meets the flame, different things start to happen to the flavor.

2 (3-pound) chickens, backbones and breast-bones removed
½ cup olive oil
Kosher salt and freshly ground black pepper
Peel of 1 lemon, cut into strips
8 sprigs fresh tarragon

2 cups apple-wood chips, soaked in water
32 oysters, shucked but in shells with their liquor
Lemon-Chive Beurre Blanc (recipe follows)
4 (1½-pound) lobsters, live and chilled

1. Lay 1 chicken in a roasting pan skin side up, and rub ¼ cup olive oil over it. Season with salt and pepper to taste. Sprinkle half the lemon peel and half the tarragon over the chicken, then lay a sheet of plastic wrap over the chicken so that it adheres. Repeat the process with the second chicken, and let both marinate at least 30 minutes.

2. Bank the charcoal in your grill three times as high on one side as the other; coals on the highest side should be about 2 inches from the grate. Light the coals. When they are covered in gray ash and you can hold your hand 4 inches above the grate

for only 2 seconds, lay the chickens skin side up on the high side of the grill, and cook for 10 minutes. Pull the chickens to the middle of the grill. Cook 5 minutes more, then flip them over and place on the low-fire side of grill for 10 minutes, or until cooked through. Remove to a warm platter.

3. While the chicken cooks on low heat, scatter wood chips on the hottest side of the grill, using tongs, if necessary, to work them through the grate. When the chips begin to smolder, transfer the oysters, 6 to 8 at a time, to the hot side of the grill. Cover the oysters with a stainless steel bowl, let cook 1 minute, or until the liquor bubbles. Transfer the oysters to a platter. Drizzle with lemon-chive beurre blanc and serve. Repeat with remaining oysters.

4. Place 1 lobster on a cutting board. Using a heavy chef's knife, kill the lobster with a swift stroke through the middle of the head, then continue the cut, cleaving the lobster in two lengthwise. Repeat with the other lobsters. Lay the lobster parts shell-side down on the grill so that the claws only are on the hottest side. Cook 6 minutes, then make a cut in each claw. Cook the lobsters 6 minutes more, or until the meat is opaque. Remove the chickens and lobsters from the grill and serve.

Yield: 8 servings

Time: About 1 hour, plus 30 minutes' marinating

Matt Lee and Ted Lee

➤ PEARL OYSTER BAR'S LEMON-CHIVE BEURRE BLANC

Adapted from Rebecca Charles

> 1/3 cup white wine
> 1/3 cup white wine vinegar
> 3 shallots, finely chopped
> 3 sticks butter
> 1 tablespoon plus 1 teaspoon lemon zest
> 1 tablespoon plus 1 teaspoon chopped chives

In a stainless steel saucepan over medium heat, combine the wine, vinegar and shallots. Bring to a simmer, and reduce until there are 2 tablespoons of liquid. Reduce the heat and add the butter, 1 tablespoon at a time, whisking until each piece melts. Whisk in the zest and chives. Turn off the heat, transfer to ramekins and keep in a warm place.

Yield: ¾ cup; enough for drizzling on 32 oysters and meat of 4 lobsters

Time: 25 minutes

Matt Lee and Ted Lee

NEW ENGLAND CLAMBAKE STOVE-TOP STYLE

1 pound semihot sausage
2 cups dry white wine
2 stalks celery, cut into 1-inch pieces
1 medium onion, chopped
1 bay leaf
4 dozen soft-shell (steamer) clams, about
    6 pounds, rinsed
2 dozen mussels, about 2½ pounds, rinsed,
    optional: if not available, add 2 dozen more
    clams
2 bunches scallions, trimmed

6 ears corn, husked
18 new potatoes
6 (1- to 1¼-pound) lobsters
½ pound unsalted butter

1. In a frying pan, brown the sausage over medium-high heat, 8 to 10 minutes.

2. Pour 1 cup of the wine and ½ cup water into a pot (see Note). Add the celery, onion and bay leaf. Cover and bring to a boil.

3. Add the clams first to the pot, then the mussels, 1 bunch of scallions and the corn, in that order. Cover and simmer 15 minutes over high heat. Set aside, covered.

4. In a second pot, put the remaining 1 cup wine, 1 cup water, the potatoes and 1 bunch of scallions. Cover and cook over medium-high heat for 10 minutes.

5. Add the lobsters to the second pot, cover and cook over medium-high heat for 15 minutes.

6. Melt the butter in a pan and pour into small serving bowls.

7. On a large platter, lay down a bed of mussels, clams, potatoes, scallions, sausage, celery and onions. Place the corn around the perimeter. Place the lobster in the center. Combine the broth from the two pots and pour into individual cups. Serve.

Note: This recipe calls for two large (10- to 12-quart) pots. If you have a large enough pot, all ingredients can be cooked together. In this case combine steps 3 and 4, leaving out the water, and place the potatoes on top of the mussels. Add the lobsters after 15 minutes and cook 15 minutes more.

Yield: 6 servings

Time: 1 hour 30 minutes

Bryan Miller

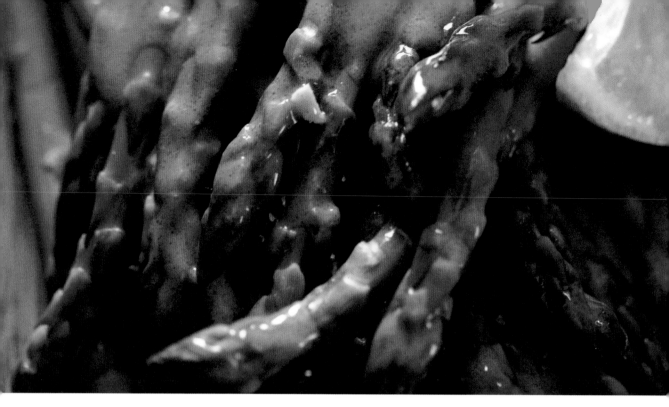

MARIO BATALI'S SLOW-COOKED SWORDFISH

Adapted from Zach Allen

This exceptional entrée is astonishingly easy to prepare and also makes a fine appetizer or part of an antipasto platter. The fish is cubed, then sprinkled with sugar, salt, chilies and lime, and completely covered in olive oil. In the slow oven, it more percolates than bakes, as the flavors in the oil infuse the fish. Before serving, the cubes of fish are sprinkled with olive oil, coarse salt and lemon juice.

1½ pounds swordfish steak, ½ inch thick, trimmed of skin and cut in 1-inch squares, or any firm-fleshed fish

1 teaspoon sugar

Kosher salt or sea salt

3 Thai chilies

Zest of 1 lime, in long strips

1½ cups best-quality olive oil, or as needed

Freshly squeezed lemon juice to taste

1. Preheat the oven to 225 degrees. Arrange the fish pieces in a 9-inch square metal baking pan in a single layer. Sprinkle with the sugar and salt, and scatter the chilies and lime strips over all. Pour just enough oil on top to cover the fish. Stir gently. Cover the pan with foil, crimping the edges to seal.

2. Bake just until the swordfish is cooked through and very tender, about 40 minutes. Allow the fish to cool in the pan.

3. When ready to serve, remove the fish from the oil. Scrape off any fat clinging to its sides and discard it. Arrange the fish on a serving platter. Discard the chilies and lime. Sprinkle with fresh olive oil and a little more salt and drizzle with lemon juice to taste.

Yield: 6 appetizer servings, or 4 main-course servings

Time: 1 hour, including 40 minutes' cooking

Amanda Hesser

ERIC RIPERT'S SEAFOOD PAELLA

Paella has infinite advantages as party food. Much of it can be made ahead. It's best served buffet style. It can serve 6 or 16. And it does not have to be piping hot. Think of it as a risotto without the stirring. Eric Ripert, the chef at Le Bernardin, understands the paella effect. He saves it for entertaining at home in Sag Harbor, N.Y., where his paella often combines monkfish, shrimp, mussels and sausage.

Paella is particularly accommodating for the home cook because it's so flexible. No single list of ingredients defines it. You can even serve cold paella like a salad, in summer, preparing the saffron rice with peppers and chorizo in advance and, just before serving, spreading it on a large platter and topping it with chilled seafood in a vinaigrette dressing.

6 cups stock, half chicken and half seafood or shrimp
½ tablespoon saffron threads
12 monkfish medallions (about 1½ pounds total)
4½ tablespoons extra virgin olive oil
Salt and freshly ground black pepper
1 onion, chopped
6 garlic cloves, chopped
¼ pound chorizo, skin removed, sliced ¼ inch thick
3 cups short-grain rice, preferably Spanish (see Note)
2 cups fresh green peas
1 small red bell pepper, seared over a flame to blacken skin, then peeled, cored and cut in strips
1 small green bell pepper, seared over a flame, peeled, cored and cut in strips
18 large shrimp, peeled and deveined (about 1 pound)
1 pound medium mussels
¼ cup thinly sliced scallions

1. Place the stock in a saucepan and bring to a simmer. Remove from heat and add saffron. Set aside. Rub monkfish with ½ tablespoon olive oil and season with salt and pepper. Set aside.

2. Preheat the oven to 400 degrees. Heat the remaining oil in a 17-inch paella pan, placed over 2 burners if necessary, or divide between two pans. Add the onion and garlic and cook over low heat until soft. Add the chorizo and sauté briefly. Add the rice and stir to coat.

3. Add the stock and stir. Simmer 10 minutes. Check seasoning, adding salt and pepper if necessary. Stir in the peas and place strips of the peppers, alternating colors, around the pan like spokes on a wheel. Place the shrimp and monkfish around the pan; add the mussels, hinge-side down.

4. Place in the oven and bake until the shrimp and monkfish are cooked and the mussels have opened,

about 15 minutes. Discard any unopened mussels. Remove from the oven, cover loosely with foil and set aside 10 minutes. Scatter scallions on top and serve.

Yield: 8 servings

Time: 1¼ hours

Note: Do not attempt to make paella without the proper pan and the proper rice. The pan should be fairly shallow, with a flat bottom, sloping sides and two handles, and made of steel, not stainless and not thick. A skillet that is not nonstick or too heavy can be used instead of a fancy heavy-duty pan. The pan should be washed and dried, then coated lightly with vegetable oil before using. It will darken with use, but a coating of oil each time it's washed and dried will prevent rust. The rule of thumb when it comes to paella pans is that half the diameter equals approximately the number of servings. Burners on most home stoves can accommodate a pan no larger than 13 inches across; to make a larger quantity, divide the recipe and use two pans. As for the rice, it must be short grain. Spanish rices, labeled *bomba,* Calasparra or Valencia, are best, although Goya brand short grain and even Italian Arborio rice can be used. Depending on the other ingredients, you should calculate ⅓ to ½ cup of rice per person. Usually twice the quantity of liquid as rice is needed. But, again, do not attempt to make paella without the proper pan and the proper rice. Pans and rice are available at specialty food markets (see Sources, page 259).

Florence Fabricant

MARK BITTMAN'S GRILLED CHICKEN, JAPANESE STYLE

This sauce is slightly sweet but it will just cling, not burn, if the chicken is properly grilled. You may also use only chicken wings and serve them as an appetizer.

¼ cup soy sauce
2 tablespoons sake or white wine
2 tablespoons mirin (or use 1 tablespoon honey mixed with 1 tablespoon water)
3 scallions, trimmed and roughly chopped
1 tablespoon minced garlic
1 tablespoon minced fresh ginger
3 pounds chicken wings, thighs and/or drumsticks

1. Mix all the ingredients together in a large baking dish, casserole, or heavy plastic bag. Cover and refrigerate for at least 2 hours, or as long as overnight, turning occasionally.

2. Start a charcoal or wood fire or heat a gas grill. The fire should be moderately hot, part of the grill should be kept cooler than the rest, and the rack should be 4 to 6 inches from the heat source.

3. Place the chicken skin side up on the coolest area of the grill. When the fat has rendered a bit, turn the chicken over. After 20 minutes or so, move the chicken to the hottest part of the grill and cook until the meat is done and the skin is nicely browned.

Yield: 4 main-course servings

Time: 45 minutes, plus at least 2 hours' marinating

Mark Bittman

MARK BITTMAN'S GRILLED CHICKEN WITH MEDITERRANEAN FLAVORS

Mark Bittman considers this the model for grilled chicken recipes, a dish that seems perfect for outdoor eating.

> Salt and freshly ground black pepper
> 1 teaspoon fresh thyme leaves
> 1 teaspoon chopped fresh rosemary leaves
> ½ teaspoon chopped fresh lavender leaves, optional
> ¼ cup roughly chopped fresh flat-leaf parsley
> Extra virgin olive oil as needed
> 8 bay leaves
> 8 chicken thighs or drumsticks, or a combination
> 2 lemons, cut into wedges

1. Start a charcoal or wood fire or heat a gas grill. The fire should be only moderately hot, part of the grill should be kept cooler than the rest and the rack should be 4 to 6 inches from the heat source.

2. In a small bowl, combine the salt, pepper, thyme, rosemary, lavender and parsley. Add enough olive oil to make a paste. Loosen the skin of the chicken and slide a bay leaf between the skin and meat, then insert a portion of the herb mixture. Push the skin back onto the meat and sprinkle with salt and pepper.

3. Place the chicken skin side up on the coolest area of the grill. When the fat has rendered a bit, turn the chicken over. After 20 minutes or so, move the chicken to the hottest part of the grill, brush with a bit of olive oil and cook until the meat is done and the skin is nicely browned. Serve with lemon wedges. (The bay leaf is not edible.)

Yield: 4 servings

Time: 45 minutes

Mark Bittman

MARK BITTMAN'S GRILLED CHICKEN WITH CHIPOTLE SAUCE

The chicken is grilled with virtually no flavorings at all, then served with its dipping sauce, or with just a garnish of lime wedges and chopped cilantro.

> 2 tablespoons lard or neutral oil, like corn or canola, plus more for brushing chicken
> 1 medium white onion, peeled and chopped
> 2 dried chipotle chilies, or to taste
> 2 cups cored and chopped tomatoes
> 8 chicken thighs, legs or drumsticks
> 2 garlic cloves, cut in half
> Salt and pepper
> Chopped cilantro leaves, for garnish
> Lime wedges, for garnish

1. Start a charcoal or wood fire or preheat a gas grill; the fire should be moderately hot, part of the grill should be cooler than the rest and the rack should be 4 to 6 inches from the heat source.

2. Put lard or oil in a medium saucepan or skillet and turn the heat to medium. When hot, add the onion and cook, stirring occasionally, until it begins to brown, 5 to 10 minutes. Add the chilies, tomatoes and ½ cup water. Adjust the heat so the mixture simmers steadily but not violently. Cook about 15 minutes, stirring occasionally, or until the chilies are soft and the tomatoes break up. Taste and add more salt and pepper if necessary. When the chipotle sauce is ready, cool for a few minutes, then remove the stems from the chipotles, put the mixture in a blender and purée. (The sauce may be made up to a couple of days in advance.)

3. Meanwhile, rub the chicken with the cut side of the garlic cloves, brush on the oil and season to taste with salt and pepper.

4. Place the chicken skin side up on the coolest area of the grill. When the fat has rendered a bit, turn the chicken over. After 20 minutes or so, move the chicken to the hottest part of the grill. When the chicken is just about done, brush it with chipotle sauce on both sides, and cook just another minute or two. Serve, garnished with cilantro and lime wedges.

Yield: 4 servings

Time: 45 minutes

Mark Bittman

BARBECUED CHICKEN FOR A CROWD

Adapted from Alexander Smalls

For smaller gatherings you can reduce the ingredients proportionally.

5 cups white vinegar
1 tablespoon whole cloves, plus 2 teaspoons ground
Salt and freshly ground pepper
15 pounds chicken pieces
1/4 cup vegetable oil
3 cloves garlic, minced
3 cups ketchup
1 cup dark brown sugar, well packed
1/2 cup prepared mustard
1/4 cup Worcestershire sauce
Juice of 1 lemon
1 small onion, grated
1 tablespoon Tabasco sauce
3 teaspoons chili powder
1 teaspoon celery seeds

1. The night before serving, combine the vinegar with 10 cups water, the whole cloves, salt and pepper. Add the chicken and marinate, refrigerated, overnight.

2. To make the sauce, heat the oil in a large pan and sauté the garlic until golden. Add all the remaining ingredients and a dash of salt, and bring to a simmer, stirring constantly. Cook over medium-low heat for 45 minutes, stirring occasionally. Remove and cool. This sauce may be made ahead, refrigerated and reheated when ready to grill.

3. Forty-five minutes before cooking, light the charcoal fire.

4. Remove the chicken and discard the marinade. Cook the chicken over low heat for about 30 minutes, turning to cook evenly on each side. Brush the pieces with the sauce and cook 30 minutes more, basting and turning occasionally. Serve the chicken hot or at room temperature, with the remaining sauce on the side.

Yield: 20 servings

Time: 1 hour preparation time; grilling time: 1 hour; overnight refrigeration

Sara Rimer

RICHARD KRAUSE'S CRISP GRILLED CHICKEN WITH GRILLED TOMATO SAUCE

6 halves of chicken breasts, boned, with skin
    and wing joint
Juice of 1 lemon
3 cloves garlic, peeled and sliced thin
6 shallots, peeled and sliced thin
1/4 cup fresh flat-leaf parsley leaves
3 pounds ripe tomatoes
2/3 cup extra virgin olive oil
1/4 cup chopped fresh basil leaves
1 tablespoon chopped fresh marjoram or
    oregano
2 tablespoons balsamic vinegar
Salt and freshly ground pepper

1. Preheat the grill. Rub the chicken with the lemon juice. Slip the garlic, half the shallots, and half the parsley leaves under the skin of the chicken. Refrigerate until ready to cook.

2. Cut each tomato in half horizontally, and remove the cores. Brush the cut sides of the tomato halves with 2 tablespoons of the olive oil. Sear them on the grill (using a fine-screen grate so they do not fall through), turning them once, until the skins can be slipped off easily. Alternatively, they can be seared on top of the stove in a nonstick pan.

3. Coarsely chop the tomatoes, and combine them with the basil, marjoram and remaining shallots and parsley. Add the remaining oil and the vinegar, and season to taste with salt and pepper. Set aside at room temperature until ready to serve.

4. Grill the chicken, skin side down, over hot coals for about 8 minutes, or until the skin is crisp but not blackened. Turn and grill the other side for 4 to 6 minutes, until the chicken is cooked through. To serve, spread the tomato sauce on a platter or on individual plates, and place the grilled chicken, skin side up, on top.

Yield: 6 servings

Total time: 45 minutes

Florence Fabricant

JULIE SAHNI'S EASY TANDOORI CHICKEN

2 whole boneless, skinless chicken breasts, split

For the Marinade

1 1/2 cups plain yogurt
4 tablespoons lemon juice
8 medium cloves garlic, minced
1 (1/2-inch) piece fresh ginger, peeled and minced
2 tablespoons ground cumin
2 teaspoons ground coriander
1/2 teaspoon ground cardamom
1/4 teaspoon ground cloves
1 teaspoon cayenne pepper
1/2 teaspoon freshly ground black pepper
Kosher salt to taste
2 tablespoons vegetable oil

For the Garnish

2 medium tomatoes, thinly sliced
1 medium cucumber, thinly sliced
1 medium red onion, thinly sliced
1/2 small bunch fresh cilantro, leaves only
2 lemons, quartered

1. Prick holes in the chicken with the tines of a fork. In a large bowl, mix together the marinade ingredients. Add the chicken and marinate, covered, overnight in the refrigerator, turning occasionally.

2. Heat the grill. Remove the chicken from the marinade. Scrape off excess and reserve. Brush the grill with oil. Grill the chicken for 5 minutes. Turn and baste with the sauce. Continue to turn and baste, using as much sauce as desired, until the juices run clear when pricked with a knife, about 12 to 15 minutes.

3. Serve garnished with slices of tomato, cucumber, onion, cilantro sprigs and lemon.

Yield: 4 servings

Time: 1 hour, plus overnight marinating

Florence Fabricant

NIGELLA LAWSON'S BUTTERMILK ROAST CHICKEN

The chicken can marinate in a freezer bag in the refrigerator for up to two days, so there is something ready to pop into the oven without further preparation. Prepare double the recipe, and you'll have one bird for a quick, hot meal and the other to refrigerate and serve chilled a day or so later—plain, sliced in sandwiches, or as the base for a salad, such as Chicken Salad with Walnut Skordalia (see recipe, page 89). Nigella Lawson: "I sometimes use lemon juice and oil, along with some garlic and maybe a quartered onion, to marinate the chicken. But using buttermilk, instead, for the necessary acidic component, makes this chicken less Mediterranean and more down home. If you want to substitute maple syrup for the honey, you can. Although I try to remove excess buttermilk from the chicken before roasting it, I leave some on so that the chicken browns better, even turning barbecue-black in parts."

1 (4-pound) chicken
2 cups buttermilk
¼ cup, plus 2 tablespoons vegetable oil
2 cloves garlic, lightly crushed
1 tablespoon crushed black peppercorns
1 tablespoon Maldon or other sea salt
2 tablespoons fresh rosemary leaves, roughly chopped
1 tablespoon honey

1. Butterfly the chicken by placing it breast side down and using heavy-duty kitchen shears to cut along both sides of the backbone. Discard the backbone, turn the chicken over and open it like a book. Press gently to flatten it.

2. Place the chicken in a large freezer bag. Add the buttermilk, ¼ cup oil, garlic, peppercorns, salt, rosemary and honey. Seal the bag securely and refrigerate overnight or up to two days.

3. Preheat the oven to 400 degrees. Remove the chicken from the marinade and place on a rack so the excess can drip off. Line a roasting pan with foil and place the chicken in the pan. Drizzle with the remaining 2 tablespoons oil. Roast for 45 minutes, then reduce the heat to 325 degrees. Continue roasting until well browned and the juices run clear when the chicken is pierced where leg joins thigh, about another 20 minutes.

4. Place the chicken on a carving board and allow it to rest for 10 minutes before cutting it into serving pieces. Place a portion on each of four plates, and drizzle each serving with pan juices.

Yield: 4 servings

Time: 1 hour 30 minutes, plus overnight marinating

Nigella Lawson

SIMPLE SMOKE-ROASTED WHOLE CHICKEN

²/₃ cup mixed herbs: parsley, sage, rosemary
   and thyme or any combination, all
   roughly chopped
2 tablespoons minced garlic
3 tablespoons olive oil
1 teaspoon red pepper flakes
1 tablespoon kosher salt
1 tablespoon freshly ground black pepper
2 whole chickens, 3 to 3 ½ pounds each
Salt and freshly ground black pepper to taste

1. In a small bowl, combine the herbs, garlic, oil, pepper flakes, salt and pepper, and mix well. Starting at the tip of the breastbone, loosen the skin from the breasts of the chickens, being careful not to tear the skin. Gently rub the herb mixture under the skin. Rub the outside of the chickens with any remaining mixture and sprinkle with additional salt and pepper if desired.

2. In a covered grill, build a small fire to one side, making sure that all the wood or charcoal becomes engulfed in flames. When the flames die down, and you are left with flickering coals, place the chickens on the grill over the side without fire. It is important that the chickens do not come in contact with the flames at any time during cooking.

3. Cover the grill, vent slightly and cook, checking the fire every 20 minutes or so and adding a bit more fuel as necessary to keep the fire going, for about 2 hours. Check the chickens for doneness by piercing a thigh with a fork. When the juices run clear, the birds are done.

Yield: 6 servings

Total time: 2 hours 15 minutes

John Willoughby and Chris Schlesinger

MAKE-AHEAD, TANDOORI-STYLE BAKED CHICKEN

A fiery jalapeño and ginger-spiked yogurt marinade gives life to this version of tandoori chicken, which is best served the day after it is prepared. Because the flavor is so intense, the chicken doesn't need additional sauces or other condiments and can be transported easily to a picnic.

½ cup plain yogurt
¼ cup fresh cilantro leaves
2 tablespoons freshly squeezed lime juice
1 tablespoon ground cumin
1 teaspoon kosher salt
1 teaspoon ground coriander
½ teaspoon freshly ground black pepper
¼ teaspoon ground cardamom
⅛ teaspoon cayenne pepper
1 small onion, peeled and cut into chunks
1 jalapeño pepper, stemmed, and seeded if
   desired
1 (1-inch) piece ginger, peeled and sliced
   into coins
2 garlic cloves, peeled
4 pounds skinless chicken drumsticks and
   thighs, rinsed and patted dry
Vegetable oil, for brushing
Lime wedges, for garnish

1. For the marinade: Combine all the ingredients except for the chicken, oil and lime wedges in a food processor and purée until smooth.

2. With a sharp knife, make several incisions on each chicken piece to help the marinade penetrate the meat. Transfer the chicken to a large glass or ceramic baking dish and pour in the marinade, turning the chicken pieces to coat. Cover the dish with plastic wrap and transfer to the refrigerator for at least 4 hours or overnight.

3. Preheat the oven to 450 degrees. Remove the chicken pieces from the marinade. Transfer the chicken to a roasting pan and drizzle with vegetable oil. Roast, basting occasionally, until the juices run clear and the meat is just cooked through, about 25 minutes. Let cool completely, then wrap and refrigerate, preferably overnight. Bring to room temperature for at least 1 hour before serving. Serve with lime wedges.

Yield: 6 servings

Time: 50 minutes, plus 4 to 12 hours' marinating, plus 1 hour to bring to room temperature

Melissa Clark

JIMBOJEAN'S JERK CHICKEN

A Jamaican marinade but also a method of barbecuing—preferably outdoors in an oil-drum grill—jerk is a bit of fire laced with spice, a sauce of chilies, thyme and the vaunted "secret ingredient." The marinade is used to infuse chicken, but there's always goat, should you have one around the house, or pork, lamb or fish. It's the sauce that matters.

3 medium cloves garlic, chopped
2 bunches scallions, chopped
1 medium white onion, chopped
1 green, yellow, or red Scotch bonnet pepper, stemmed and chopped (with seeds)
3 tablespoons fresh thyme, chopped, or 1 tablespoon dried thyme
1 tablespoon ground allspice
10 whole cloves
1 tablespoon molasses
1 tablespoon white or cider vinegar
1 teaspoon salt
Pinch of Accent, optional
1 (5-pound) chicken, quartered
½ cup beer

½ cup ketchup
Oil, for greasing the rack

1. Blend the garlic, scallions, onions, pepper, thyme, allspice, cloves, molasses, vinegar, salt and Accent, if using, in a food processor until smooth.

2. Place the chicken in a glass baking dish. Coat with marinade over and under the skin. Cover and marinate in the refrigerator at least 4 hours but preferably overnight, turning the pieces occasionally.

3. Remove and discard the marinade from under the chicken's skin. Pour the remaining juices and marinade from the baking dish into a bowl. Add the beer and ketchup; mix.

4. Cut the chicken quarters at the joints to make 8 pieces. Brush with the basting sauce and place skin side down on a hot, oiled grill rack or skin side up on an oiled rack in a broiler pan lined with heavy-duty foil. Cook until the skin is crisp and the meat is cooked through, 30 to 40 minutes, turning and basting every 10 minutes.

Yield: 6 servings

Time: 30 minutes' preparation, 40 minutes' cooking, plus 4 hours' marination

Dulcie Leimbach

GRILLED DUCK BREASTS WITH NECTARINE—GREEN GRAPE CHUTNEY

1 tablespoon olive oil

1 large red onion, peeled and finely diced

3 nectarines, pitted and diced

1 cup green grapes, halved

1 cup cider vinegar

½ cup brown sugar, packed

Pinch of ground allspice

Pinch of ground mace

1 tablespoon roughly chopped fresh basil

Salt and freshly ground black pepper

4 duck breasts (8 to 10 ounces each)

1. In a medium sauté pan, heat the oil over medium heat until hot but not smoking. Add the onion and sauté, stirring occasionally, until transparent, 5 to 7 minutes. Add the nectarines and grapes, and cook, stirring, until the nectarines are a bit browned, about 4 minutes. Add the vinegar, sugar, allspice, mace, basil and salt and pepper to taste. Bring the mixture just to a boil, reduce the heat to low and simmer 10 minutes. Remove from heat and set aside.

2. Meanwhile, build a small fire in one side of a grill, using enough coals to fill a shoe box. Salt and pepper the duck breasts well and place them on the grill, with the fat side down, along the edge of the fire. Cook them for 6 minutes, being careful of flare-ups caused by fat dripping into the fire. If flare-ups do occur, move the breasts so that they are not directly over the flames. You want them to cook slowly, allowing the fat to drip off at an even pace and giving the skin time to crisp. Flip the breasts over and cook 5 to 7 minutes more. When the duck breasts are nicely browned and as firm to the touch as the heel of your hand, they are medium rare.

3. Pull the duck breasts off the fire, allow to cool for about 4 minutes, then slice them thinly on the bias and serve with the reserved chutney.

Yield: 4 servings

Time: 40 minutes

John Willoughby and Chris Schlesinger

GRILL-ROASTED WHOLE CORNISH HENS WITH ORANGE, OREGANO AND CUMIN

2 oranges, unpeeled, cut in ½-inch slices

2 onions, peeled, halved and cut into thick slices

2 tablespoons olive oil

Salt and freshly ground black pepper

4 Cornish game hens (about 1¼ to 1½ pounds each)

½ cup chopped fresh oregano

¼ cup minced garlic

½ cup toasted cumin seeds (or ¼ cup ground cumin)

1. Build a fire in half of a covered grill, using enough charcoal to fill a shoe box. The fire is ready for cooking when the flames have died down and you are left with flickering coals.

2. In a small bowl, combine the oranges, onions, oil, salt and pepper and mix well. Stuff the cavity of each bird with ¼ of this mixture.

3. In a small bowl, combine the oregano and garlic; mix well. With your fingers, loosen the skin from the breasts of the birds, starting at the tip of the breastbone and being careful not to tear the skin. Gently rub the oregano and garlic mixture under the skin, pushing it down as far as you can. Sprinkle the outside of the hens with cumin seeds and salt and pepper.

4. When the fire is ready, place the hens on the side of the grill with no fire; do not allow the hens to come in contact with flames at any time. Cover the grill, and vent slightly. Cook for 45 minutes to 1 hour, checking the fire every 15 minutes or so, adding fuel, if necessary, to keep the fire going. The birds are done when the thigh is pierced at the thickest part and the juices run clear. Remove from the grill, discard the stuffing and serve.

Yield: 4 servings

Time: 1½ hours, including 45 to 60 minutes on a grill

John Willoughby and Chris Schlesinger

STEVEN RAICHLEN'S BRINED TURKEY, SMOKED OUTDOORS

Adapted from *BBQ USA* by Steven Raichlen

Steven Raichlen: "Smoking produces a bird of incomparable succulence, especially when combined with another traditional American barbecue technique, brining. Given turkey's tendency to dry out, this is no small attraction. The brining keeps the bird moist; the mild smoky heat makes it exceptionally tender and flavorful. Then there's the simplicity of the method: once you put the bird in the smoker or on the grill, you pretty much leave it there until it is done. If you have an outdoor smoker, follow the manufacturer's instructions. A charcoal grill with a high lid also produces a magnificent smoked turkey. You can cook a turkey on a gas grill, but it is hard to achieve a pronounced smoke flavor, even on one with a smoker box and a dedicated burner. If you want to make a smoked turkey outdoors, I suggest you invest in an inexpensive charcoal grill. Smoking with charcoal involves indirect grilling. It's simple enough: You rake the lighted coals into two mounds at opposite sides of the grill, placing an aluminum foil drip pan in the center. When it is time to cook the bird, place it in the center of the grate over the drip pan and toss a handful of soaked hardwood chips on each mound of coals. In many parts of the country the traditional wood for smoking is hickory, but I'm partial to the lighter, milder flavor of fruitwoods like apple or cherry. Look for wood chips at a barbecue-supply store or specialty food stores. Remember to soak them in water, apple cider or beer for at least an hour beforehand. Soaking allows the chips to smolder rather than burn, generating fragrant clouds of flavorful wood smoke."

1 (10- to 12-pound) turkey, brined
    (recipe follows)
2 tablespoons melted unsalted butter

1. Set up an outdoor grill for indirect grilling, placing a large foil drip pan in the center. (If using a smoker, light and set it up according to the manufacturer's instructions and heat to 275 degrees.)

2. Drain the bird. Blot dry inside and out and truss if desired. Place in the center of the grill grate, over the drip pan and between mounds of natural lump charcoal. Toss ½ cup of soaked wood chips on each mound of coals. Place the lid on the grill. Adjust the vents to keep the temperature between 325 and 350 degrees.

3. Grill the turkey until darkly browned and cooked through, 2½ to 3 hours. Baste the turkey with melted butter after the first hour and every hour thereafter. If the skin starts to brown too much, loosely tent the bird with foil. Use an instant-read thermometer to test for doneness; the turkey is ready when the internal temperature of the thigh is 180 degrees. Replenish the charcoal every hour, adding 8 to 10 lumps of charcoal to each mound of coals and leaving the grill uncovered for a few minutes to allow the charcoal to light. After 1 hour, add 1½ cups of soaked wood chips.

4. Transfer the turkey to a platter, loosely tent with foil and let rest for 10 minutes before carving. Reserve any drippings in the drip pan for gravy.

Yield: 10 to 12 servings

Time: 2½ to 3 hours after turkey is brined

Steven Raichlen

BRINED TURKEY

Adapted from *BBQ USA*

> 1¼ cups salt
> 1¼ cups sugar
> 2 bay leaves
> 1 medium onion, peeled and halved
> 2 whole cloves
> 1 (10- to 12-pound) turkey, washed,
>   giblets removed

1. Place the salt, sugar and 1 quart of hot water in a large deep pot and whisk until salt and sugar crystals dissolve. Whisk in 4 quarts of cold water. Pin the bay leaves to the onion halves with the cloves and add them to the brine. Let the mixture cool to room temperature.

2. Add the turkey, placing a large heavy pot or sealed Ziploc bag filled with cold water on top to keep the bird submerged. Place the pot in the refrigerator and marinate overnight.

Yield: Enough brine for a 12-pound turkey

Time: 15 minutes, plus overnight marinating

Steven Raichlen

NIGELLA LAWSON'S SUMMER-BRINED ROAST TURKEY

Nigella Lawson: "My summer, brined turkey is the best way to cook the bird for the warmer months. The glorious thing about brining is that it has the effect of keeping meat moist while infusing it with flavor. Best of all, the shopping list is light: besides water, salt and sugar, all you need are some bay leaves, peppercorns, wine vinegar, honey, mustard seeds, a little allspice (but much less than I would use at Thanksgiving), onion, garlic, and celery. You find a large pan, stick the turkey in it and cover it with the brine. If it is difficult to fit the pan into the refrigerator for a day, there is always that glorious American standby, a cooler filled with ice. And this, really, is the main work of the weekend. Because brining makes the bird fabulously moist, you do not have to bother with the usual fandango of cooking the turkey for most of the time breastside down and then hoisting it around, right side up, to brown for 30 to 40 minutes at the end.

> 1 (14-pound to 15-pound) turkey, giblets
>   discarded, rinsed
> 1 cup sea salt
> 1 cup light brown sugar, packed
> ½ cup honey
> ½ cup white wine vinegar
> 4 bay leaves
> 2 tablespoons Worcestershire sauce
> 2 tablespoons yellow mustard seeds
> 1 tablespoon allspice berries
> 2 tablespoons black peppercorns
> 2 onions, peeled and quartered
> 3 to 4 celery stalks
> 2 cloves garlic, peeled and lightly smashed
> Oil for roasting pan

1. Place the turkey in a large, deep pot that will hold it snugly. In a pitcher of water, combine the salt,

Nigella Lawson's Summer-Brined Roast Turkey

sugar, and honey. Stir until dissolved, and pour over turkey. Add the vinegar, bay leaves, Worcestershire sauce, mustard seeds, allspice berries and peppercorns. Add the onions, celery, garlic and enough water to cover the turkey. Leave in a cool place overnight.

2. Heat the oven to 400 degrees. Lightly oil the bottom of the roasting pan. Remove the turkey from the brine, and place it in the pan. Roast, uncovered, for 30 minutes, then reduce the oven temperature to 350 degrees and roast for 2½ hours.

3. Allow the turkey to rest out of the oven for 15 minutes before carving. If desired, reheat the pan juices, and spoon over the meat.

Yield: 8 to 10 servings

Time: About 3½ hours, plus overnight marinating

Nigella Lawson

CRAIG CLAIBORNE'S MISSISSIPPI-STYLE FRIED CHICKEN

Craig Claiborne's recipe for the fried chicken of his southern childhood.

2 (2- to 2½-pound) chickens, cut into serving pieces
2 cups milk, approximately
¾ teaspoon Tabasco sauce
1½ cups flour
Salt, if desired
1 tablespoon freshly ground pepper
2 cups lard or corn oil for frying
½ cup butter

1. Put the chicken pieces in a mixing bowl and add enough milk to cover. Stir in the Tabasco and refrigerate for at least 1 hour, or overnight.

2. Combine the flour, salt and pepper in a flat baking dish or, preferably, in a large, heavy paper bag or strong plastic bag. Drain the chicken pieces, but don't pat them dry. Put them in the dish or the paper or plastic bag with the flour. Turn the pieces or shake to coat them thoroughly.

3. Heat the lard or oil with the butter in a heavy skillet, preferably cast-iron, large enough to hold half of the chicken pieces in one layer so they don't touch. Add half of the chicken pieces, skin side down, in one layer. Turn the heat to high and cook uncovered until golden brown.

4. Turn the pieces and reduce the heat to medium-low. Cook until golden brown. The total cooking time should be 20 to 25 minutes. Remove the cooked pieces of chicken and drain on paper towels. Repeat the process with the remaining chicken. Serve immediately or the following day.

Yield: 6 servings

Time: 60 minutes, plus refrigeration for at least 1 hour

Craig Claiborne

MARK BITTMAN'S RICE KRISPIES CHICKEN

Adapted from *How to Cook Everything*

Mark Bittman's refinement of the classic 1950s Rice Krispies chicken is the ultimate version of shake-and-bake. By soaking the chicken in an acidic, spicy marinade for a while, then turning it in crumbs of Rice Krispies (or corn flakes, which are sold precrushed) both flavor and crispness are assured. A drizzle of melted butter just before cooking improves the coating enormously and gives the chicken pretty good staying potential.

> 4 garlic cloves, peeled and minced
> 1 small onion, peeled and sliced
> 1 teaspoon dried oregano
> 1 tablespoon ground cumin
> ¼ cup fresh orange juice
> ¼ cup fresh lime juice (or use all orange juice)
> 1 good chicken, cut into serving pieces, or use 8 to 10 leg pieces (drumsticks and thighs), trimmed of excess fat

Opposite:
Mark Bittman's Rice Krispies Chicken

> 4 tablespoons melted butter
> 2 cups Rice Krispies, lightly crushed, or corn-flake crumbs

1. In a large bowl, combine the garlic, onion, oregano, cumin and juices. Add the chicken and toss; let it sit while you heat the oven, or marinate it, refrigerated, for up to a day.

2. Heat the oven to 425 degrees. Spread half the butter on a 9- × 12-inch baking dish. Put the Rice Krispies or corn flakes on a plate and roll the chicken in them, patting to help the crumbs adhere. Carefully transfer to the baking dish.

3. Drizzle the chicken with the remaining butter and bake, rotating the pan so the pieces brown evenly, until they are browned and cooked through, 30 to 40 minutes. Serve hot.

Yield: 4 servings

Time: 60 minutes, plus optional marinating for up to 1 day

Mark Bittman

NIGELLA LAWSON'S MAPLE CHICKEN 'N' RIBS

Nigella Lawson: "Chicken and ribs work well in conjunction: the relatively lean chicken is enhanced in taste and texture by the pork ribs, which give off flavorsome fat as they roast. You can use whatever ribs you like; meaty ones are best, but as long as the ribs are separated, rather than in a slab, they'll do just fine. As for the chicken, I implore you to use thighs, bone in, skin on instead of breasts, because darker meat holds up much better to this kind of roasting. If you like, add a fiery sprinkling of dried red pepper flakes to the marinade, too (or replace the vegetable oil with chili oil). A baked potato, plonked on a side plate with sour cream flecked with chives (butter for the youngsters) to dollop inside it, is the perfect accompaniment. Otherwise, you could serve a green salad and some good country bread."

   1 cup apple cider or juice, as sharp as possible
   ¼ cup maple syrup
   2 tablespoons vegetable oil
   2 tablespoons soy sauce
   2 star anise
   1 cinnamon stick
   6 unpeeled garlic cloves
   ½ teaspoon red pepper flakes, optional
   8 pork spareribs
   6 chicken thighs with skin and bone

1. In a pitcher or mixing bowl whisk together the apple cider, maple syrup, vegetable oil and soy sauce. Add the star anise, cinnamon stick, garlic and red pepper flakes.

2. In a large freezer bag or bowl combine the pork and chicken. Pour in the apple cider mixture, and seal the bag or cover the bowl. Refrigerate overnight or up to 2 days.

3. Remove the marinated mixture from the refrigerator, and heat the oven to 400 degrees. Pour the contents of the bag or bowl (including the liquid) into a large roasting pan. Turn the chicken pieces skin side up.

4. Roast until the chicken is opaque throughout and the ribs are tender, about 1¼ hours; 35 to 40 minutes into roasting turn the ribs over, but leave the chicken skin side up. Serve hot.

Yield: 4 to 6 servings

Time: 1 hour 30 minutes, plus up to 2 days' marinating

Nigella Lawson

RAO'S CHICKEN SCARPARIELLO

Adapted from *Rao's Cookbook*

   1½ cups vegetable oil
   2 (2½-pound) chickens, rinsed, patted dry,
       spines removed and each cut into 12 pieces
   4 links Italian sausage (2 hot and 2 sweet),
       in the casings, cut into 1-inch pieces
   2 large bell peppers (red, yellow or green),
       seeded and cut into thin strips
   2 jalapeño peppers, seeded and cut into thin
       rounds
   1 large sweet onion, cut in half lengthwise
       and sliced
   1 teaspoon minced garlic
   6 to 8 hot vinegared cherry peppers,
       left whole
   2 to 3 small potatoes, peeled, boiled and
       sliced (optional)
   ½ cup chicken broth
   ½ cup dry white wine
   ½ cup red wine vinegar
   1 tablespoon dried oregano leaves
   Salt and pepper to taste

1. Heat the oil in a Dutch oven over medium-high heat. In batches, brown the chicken, about 5 minutes on each side. Remove the chicken and drain on paper towels. Add the sausage and sauté until brown. Remove with a slotted spoon and drain. In the same pan, sauté the bell peppers, jalapeños, onion and garlic until soft and beginning to brown, about 5 minutes. Remove and drain.

2. Pour the oil from the pan. Return the sausage, chicken and vegetables to the pan. Add the cherry peppers, potatoes, chicken broth, wine, vinegar, oregano, salt and pepper. Cover and simmer until the chicken is cooked through, about 10 minutes. Uncover and continue cooking until the sauce has reduced slightly, about 10 minutes.

Yield: 6 servings

Time: 1 hour 15 minutes; refrigerate overnight after cooking, if desired

Note: This is even better if prepared a day ahead. Prepare until the chicken has cooked through, then let cool and refrigerate. Reheat, covered, until heated through. Uncover and continue simmering until the sauce is reduced slightly.

Jason Epstein

ZUNI CAFÉ'S ROASTED FILLET OF BEEF WITH BLACK PEPPER

Adapted from Judy Rodgers

This is a showcase dinner party or buffet entrée that should be marinated in a refrigerator for one to two days before cooking. Since it is best served at room temperature, you can make it several hours in advance. Judy Rodgers: "If you want a sauce, some fresh, chunky salsa will do. Sometimes I make a horseradish sauce with fresh grated horseradish, mascarpone, cream and black pepper. But mostly I like to let the meat stand on its own. And I think it's more delicious tepid than hot. It's great for summer, with a big tomato salad. And any leftovers are fabulous for sandwiches."

1 whole fillet of beef (about 5 1/2 pounds)
1 tablespoon fine sea salt, approximately
1 tablespoon crushed black peppercorns
2 tablespoons extra virgin olive oil

1. Trim the meat, removing excess fat and silver skin. Cut off about 4 inches of the narrow end, about 1 pound, and reserve for another use.

2. Place the fillet on a large sheet of parchment paper. Dust all over with salt, using 3/4 teaspoon salt to a pound of meat. Roll in the peppercorns. Tie with butcher's string at 2-inch intervals. Wrap the meat loosely in parchment, and refrigerate at least 24 hours and up to 48 hours.

3. Remove the fillet from the refrigerator an hour before cooking. Rub it all over with oil. Preheat the oven to 400 degrees. Sear the fillet on all sides in a heavy roasting pan over two burners, under a broiler or on a grill. Or cut in half and sear in two pieces in a large, heavy skillet.

4. Place the meat in the oven in the roasting pan. Roast 15 minutes. Test with an instant-read meat thermometer: if the thickest part registers about 105 degrees, the meat will be very rare when finished. For medium rare, roast 20 to 25 minutes, until the thermometer registers 115 degrees. For medium, roast longer, to 125 degrees. At these temperatures, the meat will be slightly undercooked, but will continue to cook after it is removed from the oven. Place the meat on a cutting board.

5. If serving immediately, allow it to rest 15 minutes. Remove the string, cut the meat in 1/2-inch-thick slices, arrange on a platter and serve.

6. If serving later, allow the meat to rest to room temperature or refrigerate and bring to room temperature before serving time.

Yield: 10 to 12 servings

Time: 2 hours, plus refrigeration for 1 to 2 days

Florence Fabricant

THAI STEAK WITH CORIANDER PESTO

Adapted from Nongkran Daks, Thai Basil, Chantilly, VA.

5 coriander roots
4 cloves garlic
2 teaspoons whole peppercorns
4 teaspoons neutral oil
2 tablespoons fish sauce
2 tablespoons soy sauce
2 pounds flank steak, scored on both sides in diamond pattern on the diagonal

1. Wash the coriander roots thoroughly. Combine in a blender with the garlic, peppercorns and oil, and process to make a thin paste. Add the fish sauce and soy sauce.

2. Spoon into a bowl large enough to hold the steak and rub the paste on both sides of the meat. Refrigerate, covered, and allow to marinate for at least 4 hours or overnight.

3. Cook on a hot grill 3 to 4 minutes on each side for medium rare; or heat a pan over medium-high heat on the stove until hot, pour in a tablespoon of oil and brown meat 3 to 4 minutes on each side for medium rare. Slice thinly on the diagonal. Serve immediately or at room temperature.

Yield: 6 to 8 servings

Time: 20 minutes, plus marinating at least 4 hours

Molly O'Neill

GRILLED MARINATED TENDERLOIN

2 bay leaves
1 onion, thinly sliced
2 cloves garlic, peeled
2 tablespoons black pepper, plus additional pepper for seasoning to taste
¼ cup fresh thyme, or 2 tablespoons dried
6 sage leaves, or 1 teaspoon dried
¼ cup dry red wine
2 tablespoons olive oil
1 beef tenderloin (about 4 pounds) cleaned so that all fat and membrane is removed, and the center cut (chateaubriand) is separated from the tips
Salt

1. In a large bowl, combine the bay leaves, onion, garlic, 2 tablespoons black pepper, thyme, sage, red wine and olive oil. Add all the pieces of meat and marinate for at least 1 hour or in the refrigerator overnight, turning occasionally.

2. Prepare the grill.

3. Remove the beef from the marinade and pat dry. Discard marinade. Season each piece very well with salt and black pepper and grill about 20 minutes for rare, or to desired doneness.

Yield: 8 servings

Time: Preparation time: 15 minutes, plus at least 1 hour for marinating; cooking time: 20 to 30 minutes

Molly O'Neill

MARK BITTMAN'S GRILLED ROAST BEEF

Mark Bittman: "One of the greatest crowd-pleasers, assuming the crowd has plenty of carnivores, is the standing rib roast. Unless you choose a super-lean cut, the internal meat will be fatty enough to self-baste; it will not dry out easily. Thus it can be cooked unadorned, without liquid, in a dry oven or in the outdoor equivalent, over indirect heat on a grill. A grill using wood or hardwood charcoal is ideal, but briquettes or even gas will do. With these last two options, soaked wood chips over the flames will add an intense grilled flavor. All that matters is that the internal heat of the grill reaches 450 to 600 degrees when it is covered (easily achieved with half the burners on in a gas grill, or with a moderately hot charcoal fire) and that the meat not be cooked beyond 125 degrees. An instant-read thermometer guarantees success. After grilling a number of roasts, I recommend salt, pepper and perhaps a suspicion of garlic as a perfectly fine seasoning. You can go in other directions—curry or chili powder, or your favorite spice rub—but to my taste anything else detracts from the roast's stark and wonderful meatiness. To save time, buy a roast of sirloin strip, also known as New York sirloin. This is a piece usually cut for familiar steak, but in this case left whole. A 3- to 4-pound piece will cook in less than an hour."

1 (5- to 7-pound) standing rib roast, prime meat preferably, or choice
Salt and freshly ground black pepper
1 clove garlic

1. Prepare a grill for indirect cooking. If gas, turn only one side on, or just the front or back burner, depending on the grill's configuration. Placing an aluminum tray of soaked wood chips over the flames to impart a wood flavor to meat is optional. If grilling over wood or charcoal, build a fire on one side of the grill only.

2. Sprinkle the meat liberally with salt and pepper. Cut the garlic clove and rub it all over the meat. If you want intense garlic flavor, cut slivers of garlic and use a sharp, thin-bladed knife to insert them into the meat.

3. Place the roast directly on the cool side of the grill and cover. Monitor the meat's temperature and keep the fire alive, checking every 30 minutes or so. The target internal temperature for the meat is just over 120 degrees for rare, 125 degrees for medium-rare (the meat's temperature will climb about 5 degrees after you take it off the grill). A 5-pound roast will be done in under 2 hours; a 7-pounder in just over 2 hours. Let the meat rest before slicing and serving.

Yield: 6 servings

Time: 2 to 2½ hours

Note: For faster grilled roast beef, start with a boneless sirloin roast (3 to 4 pounds). Proceed as above; cooking time will be about 45 minutes.

Mark Bittman

BARBECUED SPARERIBS WITH BEER AND HONEY

Adapted from *The Best of Craig Claiborne*

Overnight marinating is the secret of the intense flavor of these ribs, which can be grilled over charcoal or broiled indoors.

8 pounds spareribs, cut into serving pieces
3 cups beer
1 cup honey
1½ teaspoons dry mustard
2 teaspoons chili powder
2 teaspoons sage
1 tablespoon salt
2 tablespoons fresh lemon juice

1. Place the ribs in a large shallow pan. Mix the remaining ingredients and pour over the ribs. Let stand in the refrigerator 24 hours, turning at least once.

2. If charcoal broiling, prepare the grill.

3. Remove the ribs from the marinade. Reserve the liquid. Place flat on the rack of a medium-hot charcoal grill. You can also prepare these on a gas grill, heated to medium, and cook them indirectly by turning off the burner directly below the ribs. Use high direct heat for the last few minutes to crisp the ribs. To cook in a broiler, place the ribs about 4 inches from the heat. Broil, turning frequently and brushing with the marinade, until brown, about 1 hour and 15 minutes, or bake in a preheated 350-degree oven about 1½ hours, or till the ribs are brown and glazed, basting frequently.

Yield: 8 servings

Time: 10 minutes' preparation, overnight marinating and 1½ hours' cooking

BARBECUED SPARERIBS CANTONESE STYLE

Although not authentically Chinese, the mixture of honey, ketchup and soy sauce gives the ribs a dark, lacquerlike glaze. In an earlier version of this recipe in *The Times*, the ribs were first roasted for 55 minutes in an oven set at 350 degrees, then finished on the grill. This method lessens the possibility that they will char, spoiling the lacquered look. The choice is yours.

½ cup honey
½ cup soy sauce
2 cloves garlic, crushed
3 tablespoons ketchup
4 pounds pork spareribs, cut into serving pieces (see Note)

1. In a pan large enough to fit the ribs, combine the honey, soy sauce, garlic, ketchup and ½ cup water. Marinate the spareribs in this mixture in the refrigerator for several hours, turning a few times.

2. Preheat a gas or charcoal grill to low. Arrange the spareribs on a hinged grill basket and cook over a low flame, basting occasionally, for 1½ hours, or until the ribs are shiny brown and fork-tender. As the meat cooks, the basket should be turned frequently so that neither side gets charred.

Note: You may also cook the ribs in whole racks and separate them later.

Yield: 4 servings

Time: 10 minutes' preparation, several hours' marinating, 1½ hours on a grill

Amanda Hesser

ROBERT PEARSON'S FAMOUS BARBECUE SAUCES (MILD, MEDIUM AND HOT)

1 large Spanish onion, finely diced
4 cups water
14 ounces ketchup
10 ounces tomato purée
5 ounces Worcestershire sauce
2 tablespoons cider vinegar
5 ounces dry white wine
1 tablespoon brown sugar
1 tablespoon ground cumin
1 tablespoon ground coriander
1 tablespoon powdered garlic
Chilies, depending on degree of hotness (see Step 3)

1. Place the onion and water in a medium saucepan and bring to a boil. Boil for 2 minutes.

2. Add the remaining ingredients, except the chilies, and return to a boil. Reduce the heat and simmer for 10 minutes.

3. To make sauce of various degrees of hotness, continue as follows: Mild sauce: add 6 tablespoons ground ancho chili. Medium-hot sauce: add the ground ancho chili and 4 tablespoons ground New Mexican chilies. Hot sauce: add 4 tablespoons ground guajillo chilies and 2 cups of water. Very hot sauce: add 4 tablespoons of ground guajillo, 2 cups of water and 4 tablespoons ground arbol chili.

4. To finish the sauce, add the chilies (and water where indicated) and simmer 2 minutes longer, stirring often. Put the sauce in a blender or food processor and process for 4 minutes, until the mixture is completely smooth. (Refrigerate up to 2 weeks, if desired.)

Yield: Mild and medium-hot sauces make 8 cups; hot and very hot sauces make 10 cups

Time: 25 minutes

Marian Burros

BILL COLLINS'S BARBECUED LEG OF LAMB, GRILLED OR SMOKED

> 1 whole leg of spring lamb (about 5 pounds), or a boned and butterflied leg of lamb (about 4 pounds)
> 5 cloves garlic, peeled and cut in thin slivers
> ½ cup hearty dry red wine, such as zinfandel
> ½ cup red wine vinegar
> ¼ cup extra virgin olive oil
> 1 clove garlic, peeled and crushed
> 1 to 3 teaspoons salt
> ¼ teaspoon cayenne pepper

1. If you plan to smoke the lamb, use the whole leg. For grilling use a boned leg, butterflied.

2. Trim the excess fat from the lamb. Using a small knife, make narrow slits to a depth of about 1 inch in the meat and insert the slivers of garlic. Put the lamb in a dish.

3. Combine the remaining ingredients, pour over lamb and marinate it in the refrigerator 10 to 12 hours. Use the smaller amount of salt in the mari-

nade if the lamb is going to be grilled. The larger amount, 3 teaspoons, is necessary for smoking.

4. Remove the lamb from the refrigerator and allow it to come to room temperature. Remove the lamb from the marinade. To smoke the lamb, cook in a smoking pit using mesquite at 240 degrees for about 2½ hours. The butterflied lamb can be grilled over hot coals to the desired degree of doneness, about 30 minutes for medium rare.

Yield: 8 servings

Time: Preparation time: 15 minutes; Cooking, grilled or smoked time: 30 minutes if grilled, 2½ hours if smoked; Refrigeration time 10 to 12 hours

Florence Fabricant

TANDOORI-STYLE WHOLE LEG OF LAMB

> 1 boneless leg of lamb (about 4 to 5 pounds)
> Salt and freshly ground black pepper
> ¼ cup roughly chopped fresh cilantro
> ¼ cup minced ginger
> ¼ cup minced garlic
> ¼ cup ground cumin
> ¼ cup cayenne pepper
> 2 tablespoons ground coriander
> 2 tablespoons ground cardamom
> 1 tablespoon ground cinnamon
> 1 tablespoon ground cloves
> ¼ cup kosher salt
> ¼ cup olive oil
> ½ cup plain yogurt

1. Trim any excess fat from the lamb. With a mallet or heavy frying pan, pound the lamb at its thickest points until it is uniformly about 3 inches thick. Sprinkle with salt and pepper and set aside.

2. In a medium bowl combine the rest of the ingredients and mix well. Rub the lamb all over with

this mixture, place it in a roasting pan, cover it with plastic wrap and refrigerate for 1 to 3 hours.

3. When you are ready to cook, build a fire to one side of a covered grill, using enough coals to fill a shoe box. When the flames have died down and the coals are covered with gray ash, spread one-third of them on the empty side of the grill. Place the lamb on the grill directly over the coals and cook for about 15 minutes per side for medium rare. If the lamb begins to overcook on the exterior or if you have flare-ups while cooking, move the lamb to the cooler part of the fire and continue cooking.

4. When an instant-read meat thermometer placed in the center of the lamb registers 124 degrees, remove the meat from the grill, allow it to rest for about 15 minutes, slice thinly and serve.

Yield: 10 servings

Time: 50 minutes, plus 1 to 3 hours' marinating time

John Willoughby and Chris Schlesinger

PATRICK CLARK'S MUSTARD-BARBECUED LAMB CHOPS

5 cloves garlic, peeled and sliced
2 sprigs fresh rosemary
2 sprigs fresh thyme
1 tablespoon dried oregano
20 black peppercorns, cracked
½ cup olive oil
12 rib lamb chops, trimmed of fat
1 tablespoon canola oil
1 small red onion, peeled and diced
½ carrot, peeled and diced
2 cloves garlic, peeled and crushed
½ serrano chili, seeded

¼ cup red wine vinegar
½ cup ketchup
1½ tablespoons Dijon mustard
1 tablespoon honey

1. Combine the garlic, herbs, peppercorns and olive oil. Pour over the lamb and refrigerate overnight.

2. To make the sauce: heat the canola oil in a medium saucepan over medium-high heat. Add the onion, carrot and garlic and sauté until softened, about 3 minutes. Add the chili and vinegar and stir 1 minute. Add the ketchup, mustard and honey. Turn the heat to low and simmer 25 minutes. Let cool slightly and purée in a blender. Strain. Thin with a little water, if needed.

3. Start a charcoal grill. Wipe the marinade off the lamb and grill the meat until medium rare or to desired doneness. About a minute before the lamb is done, brush the lamb on both sides with the sauce. Serve with additional sauce.

Yield: 4 servings

Time: 50 minutes' preparation, overnight marinating, grilling to taste

Molly O'Neill

SYRIAN BEEF KEBABS

Adapted from Lisa Ades

2 pounds fatty ground beef, such as chuck
4 tablespoons tomato paste
⅔ cup minced onion
2 teaspoons salt
Juice of 1 lemon
½ teaspoon ground cinnamon
2 dashes cayenne pepper
1 tablespoon ground allspice
⅓ cup pine nuts
Oil, for brushing on the grill rack

Continued

Lemon wedges and pita bread, for serving
Lemony Cucumber Salad, for serving
(recipe follows)

1. Combine all the ingredients except the oil,
lemon wedges, pita and salad in a bowl and knead
very well into a paste.

2. Hold a flat metal skewer—not nonstick, and at
least 12 inches long—point up in one hand. Dip
your other hand in a bowl of water, take a handful of the meat mixture and form it around the
base of the skewer in a small sausage shape with
pointed ends. Repeat, working your way up the
skewer. Each skewer should hold 3 or 4 kebabs.
(You can also just form the meat into 8 patties.)

3. Lay the finished skewers on a sheet pan, and
smooth the kebabs with your fingers, making sure
they are fairly smooth and secured on skewers.
Refrigerate at least 1 hour.

4. Prepare a charcoal grill, or turn a gas grill to
medium-low. Spray or brush oil on the clean grill
rack, and set within a few inches of the fire. The
fire should not be too hot, and the rack should be
at least several inches from the heat source.

5. When the rack is heated through, gently squeeze
the kebabs to be sure they are secure on the skewers, and place the skewers on the grill. The meat
should start sizzling gently; it should not spit and
turn black. Cook undisturbed until deep brown, at
least 7 minutes. When the meat lifts easily from
the grill, slide a spatula under the kebabs and turn
them over. Continue grilling until browned on
both sides and juicy, but cooked through, 10 to 15
minutes total. Serve hot with lemon wedges, and
pita that has been warmed on the grill. Put a few
spoonfuls of Lemony Cucumber Salad in each pita
with the meat.

Yield: 4 to 6 servings (8 skewers)

Time: 30 minutes, plus 1 hour for chilling

Julia Moskin

LEMONY CUCUMBER SALAD

6 cups romaine lettuce (about 2 hearts)
1 seedless hothouse cucumber or 3 Kirbys,
   peeled, halved lengthwise and sliced
   ¼-inch thick crosswise
3 tablespoons olive oil
2 teaspoons lemon juice
Salt and freshly ground black pepper to taste

Toss all ingredients together. Serve chilled.

Yield: 4 to 6 servings

Time: 5 minutes

Julia Moskin

VIETNAMESE PORK KEBABS

Adapted from Corinne Trang

2 pounds fatty ground pork, such as shoulder
3 stalks lemongrass, tender white and pale
   green parts only, minced
4 shallots, minced
2 garlic cloves, minced
1 tablespoon fish sauce
2 teaspoons sugar
1 teaspoon ground turmeric
1 teaspoon freshly ground black pepper
Oil, for brushing on the grill rack
Whole lettuce leaves, fresh mint and cilantro
   sprigs, for serving
Nuoc cham, for serving (recipe follows)

1. Combine all the ingredients except the oil, lettuce leaves, herbs and naoc cham in a bowl, and
knead very well into a paste.

2. Hold a flat metal skewer—not nonstick, and at
least 12 inches long—point up in one hand. Dip

Opposite:
Vietnamese Pork Kebabs

your other hand in a bowl of water, take a handful of the meat mixture and form it around the base of the skewer in a small sausage shape with pointed ends. Repeat, working your way up the skewer. Each skewer should hold 3 or 4 kebabs. (You can also just form the meat into 8 patties.)

3. Lay the finished skewers on a sheet pan, and smooth the kebabs with your fingers, making sure they are fairly smooth and secured on the skewers. Refrigerate at least 1 hour.

4. Prepare a charcoal grill, or turn a gas grill to medium-low. Spray or brush oil on the clean grill rack, and set within a few inches of the fire. The fire should not be too hot, and the rack should be at least several inches from the heat source.

5. When the rack is heated through, gently squeeze the kebabs to be sure they are secure on the skewers, and place the skewers on the grill. The meat should start sizzling gently; it should not spit and turn black. Cook undisturbed until deep brown, at least 7 minutes. When the meat lifts easily from the grill, slide a spatula under the kebabs and turn them over. Continue grilling until browned on both sides and juicy, but cooked through, 10 to 15 minutes total. To serve, wrap a kebab in a lettuce leaf with herbs, then dip in Nuoc Cham.

Yield: 4 to 6 servings (8 skewers)

Time: 30 minutes, plus at least 1 hour chilling

➤ NUOC CHAM

> 1 serrano chili, thinly sliced
> 1 garlic clove, thinly sliced
> 3 tablespoons sugar
> 2/3 cup warm water
> 1 tablespoon fresh lime juice
> 1 tablespoon rice wine vinegar
> 5 tablespoons fish sauce

Chop the chili, garlic and sugar together until fine. Transfer to a bowl. Add the remaining ingredients. Set aside for 10 minutes before serving.

Yield: 1 cup

Time: 15 minutes

Julia Moskin

ADANA LAMB KEBABS

Adapted from *Classical Turkish Cooking*

> 2 pounds ground lamb
> 1 onion, minced
> 1/2 cup minced fresh flat-leaf parsley
> 1/4 cup minced red bell pepper
> 1 teaspoon paprika
> 2 teaspoons Aleppo pepper, or 1 teaspoon red pepper flakes
> 2 garlic cloves, minced
> 1 tablespoon whole coriander seeds, lightly crushed
> 2 teaspoons salt
> Oil, for brushing on the grill rack
> Lemon wedges and pita bread, for serving
> Cucumber Yogurt-Mint Salad, for serving (recipe follows)

1. Combine all the ingredients except the oil, lemon wedges, pita and salad in a bowl and knead very well into a paste.

2. Hold a flat metal skewer—not nonstick, and at least 12 inches long—point up in one hand. Dip your other hand in a bowl of water, take a handful of the meat mixture and form it around the base of a skewer in a small sausage shape with pointed ends. Repeat, working your way up the skewer. Each skewer should hold 3 or 4 kebabs. (You can also just form the meat into 8 patties.)

3. Lay the finished skewers on a sheet pan, and smooth the kebabs with your fingers, making sure they are fairly smooth and secured on the skewers. Refrigerate at least 1 hour.

4. Prepare a charcoal grill, or turn a gas grill to medium-low. Spray or brush oil on the clean grill rack, and set within a few inches of the fire. The fire should not be too hot, and the rack should be at least several inches from the heat source.

5. When the rack is heated through, gently squeeze the kebabs to be sure they are secure on the skewers, and place the skewers on the grill. The meat should start sizzling gently; it should not spit and turn black. Cook undisturbed until deep brown, at least 7 minutes. When the meat lifts easily from the grill, slide a spatula under the kebabs and turn them over. Continue grilling until browned on both sides and juicy, but cooked through, 10 to 15 minutes total. Serve hot with lemon wedges, and pita that has been warmed on the grill. Put a few spoonfuls of Cucumber Yogurt-Mint Salad in each pita with the meat.

Yield: 4 to 6 servings (8 skewers)

Time: 30 minutes, plus 1 hour for chilling

Julia Moskin

➤ CUCUMBER YOGURT-MINT SALAD

Adapted from *Classical Turkish Cooking*

> 2 cups whole-milk yogurt, preferably Greek (see Note)
> 1 teaspoon minced garlic
> 2 tablespoons olive oil
> ½ teaspoon salt
> 1 seedless, hothouse cucumber, peeled, halved lengthwise and sliced ¼-inch thick, crosswise
> 12 mint leaves, cut in thin ribbons, plus extra whole leaves for garnish

In a bowl, mix the yogurt, garlic, oil and salt together until smooth. Chill until ready to serve. Just before serving, mix in the cucumber and sliced mint. Add salt to taste, if necessary. Garnish with mint leaves and serve.

Yield: 4 to 6 servings

Time: 5 minutes

Note: Whole-milk yogurt is preferred; otherwise, the dressing will be watery.

Julia Moskin

BEEF SKEWERS WITH GARLIC-THYME MOJO

Adapted from Sonora, New York City

> ⅓ cup extra virgin olive oil
> 2 large garlic cloves, chopped
> 1 canned chipotle chile, puréed, or 1 dried chipotle chili, soaked in hot water, drained and minced
> 1 cup chopped fresh cilantro leaves
> 1 tablespoon soy sauce
> 1 teaspoon honey

Continued

2 pounds boneless sirloin steak, 1 inch thick
1 teaspoon chopped fresh oregano
2 teaspoons chopped fresh thyme leaves
½ cup chicken stock
Juice of 1 lime
Salt and freshly ground black pepper
1 tablespoon cold unsalted butter

1. Soak 16 wooden skewers. Preheat a grill.

2. Heat the oil in a heavy saucepan. Reserve 1 teaspoon garlic; add the rest to the oil, and cook, stirring, until golden. Add the chipotle purée, ¾ cup cilantro, soy sauce and honey. Simmer 3 minutes. Remove from heat, transfer to a medium-large bowl and let cool.

3. Trim the steak of all fat. Cut in strips ½ inch thick and 3 inches long. Add to the bowl and mix to coat. Marinate 15 minutes.

4. Combine the remaining garlic with the oregano, thyme, stock and lime juice in a small saucepan and simmer 5 minutes. Add the remaining cilantro. Season with salt and pepper. Remove from the heat.

5. Weave the steak strips onto skewers. Grill about 3 minutes on each side, to the desired degree of doneness. Arrange on a platter. Whisk the butter into the sauce, serve with the steak.

Yield: 16 skewers

Time: 45 minutes

Florence Fabricant

CURRIED MUSTARD PORK

Adapted from *Cooking for the Weekend*

The flavor of the curried mustard becomes more piquant as the meat cools and rests. It can be served as the centerpiece of a dinner buffet. Leftover meat is versatile: wrapped in flour tortillas and garnished with a tomatilla salsa, or finely chopped and added to potato salad, or sliced thin and layered on bread with mustard mayonnaise or used as a cold topping for pita bread, hot from the oven or grill.

½ cup Dijon mustard
¾ teaspoon curry powder
Freshly ground pepper to taste
2 (2½-pound) boned and rolled pork loins
2 bunches fresh spinach, wilted

1. Stir together the mustard, curry powder and pepper. Rub the mixture all over the pork loins, and let stand until the pork comes to room temperature.

2. Preheat the oven to 350 degrees. Put the pork loins in a large roasting pan, and roast until they reach an internal temperature of 160 degrees, about 1 hour 10 minutes. Let stand 10 minutes. Remove the string.

3. Cut slices off one loin, and put the slices and the remaining loin on a platter. Surround the platter with wilted spinach, and serve, cutting more slices as needed or allowing guests to cut their own.

Yield: 8 servings, plus leftovers

Time: 1 hour 20 minutes, plus standing time

Molly O'Neill

WOOD-GRILLED VEAL CHOPS WITH MARIO BATALI'S LEMON-OREGANO JAM

4 veal chops, 1-inch thick and about
    12 ounces each
3 tablespoons extra virgin olive oil
Coarse sea salt and freshly ground
    black pepper
1 lemon, halved and seeded
2 tablespoons chopped fresh
    oregano

1. Rub the chops with olive oil, and season them generously with salt and pepper. Place the chops in a baking dish, and squeeze lemon juice over them. Sprinkle the chopped oregano on both sides, turning the chops several times. Marinate for 15 minutes, while you build the fire.

2. Light the grill, and rake out the embers into a three-zone fire or a single zone with an ember-free safety zone. (In a gas grill, place wood chips in the smoker box or pouch, and preheat them until you can see smoke.)

3. Grill the chops over a hot fire until they are cooked to taste, rotating the chops 90 degrees after 3 minutes to get an attractive crosshatching of grill marks.

4. Transfer the chops to plates, and let them rest for 3 minutes. Serve them with Lemon-Oregano Jam (recipe follows) on the side.

Yield: 4 servings

Time: About 30 minutes, depending on degree of doneness

Steven Raichlen

➤ MARIO BATALI'S LEMON-OREGANO JAM

Adapted from Zach Allen

> 2 large lemons (preferably with thin rinds), washed, each cut into 8 pieces and seeded
> ¼ cup sugar
> 1½ teaspoons salt
> ½ teaspoon freshly ground black pepper
> 2 tablespoons extra virgin olive oil
> 3 packed tablespoons stemmed fresh oregano leaves

To make the jam: Place the lemon pieces, sugar, salt and pepper in a food processor, and process to a coarse purée. With the processor running, add the olive oil in a thin stream, and emulsify to a honeylike consistency. Just before serving, work in the oregano. Adjust the seasoning. (If there is extra jam, it will keep in the refrigerator for up to a week).

Yield: ½ cup

Time: 5 minutes

VEAL MILANESE

Adapted from Baldoria, New York City

> 3 eggs
> 2 tablespoons finely grated Parmesan cheese
> 1½ tablespoons chopped fresh parsley
> Salt
> Freshly ground black pepper
> 1 cup flour
> 1 to 2 cups fine bread crumbs, made with stale not toasted, country bread, crusts on
> 4 large handfuls arugula, rinsed and dried if necessary
> 2 small or 1 large very ripe tomatoes, roughly chopped
> ½ small red onion, very thinly sliced
> Extra virgin olive oil
> Juice of 1 lemon
> 4 veal chops with bones, pounded very thin, almost transparent (no thicker than a piecrust)
> Corn oil
> 1 lemon, cut into wedges, for serving

1. In a small bowl, whisk together the eggs, cheese and parsley. Season generously with salt and pepper. Pour into a large, shallow bowl or tray. Spread the flour in a second shallow bowl and the bread crumbs in a third. Set aside near the stove.

2. In a large mixing bowl, combine the arugula, tomatoes and onion. Sprinkle with olive oil and lemon juice. Season with salt, and toss until the leaves are coated. The dressing should be assertive and lemony. Set aside.

3. Working one at a time, press each veal chop into the flour on each side, then pat it off so that there is just a fine dust on the veal. Dip the chop into the egg, coating both sides, and letting as much drain off as possible. Lay the chop in the bread crumbs, tapping it gently to make sure it gets coated, but ever so thinly. Flip it over, and coat the other side.

Layer the chops between waxed paper or parchment as you go.

4. Preheat the oven to 175 degrees, and place a baking sheet on the middle rack. Place a sauté pan large enough to fit 2 chops over medium-high heat. Pour in enough corn oil to generously cover the base of the pan. When the oil shimmers (it should be very hot so the veal sizzles immediately), add a chop and sauté until browned, 2 to 3 minutes. Turn and brown the other side. Transfer to a baking sheet, and keep warm in the oven. Repeat with the other chops.

5. To serve, place the chops on each of four large plates. Place a large handful of salad on top of each, making sure each gets enough tomatoes and onion. Serve with a wedge of lemon, for squeezing over the meat.

Yield: 4 servings

Time: 20 minutes

Amanda Hesser

PIERRE HERMÉ'S BITTERSWEET CHOCOLATE SORBET

Adapted from *Desserts by Pierre Hermé*

Easy, intensely rich and elegant.

> **7 ounces good-quality bittersweet chocolate**
> **1 scant cup sugar**

1. Fill a large bowl, at least 4 to 5 quarts, with ice cubes. Have a 1- to 1½-quart metal bowl ready.

2. Place the chocolate, sugar and 2 cups water in a heavy 2-quart saucepan over low heat. Cook, stirring frequently, until the mixture reaches a boil (this can take 10 minutes or more). Keep stirring while the mixture bubbles furiously for 2 minutes, then pour it into the smaller bowl.

3. Set the small bowl into the large bowl, and add cold water to the ice cubes, taking care that no water gets into the chocolate mixture. Allow the mixture to cool, stirring from time to time; then, refrigerate until very cold.

4. Freeze in an ice cream maker, according to the manufacturer's instructions. Serve at once, or pack into a container and place in the freezer for up to 1 week.

Yield: 1 pint

Time: 25 minutes' preparation, plus cooling, refrigeration and freezing

Florence Fabricant

GIANT CHOCOLATE SHORTBREAD COOKIE

A giant chocolate cookie with a touch of Grand Marnier, which can be made ahead. You can eat it plain or dress it up with ice cream or slices of slightly sweetened fresh peaches that have been treated to a splash of Grand Marnier, if desired.

> **9 tablespoons unsalted butter, at room temperature, plus butter for greasing the pan**
> **1⅓ cups unbleached, all-purpose flour, plus flour for dusting the pan**
> **2 ounces slivered almonds**
> **3 ounces semisweet chocolate, broken into pieces**
> **½ cup sugar**
> **Salt to taste**
> **2 tablespoons Grand Marnier**

1. Preheat the oven to 325 degrees. Butter and flour a 12-inch tart pan with a removable bottom.

2. Place the almonds in a food processor or blender and chop finely. Remove and set aside. Add the chocolate and sugar to the processor and chop coarsely (or chop the chocolate with a knife and mix with the sugar).

3. Combine the almonds with the chocolate. Add the flour and salt and process briefly. Add the butter and process until the mixture resembles a coarse meal. (You may do this entire step by hand in a mixing bowl using a fork.) Add the Grand Marnier and combine until the mixture becomes crumbly.

4. Using your fingertips, spread the mixture evenly into the prepared pan. Do not press down. Bake for 30 to 40 minutes until lightly browned. Remove from the oven and cool on a rack. Unmold just before serving and cut into eight wedges.

Yield: 8 servings

Time: 1 hour, including 30 to 40 minutes' baking, plus cooling

Nancy Harmon Jenkins

AZO FAMILY'S FUDGY CHOCOLATE CAKE

Adapted from Loretta Keller, Coco500 in San Francisco

This mouthwatering cake takes about 25 minutes to bake and even less time to put together. After the batter bakes in a very hot oven, the pan is cooled a bit, then wrapped in foil and placed in the refrigerator. Ms. Keller believes the recipe may have developed when a cook feared the oven was too hot and the cake was cooking too fast, and tried to save it by putting it in the refrigerator. The result: a cake that serves 8 to 10 people, with a delightfully fudgy center.

8½ ounces (2 sticks plus 1 tablespoon) unsalted butter, plus more for greasing pan

7 ounces bittersweet chocolate (50 percent or higher cocoa), chopped
5 large eggs, separated
1 cup sugar
½ cup all-purpose flour
Pinch of salt
Whipped cream for serving (optional)

1. Place the rack in the top third of the oven and heat to 400 degrees. (For best results, use a separate oven thermometer.) Butter a 9-inch springform pan and set it aside. In a double boiler or microwave oven, melt together the 8½ ounces of butter and the chocolate. Stir to blend.

2. In a medium bowl, stir together the egg yolks and sugar. Stir in the flour. Add the chocolate mixture and stir until smooth. Using an electric mixer, whisk the egg whites and salt until stiff but not dry. Fold the whites into the chocolate mixture just until blended. Pour into the cake pan.

3. Bake for 25 minutes. Remove the cake from the oven and allow to cool for 1 hour. Wrap the cake with foil and refrigerate until firm and cold, at least 2 hours. Two hours before serving, remove the cake from the refrigerator and bring to room temperature. Slice (the center of the cake will be fudgy) and serve, with whipped cream if desired.

Yield: 8 to 10 servings

Time: 40 minutes plus 3 hours for cooling

Kim Severson

BACK TO
THE CITY

Lee Bailey was, in many ways, the single-handed creator of the country weekend. With his many books, especially his indispensable *Country Weekends*, Bailey showed us all how to get away from the hot and hectic city to a cool, bucolic retreat, even if we were only doing so in our armchair in front of an air conditioner with his beautiful book open before us. Bailey was a master of elegantly easy entertaining. He championed simpler dishes, casually arranged bouquets of flowers and table settings that spoke the word *ease* with every linen napkin. We learned how to relax with our guests on summer weekends by reading his books and visiting his elegant boutique in the original Henri Bendel store on Fifty-seventh Street, and now we owe him a debt of gratitude for the many lessons we learned. We felt that there was no more fitting way to end our book than with Lee stretched out in his hammock, offering us a classic French dish and waving good-bye until he sees us next time.

FAREWELL FARE

By Lee Bailey

As I plan food to serve on Sunday, I always try to come up with combinations that can be cooked, at least partly, in advance—preferably the day before. Experience has taught me that Sunday is the day with the greatest potential for missed schedules and changed plans. Gloomy weather can send everyone scurrying back to the city. Or a glorious day can cause guests to linger long beyond when they had expected to depart. And, of course, it is likely that they won't all leave at the same hour.

If you have a houseful, the greater the odds of upset on all scores. So you can see the wisdom of being ready to get something on the table in a hurry when necessary, and still have leftovers that will keep for those who might be staying later. Then, too, if the schedule has been a busy one, there is the distinct chance that by Sunday I'll have had enough cooking for one weekend. It is a welcome relief to be able to serve the sort of meal that doesn't require much effort.

So one of my favorite Sunday menus is built around a dish called *rigodon,* which is related to the overworked quiche, but easier. It is better made the day before and is served with a green salad and toasted sliced brioche.

This kind of lunch lets guests leave for home as they choose. And it lets me wave good-bye from the hammock.

RIGODON

This custard dish originated in Burgundy. The ingredients make it related to quiche but it is easier to make because it doesn't require a crust. It also can utilize leftover meats, such as chicken, beef, lamb, or pork, and was, I imagine, conceived as a handy way to dress these up for another go-round.

Although this dish is a perfect way to use leftovers, I prefer it made with freshly baked chicken. Since this is very easy to do, try it that way first. If you are feeling thin and/or indulgent, you could use heavy cream and whole milk to make the dish more authentic, but I like evaporated skim milk and low-fat milk respectively, which make the dish less rich. Instead of the brioche top, coarse stale bread cubes could be substituted.

4 to 5 small chicken thighs or 1½ cups cooked chicken, cubed (see Note)

Continued

¼ teaspoon salt

¼ teaspoon freshly ground pepper

1¼ cups low-fat milk (see Note)

¾ cup evaporated milk (see Note)

1 slice bacon

1 scallion, chopped, including some of
    the green part

1 tablespoon unsalted butter

1 tablespoon chicken fat, reserved from
    cooking the chicken, or an additional
    tablespoon of unsalted butter

¾ cup cubed brioche or stale bread cubes

1½ tablespoons all-purpose flour

4 eggs, lightly beaten

1 tablespoon chopped fresh flat-leaf parsley

Few drops Tabasco sauce or pinch of cayenne
    pepper

½ cup cubed fresh mozzarella

1 tablespoon freshly grated Parmesan cheese

1. If preparing chicken for this dish, instead of using leftover chicken, preheat the oven to 375 degrees.

2. Place chicken thighs skin side up, in an 8- × 8-inch casserole. (They should fit snugly.) Season the thighs with salt and pepper. Bake for 35 minutes and turn off the oven. This step can be done the day before you plan to use the chicken thighs. When cool, skin the chicken and cut it into cubes. Set aside, reserving 1 tablespoon of chicken fat.

3. When ready to prepare the Rigodon, preheat the oven to 325 degrees.

4. In a small saucepan, bring the milk and cream to a boil. Turn off the heat and set aside.

5. In a skillet, sauté the bacon over medium-high heat until crisp. Drain, crumble, and set aside. Pour off the fat from the skillet and add the scallion. Cook until wilted. Add the butter and chicken fat to the skillet and melt. Add the brioche cubes and toss over medium heat. When the cubes start to turn golden, switch off the heat and set aside.

6. In a bowl, whisk together the flour and eggs until smooth. Mix in the chicken cubes, parsley, salt, pepper and Tabasco. Add the milk (or milk and cream) mixture, and mix again.

7. Pour the mixture into a greased 8- × 8-inch casserole. (You can use the casserole that the chicken thighs were baked in. Wipe out most of the chicken fat, leaving a thin layer to coat the bottom and sides.)

8. Sprinkle with the mozzarella cubes and the toasted brioche-scallion mixture, pressing them down lightly. Top with the Parmesan cheese and crumbled bacon. Bake until set and lightly browned, about 30 minutes. Let cool at least 1 hour before serving.

Yield: 4 to 6 servings

Time: 80 minutes, plus an additional 45 minutes if roasting the chicken

Note: You can substitute 1½ cups of leftover meats, such as beef, lamb or pork, for the chicken in this dish. Also, for a richer casserole, you can substitute equal amounts of whole milk for the low-fat milk and cream for the evaporated milk.

APPENDIX: RECIPE PLANNER

This chart is intended as a shortcut to planning menus that will accommodate your needs and schedule, especially on weekends when you are likely to want to be relaxing out of kitchen range, instead of working in front of one.

The first column gives you the page on which the recipe can be found. Scanning across the other columns, you will see, at a glance, helpful information about each recipe—details such as the estimated time for preparation and cooking—whether it can be made in advance, either partially or fully; if it requires a grill, broiler, oven, stove top or no heat at all; the number of people it will serve.

How to Use the Guide

One way to maximize your leisure time is to serve meals that can be prepared quickly. To identify those, look at **COLUMN 3**, which provides the total preparation and cooking time for each recipe. X denotes a dish that can be made in 30 minutes or less; XX is for dishes that require from 30 to 60 minutes and XXX is for recipes that will take more than an hour from start to serving. V indicates that the time may vary, depending on aspects of the recipe. Any recipe with either an X or XX in **COLUMN 3** and nothing in the adjoining **COLUMN 4** may be made and on the table in an hour or less.

If you prefer more ambitious cooking but still want plenty of time for other pursuits, the solution is to make dishes that can be prepared in stages. **COLUMN 4** will point you to recipes that call for steps not reflected in **COLUMN 3**—steps that require time, but not your active presence: marinating ingredients before final cooking, for example, or resting them afterward, to ripen the flavors.

A final time factor for many recipes is how long it might take to preheat an oven or broiler or to prepare a grill. No times are given for these steps, since they are often a function of equipment and materials. But **COLUMN 5** alerts you to those methods of preparation (using a G for grill, B for broiler, O for oven, S for stove top and N when no heat step is used), so that you can factor in the extra time required. A recipe that has more than one such designation may be prepared in more than one way.

The next two columns show the number of servings given for each recipe. **COLUMN 6** is for dishes that make from 1 to 7 portions. **COLUMN 7** shows dishes for larger groups, from 8 to 25. V indicates that the number of portions will vary depending, for example, on whether you plan to serve it as an appetizer or as a main course. Using your judgment, you can either increase or decrease the ingredients (and, proportionally the cooking times)

in many of the recipes, to accommodate the number of people you will be feeding.

Since weekends often mean guests, **COLUMN 8** highlights some, but by no means all, dishes to serve when company comes and/or that are particularly suitable for buffets or dinner parties or large, informal gatherings.

Example: if you are looking for company dishes that can be prepared partially in advance, set aside and grilled just before serving: you will find them in recipes with a notation in **COLUMN 4**; a G in **COLUMN 5**; and an X in **COLUMN 8**. (If you're planning a meal for up to 7 people, look at **COLUMN 6**; for larger gatherings, see **COLUMN 7** for recipes that serve 8 or more.)

HORS D'OEUVRES AND APPETIZERS

PAGE	PREPARATION & COOKING TIME X = under 30 min. XX = 30–60 min. XXX = over 1 hour V=time varies	OTHER TIME REQUIRED BEFORE AND AFTER COOKING (marinating, etc.)	METHOD G = Grill B = Broiler O = Oven S = Stove top N = No heat	SERVINGS 1 = 7–8 V = Varies	SERVINGS 8 or more V=Varies	COMPANY'S COMING
3	FRICO'S BEAN PURÉE WITH ROSEMARY AND LEMON	V	keeps 3 days	S or N		2 cups	X
3	RICOTTA WITH GARLICKY TOMATO-BASIL SPREAD	X		N		5 cups	X
4	LE BERNARDIN'S FRESH AND SMOKED SALMON SPREAD	X	up to 7½ hours	S		8–12	X
4	TUNA TAPENADE		X	N		1 cup	X
6	PIERRE FRANEY'S LEMONY CHICKPEA AND TUNA SPREAD	X		N		2 cups	X
5	NUEVA YORK CLAM DIP	X		S		2 cups	X
9	MUSHROOM CEVICHE	X	1 hour	N	6–8		X
6	BLUE SMOKE'S DEVILED EGGS	X	refrigerate	S	5–6		X
7	FIG AND ANCHOVY CROSTINI	X		N	6		X
9	SHRIMP WITH LIME PICKLE AND MINT	X		N		8	X
9	MARINATED WHITE ANCHOVIES WITH BASIL AND LEMON ZEST	X		N	6–8		X
9	TARAMOSALATA CANAPÉS	X		N		8	X
10	ROMAINE HEARTS AND ÉPOISSES OR CAMEMBERT	X		N	6–8		X
10	CHEESE BOARD OF AGED CANTAL AND YOUNG PECORINO	X		N		8	X
10	PROSCIUTTO-WRAPPED PEACHES	X		N		8	X
10	LA CARAVELLE'S CITRUS GRAVLAX	X	12–24 hours	N		12+	X
11	SMOKED TROUT CANAPÉS WITH LEMON-CHIVE SAUCE	X		N	V		X
11	SCANDINAVIAN SHRIMP	XX	1 day or more	S		10	X

Page	Recipe						
113	ALAN HARDING'S CHILLED CUCUMBER SOUP	X	2 hours or more	N	4–6		X
112	LITTLE SPRING SOUP	X	2 hours or more	S	4		X
116	CORN AND CILANTRO SOUP WITH TOMATO GARNISH	XX	cool	S	6		
111	COCO PAZZO'S PAPPA AL POMODORO	X		S	V		
111	CHILLED YELLOW TOMATO SOUP WITH BLACK OLIVE CREAM	XX	5 hours–2 days	S		8	X
112	LEMONGRASS VICHYSSOISE	X	several hours	S	6–7		X
113	CHILLED CURRIED ZUCCHINI SOUP WITH APPLE GARNISH	X	one hour or more	S	4		
39	COCONUT MILK SOUP WITH GINGER, LEMONGRASS AND BASIL	XX		S	4		X
39	OYSTER AND CORN CHOWDER	XX		S	4–6		X
79	JASPER WHITE'S OLD-FASHIONED NEW ENGLAND CLAM CHOWDER	XX	several hours	S	6–8		X
118	SQUASH AND APPLE SOUP	XXX	may be frozen	S and O		10 cups	X
118	HARVEST SOUP	XXX		S	4		X

FISH AND SEAFOOD

Page	Recipe						
55	BLUEFISH COOKED IN FOIL	X		G/O	2		
182	CHARRED STRIPED BASS NIÇOISE	X		G	4		X
190	WOOD-GRILLED BLACK SEA BASS WITH MINT VINAIGRETTE	XX		G	4		X
191	BLACK COD (SABLE) WITH MISO	X	24 hours	B	4		X
86	FLOUNDER IN SAOR	XX	cool	S	4		X
182	HALIBUT WITH INDIAN RUB AND CORN SALSA	X	3 hours	G	4		X
54	EASY SALMON WITH HOT-MUSTARD GLAZE	X		O	4		X
183	CRAIG CLAIBORNE'S "POACHED" BAKED SALMON	XXX		O		8–12	X
184	DILL AND CUCUMBER MAYONNAISE	X	30 minutes	N		3 cups	X
186	TANDOORI-SPICED SALMON WITH YOGURT-MANGO SAUCE	XX	3 hours	G	6		X

PAGE	Recipe	PREPARATION & COOKING TIME X = under 30 min. XX = 30–60 min. XXX = over 1 hour V=time varies	OTHER TIME REQUIRED BEFORE AND AFTER COOKING (marinating, etc.)	METHOD G = Grill B = Broiler O = Oven S = Stove top N = No heat	SERVINGS 1 = 7–8 V = Varies	SERVINGS 8 or more V=Varies	COMPANY'S COMING
186	RICK BAYLESS'S SKILLET-SEARED SNAPPER WITH TOASTED GARLIC, PRUNES AND PECANS	XX		S	4		X
198	MARIO BATALI'S SLOW-COOKED SWORDFISH	XX		O	4–6		X
56	GRILLED SWORDFISH WITH PESTO-LEMON-CAPER SAUCE	X		G	6		X
189	GRILLED TROUT WITH ZESTY CUCUMBER-TOMATO RELISH	X		G/B	4		
56	RAINBOW TROUT STUFFED WITH SPINACH, PINENUTS AND DILL	X		S	4		
86	GOTHAM BAR & GRILL'S TUNA BURGERS	XX		G	4		X
188	UNION SQUARE CAFÉ'S FILET MIGNON OF TUNA	X	3½ hours	G/B	4		X
188	TUNA STEAKS WITH RED-ONION COMPOTE	XX		G	4		X
188	RED ONION COMPOTE	XX		S		2 cups	X
194	OLD STONE FISH STEW	XX		S	6		
197	NEW ENGLAND CLAMBAKE, STOVE-TOP STYLE	XXX		S	6		X
194	ERIC RIPERT'S SOFT-SHELL CRABS WITH GARLIC VINAIGRETTE	X		S	2–4		X
191	EASTERN SHORE CRAB CAKES	X		S	6 cakes		
195	PEARL OYSTER BAR'S LOBSTER MIXED GRILL	XX (incl. Beurre Blanc)	½ hour or more	G		8	X
197	LEMON-CHIVE BEURRE BLANC	X		S	¾ cup		X
193	MUSSELS WITH WHITE WINE AND CURRY LEAVES	X		S	2		
55	STEVEN RAICHLEN'S ROSEMARY-GRILLED SCALLOPS	X		G	4–6		X
192	SHRIMP STEAMED IN BEER WITH DILL	X		S		30 shrimp	
192	SPICY GRILLED SHRIMP FOR A CROWD	X	overnight	G/B		20	X

Page	Recipe			S and O		X
199	ERIC RIPERT'S SEAFOOD PAELLA	XXX			8	X
82	CRAB AND CORN SALAD, SOUTHERN STYLE	XX	cool	S	20	X
82	RICK BAYLESS'S CRAB AND GREEN BEAN SALAD	X		S	4	X
81	ITALIAN LOBSTER SALAD (*INSALATA DI ASTICE*)	XX	2 hours or more	S	6	X
79	E.A.T.'S TARRAGON LOBSTER SALAD	X	1 hour refrigeration	N	6	X
80	LOBSTER OR CRAB SALAD ROLL	X		N	3 cups, 6 rolls	X
83	GERMAINE'S FESTIVE SCALLOP SALAD	X	overnight	N	12	X
83	COLD PASTA WITH PESTO AND BAY SCALLOPS	X	overnight–2 days	S	4	X
89	GIGI SALAD WITH SHRIMP AND GREEN BEANS	XX	1 hour	S	4	X
84	MOLLY O'NEILL'S NIÇOISE SALAD WITH OLIVE-OIL MARINATED TUNA	XX	6 hours–overnight	G/B	4	X
84	TOBY CECCHINI'S TUNA SALAD	X	*keeps for 3 days*	N	2 cups	X
84	TUNA PAN BAGNA	X	1 hour or more	N	1	

POULTRY

Page	Recipe			S and O		X
91	NIGELLA LAWSON'S ROAST CHICKEN SALAD WITH SPINACH AND AVOCADO	X		N	4	X
90	WARM CHICKEN SALAD WITH ORANGE-TARRAGON DRESSING	XX		S	4	
89	MARK BITTMAN'S CHICKEN SALAD WITH WALNUT SKORDALIA	X		N	4	X
92	GRILLED CHICKEN SALAD WITH WARM CURRY DRESSING	XX (incl. dressing)	optional	G/B	4	X
92	WARM CURRY DRESSING	X		S	1 cup	X
93	CHICKEN SALAD WITH GRAPES AND TOASTED NUTS	X		N	4–6	X
92	CHICKEN (OR TURKEY) TONNATO	XX	can be refrigerated	S	6	X
93	TONNATO SAUCE	X		N	2 cups	
206	NIGELLA LAWSON'S BUTTERMILK ROAST CHICKEN	XXX	overnight–2 days	O	4	X
94	ALICE'S CHINESE BARBECUED CHICKEN	V	several hours–overnight	G/O	4	

PAGE		PREPARATION & COOKING TIME X = under 30 min. XX = 30–60 min. XXX = over 1 hour V=time varies	OTHER TIME REQUIRED BEFORE AND AFTER COOKING (marinating, etc.)	METHOD G = Grill B = Broiler O = Oven S = Stove top N = No heat	SERVINGS 1 = 7–8 V = Varies	SERVINGS 8 or more V=Varies	COMPANY'S COMING
208	SIMPLE SMOKE-ROASTED WHOLE CHICKEN WITH HERBS	XXX		G	6		X
46	SPICY GINGER AND LEMON CHICKEN	XX		S	6		
208	MAKE-AHEAD, TANDOORI-STYLE BAKED CHICKEN	XX	4 hours–overnight	O	8		X
200	MARK BITTMAN'S GRILLED CHICKEN, JAPANESE STYLE	XX	2 hours–overnight	G	4		
203	MARK BITTMAN'S GRILLED CHICKEN WITH MEDITERRANEAN FLAVORS	XX		G	4		
203	MARK BITTMAN'S GRILLED CHICKEN WITH CHIPOTLE SAUCE	XX		G	4		X
205	JULIE SAHNI'S EASY TANDOORI CHICKEN	X	overnight	G	4		
205	RICHARD KRAUSE'S CRISP GRILLED CHICKEN WITH GRILLED TOMATO SAUCE	XX		G	6		
209	JIMBOJEAN'S JERK CHICKEN	XX	4 hours–overnight	G/B	6		X
214	CRAIG CLAIBORNE'S MISSISSIPPI-STYLE FRIED CHICKEN	XX	1 hour–overnight	S	6		X
215	MARK BITTMAN'S RICE KRISPIES CHICKEN	XX	optional	O	4		X
204	BARBECUED CHICKEN FOR A CROWD	XXX	overnight	G		20	X
216	RAO'S CHICKEN SCARPARIELLO	XXX	best served next day	O	6		X
47	CHICKEN TAGINE WITH CHICKPEAS AND RAISINS	XX		S	4		
235	LEE BAILEY'S RIGODON	V	V	O	4–6		X
210	GRILLED CORNISH HENS WITH OREGANO AND CUMIN	XXX		G	4		X
210	GRILLED DUCK BREAST WITH NECTARINE–GREEN GRAPE CHUTNEY	XX		G	4		X

Page	Recipe		Time		Serves	
212	NIGELLA LAWSON'S SUMMER-BRINED ROAST TURKEY	XXX	overnight	O	8–10	X
211	STEVEN RAICHLEN'S BRINED TURKEY, SMOKED OUTDOORS	XXX	overnight	G	10–12	X

MEAT

Page	Recipe		Time		Serves	
48	'21' CLUB HAMBURGER	X	1 hour	G	1	X
49	CRAIG CLAIBORNE'S PREFERRED HAMBURGERS	X		S	4	
96	GRILLED MARINATED FLANK STEAK	X	8–24 hours	G	25	X
50	GRILLED STEAK WITH HERB SALAD	X		G	4–8	X
51	SALSA VERDE	X		N	2 cups	X
53	JIM FOBEL'S RIB-EYE STEAKS WITH WATERCRESS	X		S	4	
53	DANIEL BOULUD'S HANGER STEAK WITH SHALLOTS	X		S	6	X
95	MUSTARD-AND-CHILI-RUBBED ROASTED BEEF TENDERLOIN	XX	serve next day	O	4–6	X
219	MARK BITTMAN'S GRILLED ROAST BEEF	XXX		G	6	X
217	ZUNI CAFÉ'S ROASTED FILLET OF BEEF WITH BLACK PEPPER	V	1–2 days	O	10–12	X
218	THAI STEAK WITH CORIANDER PESTO	X	4 hours–overnight	G	6–8	
218	GRILLED MARINATED TENDERLOIN	XX	1 hour–overnight	G	8	X
95	SPICY DRY-RUBBED TRIANGLE STEAK FOR SALADS AND SANDWICHES	XX	10 minutes	O	4–6	
227	BEEF SKEWERS WITH GARLIC-THYME MOJO	XX		G	4–6	
223	SYRIAN BEEF KEBABS	X	1+ hours	G	4–6	
224	LEMONY CUCUMBER SALAD	X		N	4–6	X
49	MIDDLE-EASTERN-STYLE LAMB BURGERS WITH DRIED FIG AND MINT RELISH	X		G/B	4	
50	DRIED FIG AND MINT RELISH	X		N	3/4 cup	X
97	GRILLED LAMB FILLET WITH TOMATO-ONION CHUTNEY	X		G/B	2	

PAGE		PREPARATION & COOKING TIME X = under 30 min. XX = 30–60 min. XXX = over 1 hour V=time varies	OTHER TIME REQUIRED BEFORE AND AFTER COOKING (marinating, etc.)	METHOD G = Grill B = Broiler O = Oven S = Stove top N = No heat	SERVINGS 1 = 7–8 V = Varies	SERVINGS 8 or more V=Varies	COMPANY'S COMING
97	TOMATO-ONION CHUTNEY	X	keeps 2 days	S	⅓ cup		X
223	PATRICK CLARK'S MUSTARD-BARBECUED LAMB CHOPS	V	overnight	G	4		X
97	GARLIC-AND-HERB-RUBBED BUTTERFLIED LEG OF LAMB	XX	2 hours or more	O		12–15	X
222	TANDOORI-STYLE WHOLE LEG OF LAMB	XX	1–3 hours	G		10	X
222	BILL COLLINS'S BARBECUED OR SMOKED LEG OF LAMB	V	10–12 hours	G		8	X
226	ADANA LAMB KEBABS	X	1 hour or more	G	4–6		
227	CUCUMBER YOGURT-MINT SALAD	X		N	4–6		
54	GRILLED DOUBLE-THICK PORK CHOPS WITH SOUTHERN FLAVORS	XX		G	4		X
228	CURRIED MUSTARD PORK	XXX		O		8	X
215	NIGELLA LAWSON'S MAPLE CHICKEN 'N' RIBS	XXX	overnight–2 days	O	4–6		
220	BARBECUED SPARERIBS WITH BEER AND HONEY	XXX	24 hours	G/B/O		8	X
221	BARBECUED SPARERIBS, CANTONESE STYLE	XXX	several hours	G	4		X
224	VIETNAMESE PORK KEBABS	X	1 hour or more	G	4–6		
226	NUOC CHAM	X		N	1 cup		
229	WOOD-GRILLED VEAL CHOPS WITH MARIO BATALI'S LEMON-OREGANO JAM	XX		G	4		X
230	MARIO BATALI'S LEMON-OREGANO JAM	X		N	1 cup		X
230	VEAL MILANESE	X		S	4		X

PASTA, PIZZA, RICE AND MORE

PAGE		PREPARATION & COOKING TIME (X = under 30 min. XX = 30–60 min. XXX = over 1 hour V = time varies)	OTHER TIME REQUIRED BEFORE AND AFTER COOKING (marinating, etc.)	METHOD (G = Grill B = Broiler O = Oven S = Stove top N = No heat)	SERVINGS 1 = 7–8 V = Varies	SERVINGS 8 or more V = Varies	COMPANY'S COMING
152	JACQUES PÉPIN'S RATATOUILLE	XXX	cooling time	S	6		X
151	ANNE WILLAN'S GRATIN OF SUMMER VEGETABLES IN HERB PESTO	XXX		O	4–6		X
43	PENNE WITH GARDEN VEGETABLES	XX		S	6		
42	MARK BITTMAN'S PASTA WITH CORN, ZUCCHINI AND TOMATOES	X		S	4		
40	JAMES BEARD'S PLEASANT PASTA WITH PEAS, PARMESAN AND PROSCIUTTO	X		S	4		
46	SESAME NOODLES WITH FRESH VEGETABLES (HOT OR COLD)	X	chilling time	S	4–6		
44	NIGELLA LAWSON'S SPAGHETTI WITH RAW TOMATO SAUCE	X	30 minutes to 8 hours	S	4		X
45	SPAGHETTI WITH SCALLOPS, LEMON AND BREAD CRUMBS	X		S	4		X
42	SPRING RISOTTO	XX		S	4		X
156	RICK BAYLESS'S RED CHILI RICE	XX		S	4		X
157	PIERRE FRANEY'S INDIAN RICE WITH SAFFRON AND GOLDEN RAISINS	X		S	4		X
116	NIGELLA LAWSON'S RISI E BISI	XX		S	4		
99–102	MARK BITTMAN'S PIZZA ON THE GRILL	V	1+ hours	G		1–3 pies	X
103–106	MARK BITTMAN'S TACOS	V	V	V	6–8		X
58	WILD MUSHROOM QUESADILLAS	XX		S		8	X
98	CHARLESTON GRILL'S BAKED GRITS WITH SUN-DRIED TOMATOES	XXX		O	4		X

SALADS

Page	Recipe		Time		Serves		
120	SESAME GREEN BEAN SALAD	X	up to several hours	S	V	V	
120	MOROCCAN-INSPIRED CARROT-CILANTRO SALAD	X	up to several hours	N	V	V	
120	CELERY, BLUE CHEESE AND TABASCO SALAD	X	up to several hours	N	V	V	
120	CUCUMBER AND TOMATO RAITA	X	up to several hours	N	V	V	
128	CARMINE'S CAESAR SALAD	X		O	6–8		X
57	ALICE WATERS'S BAKED GOAT CHEESE WITH LETTUCE SALAD	X		O	4–6		X
123	NIGELLA LAWSON'S BEET AND DANISH BLUE CHEESE SALAD	X	30 minutes–4 hours	N		10–12	X
132	FESTIVE COLESLAW	X	up to 4 days	N		25	X
130	ALICE WATERS'S SPICY COLESLAW	X	2 hours	N		8–12	X
134	FRESH CORN SALAD WITH TOMATOES AND DILL	XX	1–2 hours	S		25	X
124	NIGELLA LAWSON'S SWEET-AND-SOUR DILLED CUCUMBER SALAD	X	up to 4 hours	N		10–12	
224	LEMONY CUCUMBER SALAD	X		N	4–6		X
227	CUCUMBER YOGURT-MINT SALAD	X		N	4–6		
123	MUSHROOM SALAD WITH VINEGAR AND CORIANDER	X	3 hours or more	S	4		X
129	ITALIAN TOMATO-POTATO SALAD (INSALATA PANTESCA)	XX		S	6		X
130	SHARON TURNER'S POTATO SALAD WITH GREEN BEANS AND SHELLFISH	XX	cooling time	S		12–16	
130	HOPPIN' JOHN'S POTATO SALAD	XX	chilling time	S	6		
120	POTATO, PARSLEY AND CAPER SALAD	XX	cooling time	S	V	V	
87	CAPRESE-PLUS SALAD	X	refrigeration	N	6		
88	PEACH AND TOMATO SALAD WITH CURRY VINAIGRETTE	X		N	4		X
132	TOMATO AND PITA SALAD (FATTOUSH)	X		O	6–8		
120	CORN-BREAD PANZANELLA	X	up to several hours	N	V	V	
120	SHREDDED ZUCCHINI SALAD WITH PARMESAN	X	up to several hours	N	V	V	

PAGE	Recipe	PREPARATION & COOKING TIME X = under 30 min. XX = 30–60 min. XXX = over 1 hour V=time varies	OTHER TIME REQUIRED BEFORE AND AFTER COOKING (marinating, etc.)	METHOD G = Grill B = Broiler O = Oven S = Stove top N = No heat	SERVINGS 1 = 7–8 V = Varies	SERVINGS 8 or more V=Varies	COMPANY'S COMING
134	SUZANNE HART'S COLD RICE SALAD	XX	1–24 hours	S	4		X
135	MOLLY O'NEILL'S SUMMER VEGETABLE SALAD WITH ORZO	X	several hours	S	4		X
135	CLAUDIA RODEN'S BULGUR SALAD WITH POMEGRANATE DRESSING AND TOASTED NUTS	X	30 minutes–2 hours	N		8–10	X
136	FARM-STAND TABBOULEH	XX	30 minutes	N	6		X
136	COUSCOUS SALAD	XX	overnight	S		16	X
121	BLACK-EYED PEAS AND ARUGULA SALAD	XX	overnight	S		20	X
127	MEZZALUNA'S ARTICHOKE, FENNEL AND ARUGULA SALAD	X		N	4		X
121	PEA, ASPARAGUS AND ARUGULA CHOPPED SALAD	XX		S	4		X
57	FARFALLE, ARUGULA AND TOMATO SALAD	X	keeps 3 days	N	8		
137	MOJITO SALAD	X	2 hours–overnight	N		12	
127	ROZANNE GOLD'S WATERMELON AND FETA SALAD	X		N	6		X
127	APPLE, CRANBERRY AND GOAT CHEESE SALAD	X		O	4–6		X

BREAKFAST AND BRUNCH

PAGE	Recipe	PREPARATION & COOKING TIME	OTHER TIME REQUIRED	METHOD	SERVINGS 1 = 7–8	SERVINGS 8 or more	COMPANY'S COMING
61	HONEY-ORANGE SMOOTHIE	X		N	1		
61	PLANET PINEAPPLE SMOOTHIE	X		N	2		
61	POWER BERRY SMOOTHIE	X		N	2 cups		
61	GREEN TEA SMOOTHIE	X		N	2 cups		
73	BRASSERIE ORANGE FRENCH TOAST	X	5 hours–overnight	O	6		X

Page	Recipe						
70	DAVID EYRE'S FAMOUS PANCAKE	X		O	4–6		X
70	LEMON-RICOTTA HOTCAKES	X		S	20 small		X
71	MARION CUNNINGHAM'S HEAVENLY HOTS	X		S		50–60 small	X
69	ROSE LEVY BERANBAUM'S BUTTERMILK BLUEBERRY PANCAKES	X		S	18–24	18–24	X
74	BREAKFAST CRÊPES	X		S	6		
72	MOLLIE KATZEN'S AMAZING OVERNIGHT WAFFLES	X	overnight	waffle iron	4–8		X
65	NIGELLA LAWSON'S OVERNIGHT BACON-AND-EGG BAKE	XX	overnight	O	4–6		X
65	PIPERADE	XX		S	3–4		
64	CHORIZO SCRAMBLED EGGS	X		S	2		
40	FRITATTA OF SMOKED SALMON AND LEEKS	X		S	4–6		X
64	MIGAS EGGS À LA MIKE MARKS	X		S	6		X
62	CRAIG CLAIBORNE'S BASIC OMELET AND VARIATIONS	V		S	V		X
66	JULIA REED'S MOCK CHEESE SOUFFLÉ	XX	overnight	S/O	6		X
77	NIGELLA LAWSON'S RICOTTA CRUSTLESS TART	XX		O	4–6		X
77	NIGELLA LAWSON'S ROASTED CHERRY TOMATOES	XX	cooling time	O	4–6		X
62	CRAIG CLAIBORNE'S QUICHE LORRAINE AND VARIATIONS	V		O		6–10	X
77	LEEK, MUSHROOM AND GOAT CHEESE TART	XX		O		10–12	X
62	JIM DODGE'S SIMPLE BLUEBERRY MUFFINS	XX		S/O	V	V	X
67	HASH BROWN PATTIES	XX		O		12	X
68	BROILED MAPLE-GLAZED SAUSAGE	X		O		12	X

DESSERTS

Page	Recipe						
171	HOT BLUEBERRIES	X		S	6		
168	HUBERT KELLER'S FIGS AND BLUEBERRIES IN CITRUS BROTH	X		S	6		X
165	SUMMER BERRIES WITH RASPBERRY SAUCE	X	chill	S	4		X

PAGE		PREPARATION & COOKING TIME (X = under 30 min. XX = 30–60 min. XXX = over 1 hour V=time varies)	OTHER TIME REQUIRED BEFORE AND AFTER COOKING (marinating, etc.)	METHOD (G = Grill B = Broiler O = Oven S = Stove top N = No heat)	SERVINGS 1 = 7–8 V = Varies	SERVINGS 8 or more V=Varies	COMPANY'S COMING
158	OSTERIA DEL CIRCO'S WATERMELON SOUP WITH RED BERRIES	X	2 hours or more	N	6		
168	JAMES BEARD'S DRUNKEN MELON	X	2 hours	N		8 or more	X
169	FRENCH LAUNDRY'S VANILLA ROASTED FIGS WITH WILDFLOWER HONEY	X	overnight	O	6		
166	ALFRED PORTALE'S POACHED PEACH AND RASPBERRY COUPE	V	3 hours	O	6		X
158	TOM COLICCHIO'S ROASTED SUMMER FRUIT	X		S	4		
166	LE CIRQUE'S FRUIT SALAD IN VANILLA-MINT SYRUP	X	4 hours	S	4		
166	MIXED FRUITS À LA MARGARITA	X	4 hours	S	4–6		X
165	LONDON'S RIVER CAFÉ'S STRAWBERRY SORBET	X	freeze	N	V		X
164	FROZEN BANANA ICE CREAM	X	freeze	N	6		X
231	PIERRE HERMÉ'S BITTERSWEET CHOCOLATE SORBET	XX	freeze	S		1 pt	X
171	NIGELLA LAWSON'S JUMBLEBERRY GRUNT	X	2 hours or more	O		8	X
170	BING CHERRY CLAFOUTIS	XX		O	8	8	
161	MARK BITTMAN'S FREE-FORM FRUIT TART	XX		O		8	X
174	LARRY FORGIONE'S OLD-FASHIONED STRAWBERRY SHORTCAKE	XX	crust: up to 2 days	O		6	X
172	NIGELLA LAWSON'S SUMMER BERRY CREAM CAKE	XX		O		12	X
175	BLUEBERRY CRUMB CAKE	XXX		O		8–10	X
176	SARABETH'S LEMON ROULADE	XX	cool 1–2 hours	O		8–10	X
177	LEMON CREAM CUPCAKES (LEMON FILLED)	X	10 minutes	O		12	X
231	GIANT CHOCOLATE SHORTBREAD COOKIE	XX	cooling time	O		8	
232	AZO FAMILY FUDGY CHOCOLATE CAKE	XX	cooling time	S/O	8–10		X

PAGE		PREPARATION & COOKING TIME X = under 30 min. XX = 30–60 min. XXX = over 1 hour V=time varies	OTHER TIME REQUIRED BEFORE AND AFTER COOKING (marinating, etc.)	METHOD G = Grill B = Broiler O = Oven S = Stove top N = No heat	SERVINGS 1 = 7–8 V = Varies	SERVINGS 8 or more V=Varies	COMPANY'S COMING
BEVERAGES							
23	LA CARAVELLE'S KIR ROYALE 38	X		N	1		X
23	THE RED CAT'S FRAGOLA	X	2 hours	N	4		X
23	GIN AND TONIC BY THE PITCHER	X		N	4		X
24	VODKA OR GIN GIMLET	X		N	1		X
24	THE MARTINI	X		N	1		X
25	JAMES BOND MARTINI	X		N	1		X
25	SAKETINI	X		N	1		X
25	WATERMELON MARTINI	X		N	2		X
25	FLORIDIAN	X		N	2		X
24	HORSERADISH VODKA	X	1 day	N		700 milliliters	X
26	BLOODLESS MARY	X		N	1		X
26	COYOTE CAFE'S BLOODY MARIAS	X		N		12	X
26	JUNIPEROTIVO	X		N	1		X
27	'21' CLUB'S SOUTHSIDE	X		N	2		X
27	GRAMERCY TAVERN'S KAFFIR LIME COCKTAIL	X	3+ days	S		1½ liters	X
27	RAMOS GIN FIZZ	X		N	1		X
28	THE DAIQUIRI	X		N	1		X
28	POMEGRANATE DAIQUIRI	X		N	1		X
28	TEQUILA SUNRISE	X		N	1		X

Page	Recipe		Advance Prep		Serves	Yield	
28	MANGO MOJITO	X		N	1		X
29	CHERRY CAIPIRINHA	X		N	2		X
31	COFFEE SHOP'S CAIPIRINHA	X		N	1		X
31	COFFEE SHOP'S BATIDA	X		N	1		X
31	TI-PUNCH	X		N	2		X
32	THE CUKE	X	30 minutes	N	6		X
32	THE OLD-FASHIONED	X		N	1		X
33	FIVE-SPICE RUM	X	48 hours	N		750 milliliters	X
33	PEACH SAKE	X	24 hours	N		1 liter	X
33	DANIEL BOULUD'S FRUIT PUNCH	X	overnight	N		8–10	X
34	ICED TEA CONCENTRATE	X	30 minutes	S		4 quarts	X
34	QUICK ICED TEA	X		N		2 quarts	X
34	UNION SQUARE CAFÉ'S LEMONADE WITH LEMONGRASS	X	2+ hours	S		8–10	X
36	GINGER-BERRY LEMONADE	XX	2+ hours	S		12	X
36	WATERMELON-GAZPACHO COOLER	X	2 hours	N		6	X

RECIPE BYLINES

Karen Baar
Lee Bailey
Celia Barbour
Kathleen Beckett-Young
Mark Bittman
Dana Bowen
Janet Bukovinsky
Marian Burros
Robert Farrar Capon
Toby Cecchini
Craig Claiborne
Melissa Clark
Robert Clark
Tom Colicchio
David Colman
Rena Coyle
Erica De Mane
Maura Egan
Jason Epstein
Florence Fabricant
Pierre Franey
Howard Goldberg
William Grimes
Dorie Greenspan
Sam Gugino
Trish Hall
William L. Hamilton
Suzanne Hamlin

Amanda Hesser
Moira Hodgson
John Hyland
Christopher Idone
Nancy Harmon Jenkins
Thomas Keller
Dena Kleiman
Leslie Land
Denise Landis
Nigella Lawson
Matt Lee
Ted Lee
Dulcie Leimbach
Peter Meehan
Bryan Miller
Julia Moskin
Christine Muhlke
Joan Nathan
Molly O'Neill
Jacques Pépin
Julie Powell
Joanna Pruess
Madhu Puri
Julia Reed
Steven Raichlen
Kay Rentschler
Sara Rimer
Jill Santopietro

Chris Schlesinger
Regina Schrambling
Kim Severson
Rebecca Skloot
Alex Ward
Linda Wells
Alex Witchel
John Willoughby

BIBLIOGRAPHY

Algar, Alya. *Classical Turkish Cooking*. New York: HarperCollins, 1991

Bailey, Lee. *Country Weekends*. New York: Crown, 1993

Bittman, Mark. *The Best Recipes in the World*. New York: Broadway Books, 2005

Bittman, Mark. *How to Cook Everything*. New York: Wiley, 2006

Bittman, Mark. *The Minimalist Cooks Dinner*. New York: Broadway Books, 2001

Black, Adam. *A Can of Tuna*. Dorchester, UK: Prism Press, 1995

Boulud, Daniel, and Dorie Greenspan. *Café Boulud Cookbook*. New York: Scribner, 1999

Chattman, Lauren. *Cool Kitchen*. New York: William Morrow/HarperCollins, 1998

Chattman, Lauren. *Instant Gratification*. New York: William Morrow/HarperCollins, 2000

Claiborne, Craig, and Pierre Franey. *The Best of Craig Claiborne*. New York: Times Books, 1999

Cowan, Dana, and Kate Heddings. *Food & Wine Annual Cookbook 2004*. New York: American Express Publishing, 2004

Crichton, Jennifer. *Family Reunion*. New York: Workman, 1998

Cunningham, Marion. *The Fanny Farmer Cookbook*. New York: Alfred A. Knopf, 1996

Czarnicki, Jack. *Portobello Cookbook*. New York: Artisan Books, 1997

Dojny, Brooke. *The New England Clam Shack Cookbook*. North Adams, MA: Storey Publishing, 2003

Dodge, Jim, Elaine Ratner, Lauren Jarret. *Baking with Jim Dodge*. New York: Simon & Schuster, 1991

Forgione, Larry. *An American Place Cookbook*. New York: William Morrow/Harper Collins, 1996

Gold, Rozanne. *Recipes 1-2-3*. New York: Viking Books, 1996

Hermé, Pierre, and Dorie Greenspan. *Desserts by Pierre Hermé*. New York: Little, Brown, 1998

Hurt, Alison Becker. *Kitchen Suppers*. New York: Doubleday, 1999

Katzen, Mollie. *Mollie Katzen's Sunlight Café*. New York: Hyperion, 2002

Kendall, Sadie. *Crème Fraîche Cookbook*. New York: Ridgeview Publishing Co., 1989

Kennedy, Diana. *My Mexican Kitchen*. New York: Clarkson Potter, 2003

Killeen, Johanne. *Cucina Simpatica*. New York: HarperCollins, 1991

Kurlansky, Mark. *The Big Oyster*. New York: Ballantine Books, 2006

Lawson, Nigella. *Forever Summer*. New York: Hyperion, 2003

Le Coze, Maguy. *Le Bernardin Cookbook*. New York: Broadway Books, 1998

Longbotham, Lori. *Lemon Zest*. New York: Broadway Books, 1998

McLaughlin, Michael. *Cooking for the Weekend*. New York: Simon & Schuster, 1993

Narlock, Lori Lynn, Mary C. Barber, Sara C. Whiteford, Amy Neunsinger. *The Smoothies Deck*. San Francisco: Chronicle Books, 1999

Paradissis, Chrissa. *Best of Greek Cookery*. Athens: P. Efstathiadis & Sons, 1971

Patraker, Joel, and Joan Schwartz. *Greenmarket Cookbook*. New York: Viking Books, 2000

Peck, Carole, and Carolyn Hart Bryant. Woodbury, CT: *The Buffet Book*. Ici La Press, 2002

Pellegrino, Frank. *Rao's Cookbook*. New York: Random House, 1998

Pirie, Gayle, and John Clark. *Country Egg, City Egg*. New York: Artisan Books, 2000

Portale, Alfred. *Alfred Portale's Twelve Seasons Cookbook*. New York: Broadway Books, 2000

Pyles, Stephan. *The New Texas Cuisine*. New York: Broadway Books, 1993

Raichlen, Steven. *How to Grill*. New York: Workman, 2001

Raichlen, Steven. *BBQ USA*. New York: Workman, 2001

Ripert, Eric, and Michael Ruhlman. *Return to Cooking*. New York: Artisan Books, 2002

Roden, Claudia. *The Book of Jewish Food*. New York: Knopf, 1996

Rogers, Ruth, and Rose Gray. *London River Café Cookbook*. New York: Random House, 1996

Rojas-Lombardi, Felipe. *The Art of South American Cooking*. New York: William Morrow/HarperCollins, 1991

Romaniello, Kerry Downey. *Out of the Earth*. New Bedford, MA: Spinner Publications, 1999

Trang, Corinne. *Essentials of Asian Cooking*. New York: Simon & Schuster, 2003

Vongerichten, Jean-Georges, and Mark Bittman. *Jean-Georges: Cooking at Home with a Four-Star Chef*. Cookbook. New York: Broadway Books, 1998

Waters, Alice. *Chez Panisse Café Vegetables*. New York: William Morrow/HarperCollins, 1999

Waters, Alice. *Chez Panisse Cookbook*. New York: William Morrow/HarperCollins, 1996

Willan, Anne. *From My Chateau Kitchen*. New York: Clarkson Potter, 2000

Willinger, Faith. *Red, White and Greens*. New York: HarperCollins, 1996

White, Jasper. *50 Chowders*. New York: Scribner, 2000

SELECTED SOURCES FOR INGREDIENTS AND KITCHENWARE

Adriana's Caravan (800) 316-0820 *www.adrianascaravan.com*
Bridge Kitchenware (800) 274-3435 *www.bridgekitchenware.com*
Chefshop.com (800) 596-0885 *www.chefshop.com*
Dean & DeLuca (800) 221-7714 *www.deanddeluca.com*
Entner-Stuart (800) 377-9787 *www.entnerstuartsyrups.com*
Ethnic Grocer (800) 438-4642 *www.ethnicgrocer.com*
Kalustyan's (800) 352-3451 *www.kalustyans.com*
MexGrocer (877) 463-9476 *www.mexgrocer.com*
Sahadis (718) 624-4550 *www.sahadis.com*
La Tienda (800) 710-4304 *www.tienda.com*
Williams-Sonoma (877) 812-6235 *www.williams-sonoma.com/*
Zabar's (212) 787-2000 and (800) 697-6301 (outside NYC) *www.zabars.com*

INDEX